Behavior and Passage of Juvenile Salmonids during the Evaluation of a Behavioral Guidance Structure at Cowlitz Falls Dam, Washington, 2011

By Tobias J. Kock, Theresa L. Liedtke, Brian K. Ekstrom, Ryan G. Tomka, and Dennis W. Rondorf

Prepared in cooperation with Tacoma Power

Open-File Report 2012–1030

U.S. Department of the Interior
U.S. Geological Survey

U.S. Department of the Interior
KEN SALAZAR, Secretary

U.S. Geological Survey
Marcia K. McNutt, Director

U.S. Geological Survey, Reston, Virginia: 2012

For more information on the USGS—the Federal source for science about the Earth, its natural and living resources, natural hazards, and the environment, visit *http://www.usgs.gov* or call 1-888-ASK-USGS.

For an overview of USGS information products, including maps, imagery, and publications, visit *http://www.usgs.gov/pubprod*

To order this and other USGS information products, visit *http://store.usgs.gov*

Suggested citation:
Kock, T.J., Liedtke, T.L., Ekstrom, B.K., Tomka, R.G., and Rondorf. D.W. 2012, Behavior and passage of juvenile salmonids during the evaluation of a behavioral guidance structure at Cowlitz Falls Dam, Washington, 2011: U.S. Geological Survey Open-File Report 2012-1030, 96 p.

Any use of trade, product, or firm names is for descriptive purposes only and does not imply endorsement by the U.S. Government.

Contents

Figures

Tables

Conversion Factors

Inch/Pound to SI

Multiply	By	To obtain
Length		
foot (ft)	0.3048	meter (m)
mile (mi)	1.609	kilometer (km)
mile, nautical (nmi)	1.852	kilometer (km)
yard (yd)	0.9144	meter (m)
Flow rate		
foot per second (ft/s)	0.3048	meter per second (m/s)
cubic foot per second (ft^3/s)	0.02832	cubic meter per second (m^3/s)

SI to Inch/Pound

Multiply	By	To obtain
Length		
millimeter (mm)	0.03937	inch (in.)
meter (m)	3.281	foot (ft)
kilometer (km)	0.6214	mile (mi)
kilometer (km)	0.5400	mile, nautical (nmi)

Behavior and Passage of Juvenile Salmonids during the Evaluation of a Behavioral Guidance Structure at Cowlitz Falls Dam, Washington, 2011

By Tobias J. Kock, Theresa L. Liedtke, Brian K. Ekstrom, Ryan G. Tomka, and Dennis W. Rondorf

Executive Summary

A radiotelemetry evaluation was conducted during April–October 2011 to describe movement patterns, forebay behavior, and passage of juvenile steelhead, coho salmon, and Chinook salmon at Cowlitz Falls Dam, Washington. The primary focus of the study was to describe fish behavior near a behavioral guidance structure (BGS) and floating surface collector (FSC) deployed upstream of Cowlitz Falls Dam. A secondary focus was to determine the proportion of tagged fish that were detected near spillbays 2 and 3 on the dam, because this location has been proposed for deploying weir boxes as an additional dam-based collection alternative in the future. Juvenile steelhead (*Oncorhynchus mykiss*), coho salmon (*Oncorhynchus kisutch*), and Chinook salmon (*Oncorhynchus tshawytscha*) were collected and tagged at the Cowlitz Falls Fish Collection Facility and transported upstream where they were released into the Cowlitz and Cispus Rivers. We radio-tagged and released 110 juvenile steelhead, 110 juvenile coho salmon, and 110 juvenile Chinook salmon and monitored their movements in and around the BGS/FSC complex, at the dam, and downstream of the dam. We used detection records and a Markov chain model to calculate probabilities of movement between specific areas in the forebay of Cowlitz Falls Dam. These areas are referred to as states and the Markov chain model was used to create a series of tables, called transition matrices, that contained estimated probabilities of movement between states. These probabilities were insightful for understanding how radio-tagged fish moved near the BGS, FSC, and spillbays.

Most tagged fish (89–91 percent) moved downstream of release sites (9 or 22 rkm upstream of the dam) and were detected in the dam forebay during the study period. Tagged fish that encountered the BGS on their first approach to the dam were distributed across the forebay, which supports the concept of using a BGS to concentrate fish near a collector entrance in the dam forebay. We found that 14 percent of the steelhead, 18 percent of the coho salmon, and 17 percent of the Chinook salmon encountered the FSC discovery area without BGS guidance on their first trip through the forebay. The BGS guided 36 percent of the steelhead, 22 percent of the coho salmon, and 46 percent of the Chinook salmon to the FSC discovery area when fish first entered the forebay, which resulted in 40–63 percent (by species) of the tagged fish arriving at the FSC discovery area. Movement patterns along the BGS showed that fish were likely to guide along the device, but also demonstrated the tendency of fish to move under the BGS and downstream to Cowlitz Falls Dam.

Tagged fish that arrived at Cowlitz Falls Dam were distributed across the dam face but a high percentage of each species (65 percent of steelhead; 61 percent of coho salmon; 71 percent of Chinook salmon) arrived on the northern side of the dam. Movement probabilities near spillbays 1 and 4 showed a strong preference for tagged fish to move from the outer edges of the dam towards the center of the dam where they were detected at the debris barrier (range of probabilities = 0.690–0.841). We found that 76 percent of the steelhead, 61 percent of the coho salmon, and 92 percent of the Chinook salmon were detected at spillbays 2 or 3 during the study. This behavior supports the strategy of weir box deployments in spillbays 2 and 3 for future dam-based collection options. Tagged fish that arrived at the dam commonly moved upstream and were detected at the BGS or FSC discovery area. This behavior provided a secondary opportunity for fish to encounter the FSC discovery area and we found that in total, 72 percent of the steelhead, 48 percent of the coho salmon, and 92 percent of the Chinook salmon were detected near the FSC while residing in the forebay. Overall, 88 percent of the steelhead, 76 percent of the coho salmon, and 95 percent of the Chinook salmon that entered the forebay were detected near the FSC or in spillbays 2 and 3.

Turbine passage was the most common passage route for tagged fish at Cowlitz Falls Dam during 2011. We found that 40 percent of the steelhead, 52 percent of the coho salmon, and 33 percent of the Chinook salmon passed through turbines. An additional 22 percent of the steelhead and 32 percent of the coho salmon passed through turbines or spillways when both passage routes were available. Fish collection numbers were relatively low during 2011 compared to long-term averages. In total, 37 percent of the steelhead, 14 percent of the coho salmon, and 23 percent of the Chinook salmon that entered the forebay were collected, primarily through collection flumes. The FSC collected a single radio-tagged fish (a Chinook salmon) in 2011.

Introduction

A variety of approaches have been used since 1998 to improve juvenile salmon collection at Cowlitz Falls Dam, Washington (fig. 1). Initial studies found that turbine entrainment was relatively high (45 percent; juvenile steelhead) and demonstrated that the proportion of tagged fish that entered spillbays 2 and 3, where collection flumes are located, was insufficient to meet collection goals (Adams and others, 1999). Efforts to improve collection during subsequent years included installing strobe lights in an attempt to deter fish from passing through turbines, and evaluating new spillbay entrance configurations to increase flume discovery rates by juvenile salmon (Evans and others, 2001; Hausmann and others, 2001; Kock and others, 2009). Hausmann and others (2001) found that spillbay entrances, which were 6.1 m wide and 4.9 m deep, had substantially higher flume discovery rates than spillbays configured with the original narrow-deep entrances (1.2 m wide and 11.0 m deep). Collection numbers at the flume entrances were still lower than desired so efforts were made to install new flared-rounded flume entrances to control flow acceleration upstream of the flumes. However, these modified flume entrances were tested during 2001 and 2003 and showed limited promise for substantial increases in fish collection numbers (Hausmann and others, 2001; Farley and others, 2003; Perry and others, 2004). Results from these efforts eventually lead to the development of two prototype collection devices, a fish screen and a weir box (Kock and others, 2007; Liedtke and others, 2007, 2009, 2010). The fish screen was evaluated during four collection seasons (2006–09) and had marginal collection success (Kock and others, 2007; Liedtke and others, 2007, 2009, 2010). The weir box and the fish screen were deployed simultaneously during 2009 and the weir box was more effective at collecting fish than the fish screen (Liedtke and others, 2010). Based in part on these findings, the fish screen was abandoned as a potential collection device, but the weir box continues to be considered for future evaluations. During 2010, Tacoma Power developed a prototype floating surface collector (FSC) and behavioral guidance structure

(BGS) that were located upstream of the dam (HDR, 2010). The BGS/FSC concept was based on the premise that juvenile salmon would encounter the BGS and be guided downstream to the FSC entrance for collection. Locating the FSC upstream of the dam provided two distinct advantages for juvenile salmon collection at Cowlitz Falls Dam. First, fish could be collected prior to encountering dam passage routes (that is, turbines or spillways) that contribute to lost collection opportunities at the dam. Second, the BGS/FSC could be operated simultaneously with collection devices on the dam to maximize collection numbers.

During 2011, the influences of the BGS and FSC on juvenile salmonids in the forebay of Cowlitz Falls Dam were evaluated using radiotelemetry. This evaluation focused on two specific objectives developed by Tacoma Power. The first objective was to determine the proportion of radio-tagged juvenile salmonids that encountered the FSC discovery area during 2011. The prototype FSC that was used during 2010 and 2011 is similar in concept, but different in design and scale, than the FSC that is envisioned for future collection efforts at Cowlitz Falls Dam. The prototype FSC was located approximately 60 m (200 ft) upstream of the dam near the north shore (fig. 2) and operates using less than 20 ft^3/s inflow. The proposed FSC may be located near the current FSC location, but would operate using much higher inflow (proposed minimum of 500 ft^3/s). Given the substantial differences in operating conditions between the prototype FSC and the planned FSC, high collection rates through the prototype device in 2011 were not expected. Rather, the number of juvenile salmon that encountered the prototype FSC (that is, discovery rate) in 2011 would be used to determine if anticipated discovery rates of the proposed FSC would warrant the development and operation of the device in future years. Behavioral data for juvenile salmon along the BGS also were considered to be important for the 2011 evaluation to determine if this device could effectively increase discovery rates of the FSC by juvenile salmon. The second objective for the 2011 evaluation was to determine the proportion of juvenile salmon that encountered entrances to spillbays 2 and 3 at Cowlitz Falls Dam where prototype weir boxes could be deployed during future years (fig. 2).

Methods

BGS, FSC, and Fish Collection Facility

The BGS consisted of 21 individual panels that were 6.1 m (20 ft) in length and 3.0 m (10 ft) deep. For reference, BGS panels were numbered from 1 to 21, beginning at the downstream end near the FSC (fig. 3). The BGS panels were solid steel plates supported at the surface by four large floats (fig. 3). Rubber inserts spanned gaps between individual BGS panels to provide a continuous barrier to fish passage in the upper 3.0 m of the water column. One small gap (<2 m) in the BGS was located between panels 2 and 3 where the structure was designed to break away during high flows to prevent damage to the BGS. The BGS was deployed to intercept downstream-migrating juvenile salmon and guide them towards the entrance to the FSC. Fish could move downstream of the BGS by: (1) moving between the FSC and the north shoreline; (2) moving through the space between the downstream end of the BGS and the FSC; (3) moving through the space between panels 2 and 3; (4) moving through the space between the upstream end of the BGS and the south shoreline; or (5) sounding beneath the FSC or BGS.

The FSC was located near the downstream terminus of the BGS to provide a collection location where BGS-guided fish could be collected. The FSC used during 2011 had an entrance that was 1.8 m wide and 2.0 m deep. The width and depth of the FSC decreased in a downstream direction to the point where the FSC attached to a 0.6 m diameter submerged pipe that transported collected fish from the FSC to the fish facility. Inflow to the FSC was approximately 0.57 m^3/s (18 ft^3/s) during 2011.

Collection of juvenile salmon at Cowlitz Falls Dam during 2011 (April–September) was accomplished using the FSC and two collection flumes inside spillbay 2 (fig. 2). Spillbays are numbered from north to south (fig. 2). The fish facility began operating on April 16, 2011, and was operated continuously until September 10, 2011. Collection flumes inside spillbay 2 were operated (0.60 m^3/s apiece; 20 ft^3/s) during the entire collection season. Flumes inside spillbay 3 were not operated because the FSC and spillbay 2 flumes provided the maximum amount of flow that could be handled by the fish facility. The FSC operated during most of the collection season with the following exceptions: (1) from May 15, 2011, to May 20, 2011, when high flows precluded operating the BGS, and (2) from August 30, 2011, to September 1, 2011, when the FSC was temporarily shutdown.

Fish Collection, Tagging, and Release

Juvenile steelhead, coho salmon, and Chinook salmon were collected and tagged with radio transmitters at the fish facility during 2011 (tables 1–3). Fish were collected for tagging every 5 d during the middle 95th percentile of the historical run timing for each species (April 24–June 11 for steelhead; May 12–July 9 for coho salmon; June 27–August 23 for Chinook salmon). The fish facility did not collect sufficient numbers of juvenile steelhead and coho salmon to meet the tagging request during some of the scheduled collection dates, resulting in some fish being tagged beyond the middle 95th percentile of the run for these species (tables 1–2). The 2011 run timing of juvenile Chinook salmon at Cowlitz Falls Dam was substantially later than in previous years (John Serl, Washington Department of Fish and Wildlife, oral commun., 2011). As a result, tagging of juvenile Chinook salmon was delayed for nearly a month before sufficient numbers of fish were collected to meet our tagging needs (table 3). All Chinook salmon tagging occurred during the 95th percentile of the historical run timing but within a shorter window than planned.

We used radio transmitters (Model NTC-M-2; Lotek Wireless Inc.©; Newmarket, Ontario, Canada) that had an operating life of about 50 d (based on specifications from the manufacturer and a taglife study) and weighed 0.43 g in air. All tagged fish weighed equal to or greater than 8.6 g (in air) to insure that the transmitter weight did not exceed 5 percent of the fish's body weight. We tagged 110 fish per species during the study (tables 1–3). Transmitters were surgically implanted (Adams and others, 1998) and tagged fish were held for approximately 24 h prior to release.

Following the 24 h recovery period, tagged fish were released into the Cowlitz or Cispus Rivers, upstream of Lake Scanewa (fig. 1). Tagged fish were transported in an aluminum transport container (1,189 L; oxygen supplied) to release sites on the Cowlitz and Cispus Rivers. Release sites were selected to insure that fish were released slightly upstream of the reservoir boundary in Lake Scanewa. The Cowlitz River release site was about 22 river kilometers (rkm) upstream of Cowlitz Falls Dam and the Cispus River release site was about 9 rkm upstream of the dam. When possible, release groups were split evenly between each release site on a given release date. On dates when an odd number of fish were tagged, the larger release group was released on an alternating schedule between release sites to insure that 55 tagged fish (of each species) were released at each site during the study period.

Radiotelemetry System

We established aerial monitoring arrays throughout the study area to monitor movement patterns of tagged fish in Lake Scanewa, in the forebay, and downstream of Cowlitz Falls Dam. Aerial monitoring sites were located on the Cowlitz River (19.7 rkm upstream of Cowlitz Falls Dam), Cispus River (3.4 rkm upstream of Cowlitz Falls Dam), and on Lake Scanewa (3.9 rkm upstream of Cowlitz Falls Dam; 1.3 rkm upstream of Cowlitz Falls Dam; fig. 1). Four additional aerial sites monitored the forebay of Cowlitz Falls Dam. Monitoring downstream of the dam consisted of two sites that were located in the dam's tailrace (0.2 rkm and 0.3 rkm downstream of Cowlitz Falls Dam), and one site at Taidnapam Bridge (4.8 rkm downstream of Cowlitz Falls Dam; fig. 1). Aerial monitoring sites consisted of a pair of three-element aerial antennas connected to a telemetry receiver (Model SRX 400[©]; Lotek Wireless Inc.[©], Newmarket, Ontario, Canada; Orion receiver[©]; Grant Systems Engineering, King City, Ontario, Canada).

Underwater monitoring arrays were established on the BGS, FSC, and on Cowlitz Falls Dam to monitor fine-scale movements of tagged fish. Underwater antennas were installed 1.8 m below the surface (hereafter shallow BGS antennas) on the upstream and downstream sides of each BGS panel (fig. 4). Underwater antennas also were installed 6.1 m below the surface (hereafter referred to as deep BGS antennas) on BGS panels 3–21 to detect fish that passed under the device. This configuration resulted in six shallow detection areas along the upstream and downstream sides of the BGS and FSC, respectively, and five deep detection areas beneath the BGS. Two underwater antennas also monitored the area between the FSC and the north shore for fish moving around the FSC (fig. 4). Underwater antennas were deployed 1.8 m below the surface at Cowlitz Falls Dam to monitor near-dam behavior of tagged fish (fig. 5). Detection areas at the dam included: (1) the debris barrier (antennas 23–27); (2) spillbay 1 (antenna 31); (3) spillbay 2 (antennas 30 and 33); (4) spillbay 3 (antennas 29 and 32); and (5) spillbay 4 (antenna 28; fig. 5). Underwater antennas were not deployed north of spillbay 1 or south of spillbay 4, which left approximately 18 and 32 m, respectively, that were unmonitored on the outer edges of the dam (fig. 2). Underwater antennas were range-tested prior to the study to insure that detection patterns were appropriate for study objectives (appendix A).

Data Analysis

Data Processing

A dataset was created by combining all telemetry detection records, the tagging and release data, river flow data, and dam operations data for the study period. This dataset was rigorously proofed to create a final dataset for analysis. We used the SAS statistical package (SAS, 2008) to remove non-valid detection records from the preliminary dataset. Individual detection events were removed from a fish's detection record if that detection event: (1) occurred prior to the known release time for a given fish (that is, fish that were detected during transport); (2) occurred more than 63 d (anticipated maximum tag life) after the release time for a given fish; or (3) the signal power assigned by the telemetry receiver was less than 100 on receivers monitoring aerial antennas in the forebay of Cowlitz Falls Dam. Additionally, we programmed SAS to remove detection events from a fish's detection record if there were not at least two detections within a 15-min period at a given detection location. Following preliminary processing with the automated proofing program, detection records were manually proofed by USGS staff. Manual proofers reviewed each fish's detection record to insure that the automated proofing process removed all erroneous records. If non-valid detection events were identified by the proofer, the records were removed. Following manual proofing, the dataset was considered final. In some cases, external data were available for validating detection events in the final dataset. For example, we recorded the transmitter identification for every tagged fish that was collected at Cowlitz Falls Dam during the 2011 collection season. These data were then cross-referenced with dam passage data to verify that detections were accurately recorded.

Detections and Fish Movement Patterns

Detection records were analyzed to determine the number of tagged fish using specific areas near the BGS, FSC, and the dam to understand fish distribution and movement patterns. For example, the final dataset was queried to determine the number of fish (of each species) that were detected in the forebay of Cowlitz Falls Dam. These data were then compared to the number of fish released to determine the proportion of tagged fish that successfully moved downstream from release sites to the forebay. Travel times were calculated by subtracting the release date and time (for each fish) from the first date and time of detection in the forebay of Cowlitz Falls Dam. First detection events on individual antennas on the BGS and FSC provided information about the horizontal and vertical distribution of tagged fish when they first encountered the BGS/FSC complex. The final dataset also was partitioned by diel period (that is, day or night) and dam operating condition (that is, spill or no spill) to understand trends in fish behavior under these scenarios. Diel periods were defined using sunrise/sunset data obtained from HDR (2010). Hourly dam operating conditions were assigned based on Cowlitz Falls Dam operating records. Operating conditions during the study period included: (1) two turbines operating with spill; (2) two turbines operating without spill; (3) Unit 1 operating with spill; (4) Unit 1 operating without spill; (5) Unit 2 operating with spill; (6) Unit 2 operating without spill; (7) spill only (no turbine discharge); and (8) no operations (that is, no dam discharge).

To categorize fish as having discovered the FSC for our analysis, we first had to define the spatial boundaries of the FSC. The goal of the BGS is to guide fish to an area where they encounter flow conditions created by the FSC so that they have the opportunity to be collected through the device. Hydraulic data from the forebay were not available to help determine where the extent of the FSC flow effects were during 2011 so we used two FSC discovery definitions to provide a range of observations when considering BGS guidance and FSC discovery rates. The underwater antennas used for our primary definition of the FSC discovery area included antennas 18–22 (fig. 6). These antennas monitored the FSC (antennas 20 and 22), the area between the FSC and the north forebay shore (antenna 21), and the first two BGS panels located upstream of the BGS (antennas 18–19; fig. 6). This definition will hereafter be referred to as the small FSC discovery area. The second definition of the FSC included all antennas previously described along with antennas 6, 11, and 17, which increased the spatial boundaries of the FSC to include the first six BGS panels upstream of the device (fig. 6). This definition will hereafter be referred to as the large FSC discovery area.

Markov Chain Analysis

We conducted a Markov chain analysis to describe movement patterns of tagged fish near the BGS, FSC, and Cowlitz Falls Dam. The use of Markov chain models has increased during recent years due to developments in probability theory and stochastic modeling (Grinstead and Snell, 1997; Lindsey, 2004). A Markov chain can be used to describe processes where observations can be grouped into a series of finite states where movements between states are possible. An individual movement between states is described as a "step", and the overall sum of steps within the Markov chain are represented as a series of probabilities of moving between each state. For our analysis, individual states were defined by the locations of underwater antennas in the forebay of Cowlitz Falls Dam. Steps were defined as physical movements by tagged fish between these locations. Movements between states were summarized to create tables of movement probabilities (transition matrices; Grinstead and Snell, 1997) that represented the probability of moving from a given state at time t, to another state at time $t + 1$. These transition matrices are the primary product from the Markov chain analysis in this report and probability data from these tables are used to describe movement patterns of tagged fish during the study period.

Underwater antennas were grouped to create 12 states that were used in the Markov chain analysis. We chose to group antennas, rather than use individual antenna locations to define states, for several reasons. Transition matrices become increasingly complex with increasing numbers of states and sample sizes within each state generally decrease as the number of states increase. The goal of the Markov chain analysis was to provide a probability framework to better understand behavior patterns of tagged fish near the BGS, FSC, and dam. Probability data can be very insightful for understanding movement patterns of tagged animals, but these data can be also uninformative when sample sizes are small. Grouping antennas into specific areas of interest allowed us to create a series of limited but biologically meaningful states with sufficient data to provide reliable estimates of movement patterns during the study. Using this approach, we defined 12 states. The BGS was divided into four states that included the south upstream BGS state, south downstream BGS state, north upstream BGS state, and north downstream BGS state (fig. 7). Antennas on the FSC and on the first two BGS panels upstream of the FSC were grouped to create the FSC state (fig. 7). Antennas that monitored the area between the FSC and the north forebay shore defined the north FSC gap state (fig. 7). Underwater antennas at the dam were grouped to create the debris barrier state, spillbay 1 state, spillbay 2–3 state, spillbay 4 state, fish facility state, and tailrace state (fig. 7). Tagged fish could make multiple movements between states in the forebay until they entered the fish facility state, tailrace state, or their transmitter expired.

We parsed the detection data into two datasets for the Markov chain analysis. To create these datasets, detection records were divided based on the first detection event for each fish on underwater antennas at Cowlitz Falls Dam. The first dataset consisted of the first underwater antenna detection at the dam along with all other underwater antenna detections that occurred prior to that first near-dam detection event. This dataset (hereafter approach data) consisted of detection events on the BGS, FSC, and the first detection at the dam, which comprised the first trip through the forebay for each tagged fish. This dataset was summarized to generate probabilities of fish encountering various states along the BGS and FSC, guiding along the BGS, and moving to the dam during their first trip through the forebay. The second dataset (hereafter residence data) consisted of all detection records that occurred after the initial near-dam detection event and included movements along the dam, return trips to the BGS and FSC, and passage routes used by tagged fish.

Chinook Salmon Data

Radio-tagged Chinook salmon were monitored through mid-October when all radio transmitters had expired, and the Cowlitz Falls Fish Collection Facility stopped operating on September 10, 2011. We assumed that forebay conditions changed substantially when the fish facility was not operating because flow through the FSC and surface collection flumes in spillbay 2 was no longer available for fish to orient to. Given this assumption, we did not include forebay detection records of juvenile Chinook salmon in our analyses if detection events occurred after the fish facility closed. Therefore, results that appear in this report for juvenile Chinook salmon only include data that were collected prior to the fish facility closure, with one exception. Dam passage routes were assigned for tagged Chinook salmon if tagged individuals passed the dam, or remained upstream of the dam, after the fish facility stopped operating.

Results

River Flows and Dam Operations

River flows in the upper Cowlitz River were within the normal range during April–June, but July and early August flows were nearly twice as high as flows typically observed during this period from 2000 to 2010 (fig. 8). Mean daily river flows were approximately 5,000 ft^3/s when the fish facility began operating (April 16) and peaked at 17,200 ft^3/s on May 16, 2011 (fig. 8). River flows generally ranged between 6,000 and 10,000 ft^3/s during April–June (fig. 8). However, the combined effects of a substantial snowpack, cooler than normal conditions, and a wet spring resulted in an extended runoff period, which lead to higher than normal flows during July and August (fig. 8).

Operating conditions at Cowlitz Falls Dam consisted primarily of two-turbine or one-turbine operations intermixed with spillway operations when river flows exceeded turbine capacities. Typically, Cowlitz Falls Dam operates both turbines when river flows are in the 4,000–10,000 ft^3/s range. This was the operating condition during 59 percent of the 2011 fish collection season (fig. 9). Spillbays passed additional water at the dam when river flows exceed 10,000 ft^3/s and this condition occurred on 11 percent of the days that the fish facility operated in 2011 (fig. 9). Dam operations are restricted to a single turbine when river flows are lower than 4,000 ft^3/s, which happened on 30 percent of the collection days in 2011. During July and August of some years, river flows are so low that there are periods when no turbines are operated. This allows water to be stored in Lake Scanewa and results in intermittent turbine operations. Because river flows were higher than normal during July and August 2011, intermittent turbine operations were relatively uncommon. Intermittent turbine operations happened on 5 days (August 29, September 2, September 4, September 6, and September 8) and the average length of no-flow periods at the dam was 5.4 h on each of these days.

Detections and Behavior Patterns

Forebay Detections and Travel Time

Most of the tagged juvenile salmon moved downstream from the release sites and were subsequently detected on aerial or underwater antennas in the forebay of Cowlitz Falls Dam. A total of 98 juvenile steelhead (89 percent; appendix B) were detected at Cowlitz Falls Dam during the study and their median travel time from release to the forebay was 18.4 h (range = 4.6–142.2 h). Median forebay residence (last detection event in the forebay-first detection event in the forebay) time for juvenile steelhead was 34.6 h (range = 0.07–598.3 h). A total of 91 percent (100 fish; appendix B) of the juvenile coho salmon were detected at Cowlitz Falls Dam during the study, and their the median travel time was 20.5 h (range = 3.8–406.0 h). Median forebay residence time for juvenile coho salmon was 2.7 h (range = 0.02–224.7 h) during 2011. Most juvenile Chinook salmon (90 percent; 99 fish; appendix B) arrived in the forebay of Cowlitz Falls Dam following release and their median travel time was 51.7 h (range = 13.8–501.0 h). Median forebay residence time for juvenile Chinook salmon was 191.0 h (0.04–1215.0 h).

Upstream Trips

Detection data were examined to determine how many tagged fish moved upstream into Lake Scanewa after being detected in the forebay of Cowlitz Falls Dam (hereafter upstream trips). We found that most steelhead and coho salmon remained in the forebay whereas Chinook salmon typically made numerous upstream trips following forebay entry. Most steelhead (77 percent) did not move upstream after entering the forebay of Cowlitz Falls Dam although a few fish made at least one upstream trip during the monitoring period (table 4). Nearly all coho salmon (95 percent) remained in the forebay and the five fish that did move upstream only made one trip apiece (table 4). Chinook salmon typically made numerous upstream trips during the study. Only 19 percent of the tagged Chinook salmon remained in the forebay following entry and more than one-half of the Chinook salmon (54 percent) made at least three upstream trips (table 4).

First Detections at the BGS

Forebay detection records were analyzed to determine the vertical and horizontal distribution of tagged fish when they first encountered the BGS or FSC. In total, 81 steelhead, 76 coho salmon, and 95 Chinook salmon were detected by underwater antennas on the BGS or FSC following forebay entry. Some fish were undetected at the BGS and others entered the forebay when the BGS was not in position due to high spring flows. Most fish were first detected on the shallow upstream BGS antennas (72 percent of the steelhead; 57 percent of the coho salmon; 69 percent of the Chinook salmon; figs. 10–12). Most tagged fish were first detected at the BGS (85 percent of the steelhead; 77 percent of the coho salmon, and 82 percent of the Chinook salmon; figs. 10–12) and not at the small FSC discovery area. Underwater antennas on the BGS were grouped into five zones (Zones A–E; fig. 4) and first detection events at these zones indicated that tagged fish were spread across the forebay when they first encountered the BGS. In most cases, 10–20 percent of the tagged fish that encountered the BGS were detected in each of the five BGS monitoring zones (figs. 10–12).

First detection events were grouped by diel period (day and night) and dam operating conditions to determine if fish behavior varied substantially under these conditions (figs. 13–15). Steelhead detection events occurred during three dam operating conditions, which included: (1) Unit 1 operating without spill; (2) both turbines operating without spill; and (3) both turbines operating with spill (fig. 13). Coho salmon detection events occurred during two operating conditions, which included: (1) both turbines operating without spill; and (2) both turbines operating with spill (fig. 14). All Chinook salmon detection events occurred when Unit 1 was operating without spill. Some differences were apparent in first detection events that occurred during the various diel and dam operating conditions but in most cases sample sizes within each group were relatively small (<10 fish; figs. 13–15). In general, the largest differences in the locations of first detections during day and night periods occurred at the small FSC discovery area and Zone E. For all three species, the percentage of first detections at the small FSC discovery area at night was double those that occurred during the day (figs. 13–15). For coho and Chinook salmon, Zone A showed a trend similar to the FSC, with twice as many detections at night compared to daytime periods. The opposite trend was observed at Zone E, where twice as many coho and Chinook salmon were first detected during the day compared to night (figs. 14–15). The largest difference in first detections for steelhead by dam operating condition occurred in Zone A. Fewer steelhead were detected in this zone during two turbine operations with no spill compared to the other two operations (fig. 13). The largest difference in first detections for coho salmon occurred at the FSC.

During spill conditions, 5 percent of the tagged coho salmon were first detected at the small FSC discovery area, but 28 percent of fish were first detected at the small FSC discovery area during periods without spill (fig. 14). Spill conditions also appeared to concentrate coho salmon in the center of the forebay, with fewer first detections at both the FSC and Zone E.

Effects of Release Site

We compared travel times (from release sites to the dam forebay) and first detection patterns along the BGS for tagged fish from the two release sites to determine if a release site effect was apparent during the study period. Travel times from the Cowlitz River and Cispus River release sites to the forebay of Cowlitz Falls Dam were compared (using a Wilcoxon-Mann-Whitney test) to determine if average travel times differed between the release sites. We found no difference in reservoir travel times from the two release sites for steelhead ($P = 0.077$), coho salmon ($P = 0.154$), or Chinook salmon ($P = 0.925$). First detection events along the BGS (using zones shown in figs. 10–12) were compared for each species using Fisher's exact test to determine if the horizontal distribution of tagged fish differed between release sites during the study. We found no difference in distributions of tagged steelhead ($P = 0.303$), coho salmon ($P = 0.748$), or Chinook salmon ($P = 0.871$) along the BGS based on first detection events. These results demonstrated that travel times from the two release sites were similar during our study period and that tagged fish from each release site were distributed similarly across the forebay when they first encountered the BGS. Given these findings, we did not evaluate release site effects in subsequent analyses in this report.

BGS Guidance

To determine the effectiveness of the BGS at guiding fish to the small FSC discovery area, we examined detection records of tagged fish during their initial encounter with the BGS. We found that 14 percent of the steelhead, 18 percent of the coho salmon, and 17 percent of the Chinook salmon encountered the small FSC discovery area on their first approach without BGS guidance (fig. 16). The BGS successfully guided (from the BGS to the FSC) 36 percent of the steelhead, 22 percent of the coho salmon, and 46 percent of the Chinook salmon during their first encounter with the BGS (fig. 16). In total, 50 percent of the steelhead, 40 percent of the coho salmon, and 63 percent of the Chinook salmon were detected at the small FSC discovery area on their first trip through the forebay by either encountering the small FSC discovery area directly, or being guided to the FSC by the BGS (groups A+B; fig. 16). Additionally, 26 percent of the steelhead, 25 percent of the coho salmon, and 20 percent of the Chinook salmon were partially guided by the structure (fig. 16). Partial guidance was defined as moving at least one zone closer to the small FSC discovery area from a fish's initial detection location on the BGS. One tagged steelhead and one tagged Chinook salmon encountered the BGS and moved back upstream into Lake Scanewa. The remaining tagged fish were either unguided by the BGS (15 percent of the steelhead; 17 percent of the coho salmon; 11 percent of the Chinook salmon) or were undetected at the BGS prior to arriving at the dam (8 percent of the steelhead; 18 percent of the coho salmon; 4 percent of the Chinook salmon; fig. 16).

10

We also examined BGS guidance and FSC discovery using the large FSC discovery area definition, which included the first six BGS panels located upstream of the device (fig. 6). As expected, using this larger area for FSC detection resulted in increased FSC encounters and BGS guidance rates for all species (fig. 17). In total, 74 percent of the steelhead, 55 percent of the coho salmon, and 81 percent of the Chinook salmon either encountered the large FSC discovery area directly, or were guided by the BGS on their first forebay trip (groups A+B; fig. 17). The percentage of partially guided fish and fish that were unguided by the BGS decreased. There was no change in the percentage of fish that returned upstream, or were undetected at the BGS during their first forebay trip (fig. 17).

First Detections at Cowlitz Falls Dam

We examined the pattern of first detection events of individual fish using underwater antennas on the debris barrier and along the face of the dam to determine the horizontal distribution of tagged fish when they first arrived at Cowlitz Falls Dam. Most tagged steelhead (65 percent), coho salmon (61 percent), and Chinook salmon (71 percent) were first detected on the northern side of Cowlitz Falls Dam (antennas 23, 24, 30 and 31; table 5). We also examined first detection patterns during day and night periods and under different dam operating conditions. First detection events on the northern side of the dam showed a diel trend for steelhead and coho salmon. During daytime hours, steelhead and coho salmon were more likely to be first detected on the northern side of the debris barrier (antennas 23–24) whereas nighttime detections largely occurred at spillbay 1 (tables 6–7). There are other differences in first detection events for steelhead, coho salmon, and Chinook salmon but sample sizes at several detection locations are very small so these results should be interpreted cautiously (<5 fish; tables 6–8).

Detection Patterns Near Proposed Collection Entrances

We examined several detection scenarios to understand fish behavior near the FSC and spillbays 2 and 3, which are the two most likely locations for permanent collection entrances in the future. The first scenario was the most conservative, including only detections at the small FSC discovery area and at spillbays 2 and 3 (figs. 4–6; appendix B). Under this scenario, 61 percent of the steelhead, 33 percent of the coho salmon, and 88 percent of the Chinook salmon were detected at both the small FSC discovery area and spillbays 2–3 (table 9). Conversely, 12 percent of the steelhead, 24 percent of the coho salmon, and 5 percent of the Chinook salmon were not detected at either location under this scenario. The second scenario included detections at the small FSC discovery area along with detections at spillbays 1–4 (fig. 5). This scenario resulted in marginal increases in detections at both locations for steelhead (from 61 to 70 percent) and coho salmon (from 33 to 42 percent), but only a minor increase for Chinook salmon (from 88 to 91 percent; table 9). The third scenario included the large FSC discovery area (fig. 6) area and spillbays 2–3. Results from this scenario were nearly identical to results from the second scenario for all species (table 9). The last scenario was the least conservative and used the large FSC discovery area along with spillbays 1–4. This scenario resulted in the highest proportion of tagged fish being detected near both locations for all three species under the various scenarios (80 percent for steelhead; 54 percent for coho salmon; 93 percent for Chinook salmon; table 9).

Residence Time in Forebay Areas

To determine where fish resided during the study period, we calculated elapsed residence times for individual tagged fish in distinct areas of the forebay. Detections were grouped within nine areas of the forebay based on specific antenna locations (table 10) and the entire detection history for each tagged fish in the forebay of the dam was considered for this analysis. Chinook salmon generally spent the greatest amount of time in the forebay and coho salmon generally spent the least amount of time (table 10). Chinook salmon spent the greatest amount of time near the BGS (mean = 1,725.4 mins), followed by spillbay 2 entrances (mean = 225.1 mins), and the debris barrier (mean = 134.3 mins; table 10). Steelhead spent the greatest amount of time near spillbay 3 entrances (mean = 472.2 mins), inside spillbay 3 (mean = 91.6 mins), and near spillbay 1 (mean = 79.0 mins). Finally, coho salmon spent the greatest amount of time near spillbay 1 (mean = 21.3 mins), followed by inside spillbay 3 (mean = 18.1 mins), and inside spillbay 2 (mean = 11.3 mins; table 10).

Dam Passage Routes

We found that 62 percent of the steelhead, 84 percent of the coho salmon, and 33 percent of the Chinook salmon passed Cowlitz Falls Dam and were detected in the tailrace during our study (table 11). Turbine passage was the most frequent passage route used by all species of tagged fish at Cowlitz Falls Dam during 2011. Fish that entered the tailrace could only have arrived there by passing through the turbines or spillbays, so turbine passage was assigned if tagged fish passed during a period when spillbays were not operating. We observed that 40 percent of the steelhead, 52 percent of the coho salmon, and 33 percent of the Chinook salmon that entered the dam forebay passed through turbines at the dam when the spillbays were not operating (table 11). Passage through spillbays and turbines can occur quickly because water moves through these areas at high velocities. Given our criteria for requiring at least two valid detections at a given monitoring site, and the burst rate of the transmitters that were used for the study (one transmission every 5 s), it was possible for fish to pass through turbines or spillbays without being detected. As a result, we grouped spillbay and turbine passage events into a single passage category when both turbines and spillbays were operating. We found that 22 percent of the steelhead and 32 percent of the coho salmon passed through these routes when both turbines and spillbays were operating (table 11).

We also re-examined the detection dataset by removing the criteria for two valid detections at an antenna to determine if spillbay and turbine passage routes could be distinguished during these periods. For steelhead, we found that 16 percent of the tagged fish passed through turbines compared to 6 percent through spillbays when both passage routes were available (table 12). For coho salmon, we found that 26 percent of the fish passed through turbines and 6 percent passed through spillbays (table 12). Although this analysis provided the opportunity to re-examine the data using a different set of criteria, it was still not possible to assign passage routes with complete certainty, so we urge the reader to refer to table 11 when considering passage route data from this study.

Nearly all tagged steelhead (99 percent) and coho salmon (98 percent) passed the dam during the study period, whereas nearly one-half (44 percent) of the Chinook salmon remained upstream of Cowlitz Falls Dam after their transmitters stopped functioning (table 11). The FSC only collected one tagged fish (a Chinook salmon) and almost all other tagged fish that were collected entered through collection flumes in spillbay 2. We found that 37 percent of the steelhead, 14 percent of the coho salmon, and 23 percent of the Chinook salmon were collected during 2011 (table 11).

Markov Chain Analysis

Approach Data

We examined the movement probabilities for tagged fish during their first encounter with the BGS and FSC and found that steelhead, coho salmon, and Chinook salmon responded similarly to these devices (tables 13–15). Tagged fish were most likely to first encounter the southern side of the BGS (south upstream BGS state; probabilities of 0.378 for steelhead; 0.356 for coho salmon; 0.414 for Chinook salmon), followed by the northern side of the BGS (north upstream BGS state; probabilities of 0.296 for steelhead; 0.218 for coho salmon; 0.323 for Chinook salmon), and the FSC (FSC state; probabilities of 0.102 for steelhead; 0.139 for coho salmon; 0.152 for Chinook salmon; tables 13–15).

Movement probabilities along the BGS showed that fish tended to move along the device, however, there also was a tendency for fish to pass under the BGS and move downstream to Cowlitz Falls Dam. Guidance along the BGS was defined by movements from the southern side of the BGS to the northern side of the BGS, or to the FSC. Tagged fish in the south upstream BGS state had the highest probabilities of moving to the north upstream BGS state (0.554 for steelhead; 0.522 for coho salmon; 0.462 for Chinook salmon; tables 13–15). However, tagged fish in the south upstream BGS state also had moderately high probabilities of moving under the BGS to the south downstream BGS state (0.089 for steelhead; 0.196 for coho salmon; 0.369 for Chinook salmon). Probability of movement under the BGS were higher from the north upstream BGS state to the north downstream BGS state (0.398 for steelhead; 0.322 for coho salmon; 0.437 for Chinook salmon) and all were higher than the probability of moving from the north upstream BGS state to the FSC state (0.184 for steelhead; 0.254 for coho salmon; 0.408 for Chinook salmon; tables 13–15). Steelhead and coho salmon also had relatively high probabilities of moving to the debris barrier state from the north upstream BGS state (0.174 for steelhead; 0.136 for coho salmon; tables 13–14).

Tagged fish that arrived at the FSC (from other states) displayed a range of behavioral patterns that included movements to the north shore of the forebay (north FSC gap state), returning upstream along the BGS, or moving downstream to the dam. Movement probabilities from the FSC state to the north FSC gap state were relatively high for all species (0.307 for steelhead; 0.550 for coho salmon; 0.258 for Chinook salmon; tables 13–15). However, there were species-specific differences in movement patterns from the FSC to the BGS. Juvenile steelhead moved upstream to the north BGS states at a relatively high rate (0.242 to the north downstream BGS state; 0.065 to the north upstream BGS state; 0.307 total; table 13). Chinook salmon were less likely than steelhead to return to the BGS (0.183 total; table 15) and juvenile coho salmon had a relatively low probability of moving to the BGS (0.083 total; table 14). All three species had relatively high probabilities (0.386 total for steelhead; 0.317 total for coho salmon; 0.527 total for Chinook salmon) for moving from the FSC state to the dam states (debris barrier state; spillbay 1 state; spillbay 2–3 state; tables 13–15). Transition matrices for tagged fish movements between individual antenna (ungrouped) locations from the approach dataset are presented in appendices C–E of this report.

Residence Data

Movement probabilities for juvenile steelhead showed that tagged fish moved along the dam and returned upstream to the BGS and FSC following arrival at the dam. Tagged steelhead in the debris barrier state primarily moved to spillbay 4 (0.265), spillbay 1 (0.191), spillbays 2–3 (0.167), the FSC (0.150), and the downstream zones of the north and south BGS states (0.110 and 0.066, respectively; table 16). The average number of movements per fish between these states ranged from 2.1 to 4.6, which shows that juvenile steelhead made numerous trips between these areas while present in the dam

13

forebay. Movement probabilities from spillbays 1 and 4 states to the debris barrier state (0.710 and 0.690, respectively) suggest that tagged steelhead exhibited a strong preference for moving toward the center of the dam. Once tagged steelhead were in the spillbay 2–3 state they primarily moved upstream to the debris barrier (0.555; 2.9 movements per fish) or passed the dam (0.175 to the fish facility state; 0.145 to the tailrace state; table 16). Tagged steelhead in the south downstream BGS state tended to pass under the BGS to the south upstream BGS state (0.395) or guide downstream along the BGS to the north downstream BGS state (0.327; table 16). Fish that guided downstream to the north downstream BGS state had a strong likelihood of passing under the BGS to the north upstream BGS state (0.435; 7.4 movements per fish) or moving to the FSC state (0.276; 5.4 movements per fish; table 16). Steelhead that arrived at the FSC were never collected through the device (0.000), and preferred to move back upstream to the north downstream BGS state (0.496; 6.0 movements per fish) or return downstream to the debris barrier state (0.235; 2.8 movements per fish; table 16).

Tagged coho salmon in the debris barrier state primarily moved to one of the spillbay states and had low probabilities of moving back upstream to the BGS or FSC states. Tagged coho salmon primarily moved from the debris barrier to spillbay 4 (0.362), spillbays 2–3 (0.258) or spillbay 1 (0.192; table 17). Similar to tagged steelhead, juvenile coho salmon that arrived at spillbays 1 and 4 showed a strong preference to move toward the center of the dam (debris barrier state; 0.794 and 0.815, respectively). Coho salmon that were detected in the spillbay 2–3 state were likely to pass downstream into the tailrace (0.449) or move upstream to the debris barrier (0.398). Tagged coho salmon were less likely than steelhead to move back upstream to the BGS or FSC. This observation is supported by the low probabilities of coho salmon moving from the debris barrier or spillbay states to the BGS or FSC zones (probabilities ranging from 0.000 to 0.088; table 17).

Tagged juvenile Chinook salmon exhibited similar behavior patterns to those of juvenile coho salmon during the study period. The probabilities of Chinook salmon moving from the debris barrier to the spillbay states (0.444 for the spillbay 2–3 state; 0.247 for the spillbay 4 state; 0.186 for the spillbay 1 state) were higher than to other states in the forebay (0.000–0.051 for all other states; table 18). Chinook salmon had a strong tendency to move toward the center of the dam (to the debris barrier state) from spillbays 1 and 4 states (0.736 and 0.849, respectively). Probabilities of Chinook salmon moving from the dam to the BGS or FSC were relatively low (0.000–0.145; table 18). Transition matrices for tagged fish movements between individual antenna (ungrouped) locations from the residence dataset are presented in appendices F–H of this report.

Discussion

The 2011 radiotelemetry evaluation of juvenile steelhead, coho salmon, and Chinook salmon behavior in the forebay of Cowlitz Falls Dam was insightful for understanding fish behavior and movement patterns near the BGS and FSC. Results from the study suggest that these devices achieved varying degrees of success depending on the variable and species of interest. Tagged fish from all species generally were located in the upper 3 m of the water column and dispersed across the forebay when they encountered the BGS on their first approach to the dam. Based on this distribution as fish approach the dam, the BGS could be useful to intercept fish and guide them towards the proposed collector entrance located on the north shore of the forebay, upstream of the dam. The BGS, however, was only moderately successful at guiding fish to the FSC during 2011. We found that 50 percent of the steelhead, 40 percent of the coho salmon, and 63 percent of the Chinook salmon encountered the FSC on their first trip through the forebay and 28–45 percent of those fish did so without guiding along the BGS (fig. 16). Analysis of movement probabilities for fish in various states along the BGS demonstrated tendencies of tagged fish to move along the upstream and downstream sides of the device, but these probabilities rarely exceeded 0.500, which indicates that tagged fish were equally likely to move into other states. Steelhead and Chinook salmon spent a considerable amount of time in the forebay and many Chinook salmon moved upstream of the dam during their forebay residence (table 4). This behavior provided additional opportunity for fish to locate the FSC, and 72 percent of the steelhead and 92 percent of the Chinook salmon eventually were detected near the device (table 9). Most juvenile coho salmon moved downstream after their first trip through the forebay and only 48 percent of the tagged coho salmon juveniles that arrived in the forebay of Cowlitz Falls Dam were detected near the FSC (table 9).

The interpretation of BGS guidance results during 2011 are complicated by the subjective nature of the FSC boundary definitions and the long-term vision for a FSC that will use substantially more flow than the prototype collector used during this study. High collection rates through the FSC were not required for the FSC/BGS complex to be considered successful during 2011. The goal for 2011 was high FSC encounter rates rather than high capture rates because the FSC used during this evaluation was considered temporary. In order to estimate fish encounters with the FSC, we had to subjectively define the spatial extent of the device based on underwater antennas positioned on the BGS and FSC. We chose a conservative approach and used underwater antennas mounted on the FSC, and on the first two BGS panels upstream of the FSC, to define the FSC boundaries we used to estimate FSC discovery rates and BGS guidance (that is, FSC encounter rate = 50 percent for steelhead, 40 percent for coho salmon, 63 percent for Chinook salmon; previous paragraph). However, using an expanded definition of the FSC where additional BGS panels (six panels upstream of the BGS) were included, FSC encounter rates increased by an additional 15–24 percent (figs. 16–17). Similarly, FSC and spillbay 2–3 encounter rates varied substantially based on the antenna combinations used to define these areas in table 9. The use of discovery rates estimated in 2011 to estimate collection success in the future is complicated because the proposed FSC will operate using approximately 25 times more water than the FSC used during 2011 (that is, 500 ft^3/s versus <20 ft^3/s). Given this disparity, it is difficult to determine how much BGS guidance would be required for juvenile salmon to encounter the FSC. Based on these uncertainties, we chose to calculate movement probabilities between distinct areas of the forebay to understand fish movement patterns.

The varied results for BGS guidance and FSC encounter rates support the idea of using a dam-based collection option simultaneously with a BGS/FSC complex to maximize encounter rates for juvenile salmonids at collection entrances in the forebay of Cowlitz Falls Dam. Radio-tagged fish were dispersed across the dam face on their initial encounter (table 7) but movement probabilities (0.690–0.841; tables 16–18) showed a strong tendency for all species to move from the outer edges of the dam (spillbays 1 and 4) to the center of the dam (the debris barrier). This behavior would be ideal for maximizing encounter rates of juvenile salmon at one or more collection devices, such as a weir box, located in spillbays 2 or 3. However, the debris barrier may limit spillbays 2 and 3 encounter rates as demonstrated by the relatively low probabilities of fish moving from the debris barrier to spillbays 2 and 3 (0.167 for steelhead; 0.258 for coho salmon; 0.444 for Chinook salmon; tables 16–18). Additionally, we observed that 15 steelhead, 18 coho salmon, and 19 Chinook salmon moved from the debris barrier to the tailrace, which is consistent with turbine entrainment for fish that sound beneath the debris barrier, which extends 2.7 m below the surface of the forebay (tables 16–18). Regardless of these effects, we found that 76 percent of the steelhead, 61 percent of the coho salmon, and 92 percent of the Chinook salmon were detected near entrances to spillbays 2 and 3, where weir box deployments have been proposed (table 9). We also examined the proportion of tagged fish that encountered at least one of the proposed collection locations (the FSC and spillbays 2 and 3) and found that 88 percent of the steelhead, 76 percent of the coho salmon, and 95 percent of the Chinook salmon were detected in at least one of these areas (table 9).

Past studies have shown that juvenile salmonids will guide along a BGS, when present in a dam forebay, but these studies also have shown that tagged fish will pass around or under the device, which has limited the effectiveness of these structures. Large BGS's have been deployed and tested at Lower Granite Dam on the Snake River, and at Bonneville Dam on the Columbia River where evaluations showed that 60–80 percent of the tagged fish were guided by these devices (Adams and others, 2001; Faber and others, 2010). At both locations, these devices were abandoned because they failed to guide enough fish to justify the expense required to operate and maintain these systems during periods when juvenile salmonids were passing the dams. Similarly, the BGS at Cowlitz Falls Dam has been shown to provide guidance for a portion of the fish that were studied during 2010 (HDR, 2010) and 2011, but the future of the BGS will depend on how it performs when the new FSC is in place and operating.

River flows affect collection of juvenile salmon at Cowlitz Falls Dam, so it is important to review fish behavior during 2011 in the context of the observed flow conditions. Juvenile steelhead and coho salmon out-migrate primarily during April–June each year when runoff conditions commonly result in high-flow periods at Cowlitz Falls Dam. Coho salmon are affected by high-flow periods as evidenced by the large decreases in collection efficiencies observed when river flows exceed 6,000 ft^3/s (John Serl, Washington Department of Fish and Wildlife, oral commun., 2011). Mean daily river flows exceeded 6,000 ft^3/s on 64 d (46 percent) during the collection season (April 15–August 31) in 2011, which is well above the 40 d average observed during 2000–2011. River flows that exceed 10,000 ft^3/s require spill operations at Cowlitz Falls Dam that provide an additional passage route that lacks a collection opportunity. Spill conditions were observed during 17 d (12 percent) in 2011 as compared to the 11 d average observed during the past decade. Given the higher than normal spring flows in 2011, the BGS/FSC likely guided fewer fish during 2011 than would be expected during years when spring flows are lower. For example, we found that 37 percent of the radio-tagged steelhead, and 14 percent of the radio-tagged coho salmon were collected during 2011, compared to 44 and 64 percent, respectively, during 2007, when river flows exceeded 6,000 ft^3/s on 22 d (16 percent). Conversely, higher than normal river flows during the Chinook salmon outmigration period (July–August) may have resulted in elevated performance of the BGS/FSC. River flows lower than about 1,800 ft^3/s result in no-flow periods at Cowlitz Falls Dam when the turbines are not operated. Low-flow periods during summer months typically are associated with increasing water temperatures as well, and the combination of no-flow conditions at the dam in conjunction with increasing water temperatures likely leads to decreasing collection efficiencies traditionally observed during August each year (John Serl, Washington Department of Fish and Wildlife, oral commun., 2011). During 2011, mean daily river flows fell below 1,800 ft^3/s on 1 d during the collection season, which is well below the long-term average of 27 d. Additionally, we found that 44 percent of the juvenile Chinook salmon did not pass Cowlitz Falls Dam while their transmitters were operating and this is a significant percentage in light of the long-term (about 2 months) operating life of the transmitters used during this study. Tagged fish were observed moving throughout the dam forebay and Lake Scanewa during this period so mortality does not appear to be a causal factor for this failure to pass the dam. Given this observation, a substantial number of juvenile Chinook salmon likely pass Cowlitz Falls Dam during fall or winter months because yearling Chinook salmon are rarely captured at the fish facility (John Serl, Washington Department of Fish and Wildlife, oral commun., 2011).

In summary, this evaluation was insightful for understanding juvenile salmon behavior near the BGS and for estimating proportions of tagged fish that were detected near the FSC and spillbays 2 and 3. Results from the study demonstrated that tagged fish guided along the BGS but also passed under the device readily, and moved downstream to the dam. Our use of the Markov chain analysis to describe probabilities of movement provided additional information that was insightful. However, these estimates were obtained during a single fish collection season, which included periods of atypical flow and confidence intervals for the probability estimates, in most cases, were fairly large (>20 percent; tables 13–18; appendices C–H). Encounter rates of the FSC and spillbays 2 and 3 were estimated, but these estimates varied depending on the spatial boundaries that were used to define the zones. The effects of a future FSC, which will use substantially higher flows than the prototype FSC, on BGS effectiveness and FSC discovery rates is unclear.

Acknowledgments

This study was made possible by the collaboration of many people. Keith Underwood, Mark LaRiviere, and others with Tacoma Power provided input into study design and execution that greatly enhanced the quality of the research effort. John Serl and personnel of the Cowlitz Falls Fish Facility were extremely helpful with regards to fish collection and holding operations in support of our tagging efforts. We thank Joe First and his staff at Cowlitz Falls Dam for providing logistical support for monitoring efforts at the dam. This report was improved with comments from Lynne Casal, Ian Jezorek, Keith Underwood, Matt Bleich, John Serl, and one anonymous reviewer. Funding for this research was provided through collaborative effort between Tacoma Power and Lewis County PUD.

References Cited

Adams, N. S., Johnson, G.E., Rondorf, D.W., Anglea, S.M., and Wik, T., 2001, Biological evaluation of the behavioral guidance structure at Lower Granite Dam on the Snake River, Washington in 1998: American Fisheries Society Symposium, v. 26, p. 145-160.

Adams, N.S., Plumb, J.M., Cash, K.M., Evans, S.D., Faber, D.M., Novick, M.S., Perry, R.W., and Rondorf, D.W., 1999, Behavior of juvenile salmonids at Cowlitz Falls Dam, Washington: Report by the U.S. Geological Survey to Lewis County PUD, Chehalis, Washington, USA.

Adams, N.S., Rondorf, D.W., Evans, S.D., Kelly, J.E., and Perry, R.W., 1998, Effects of surgically and gastrically implanted radio transmitters on growth and feeding behavior of juvenile Chinook salmon: Transactions of the American Fisheries Society, v. 127, p. 128-136.

Faber, D.M., Ploskey, G.R., Weiland, M.A., Deng, D., Hughes, J.S., McComas, R.L., Kim, J., Townsend, R.L., Fu, T., Skalski, J.R., and Fischer, E.S., 2010, Evaluation of a behavioral guidance structure at Bonneville Dam second powerhouse including dam passage survival of juvenile salmon and steelhead using acoustic telemetry, 2008: Report by Pacific Northwest National Laboratory for the U.S. Army Corps of Engineers, Portland, Oregon, USA.

Farley, J.M., Perry, R.W., Shurtleff, D.J., Feil, D.H., Rondorf, D.W., Morrill, C.M., and Serl, J.D. 2003, Migration behavior of juvenile salmonids and evaluation of a modified flume entrance at Cowlitz Falls Dam, Washington, 2001: Report by the U.S. Geological Survey to Lewis County PUD, Chehalis, Washington, USA.

Grinstead, C.M., and Snell, C.M., 1997, Introduction to probability: American Mathematical Society Publishing, Providence, Rhode Island, USA.

Hausmann, B.J., Feil, D.H., Rondorf, D.W., Morrill, C.F., and Serl J.D., 2001, Evaluation of an experimental baffle panel configuration to improve fish collection efficiency at Cowlitz Falls Dam, Washington, spring 2000: Report by the U.S. Geological Survey to Lewis County PUD, Chehalis, Washington, USA.

HDR, 2010, Cowlitz Falls behavioral guidance structure evaluation: Report by HDR to Tacoma Power, Tacoma, Washington, USA, accessed September 2011, at *http://aa.usno.navy.mil/data/docs/RS_OneYear.php.*

Kock, T.J., Evans, S.D., Liedtke, T.L., Rondorf, D.W., and Kohn, M., 2009, Evaluation of strobe lights to reduce turbine entrainment of juvenile steelhead (*Oncorhynchus mykiss*) at Cowlitz Falls Dam, Washington: Northwest Science, v. 83, no. 4, p. 308-313.

Kock, T.J., Liedtke, T.L., Kritter, M.A., and Rondorf, D.W., 2007, Behavior and passage of juvenile salmonids during evaluation of a fish screen at Cowlitz Falls Dam, 2006: Report by the U.S. Geological Survey to Tacoma Power, Tacoma, Washington, USA.

Liedtke, T.L., Kock, T.J., Ekstrom, B.K., and Rondorf, D.W., 2009, Behavior and passage of juvenile salmonids during the evaluation of a fish screen at Cowlitz Falls Dam, Washington, 2008: Report by the U.S. Geological Survey to Tacoma Power, Tacoma, Washington, USA, Tacoma Power Report Series Number 2009-01.

Liedtke, T.L., Kock, T.J., Ekstrom, B.K., Royer, I.M., and Rondorf, D.W., 2010, Juvenile salmonid collection efforts in the upper Cowlitz River basin: 2009 evaluations: Report by the U.S. Geological Survey to Tacoma Power, Tacoma, Washington, USA, Tacoma Power Report Series Number 2010-01.

Liedtke, T.L., Kock, T.J., Kritter, M.A., Ekstrom, B.K., and Rondorf, D.W., 2007, Behavior and passage of juvenile salmonids during the evaluation of a fish screen at Cowlitz Falls Dam, Washington, 2007: Report by the U.S. Geological Survey to Tacoma Power, Tacoma, Washington, USA.

Lindsey, J.K., 2004, Statistical Analysis of Stochastic Processes in Time: Cambridge University Press, New York, New York, USA.

Perry, R.W., Braatz, A.C., Farley, J.M., Rondorf, D.W., Morrill, C.M., and Serl, J.D., 2004, Migration behavior of juvenile salmonids and evaluation of a modified box entrance at Cowlitz Falls Dam, Washington, 2003: Report by the U.S. Geological Survey to Lewis County PUD, Chehalis, Washington, USA.

SAS, 2008, SAS Version 9.2: SAS Institute, Inc., Carey, North Carolina, USA.

Figure 1. Schematic of the upper Cowlitz River showing location of Cowlitz Falls Dam, fixed monitoring sites (empty circles) and release locations (filled circles) used during a radiotelemetry evaluation of juvenile steelhead, coho salmon, and Chinook salmon in 2011.

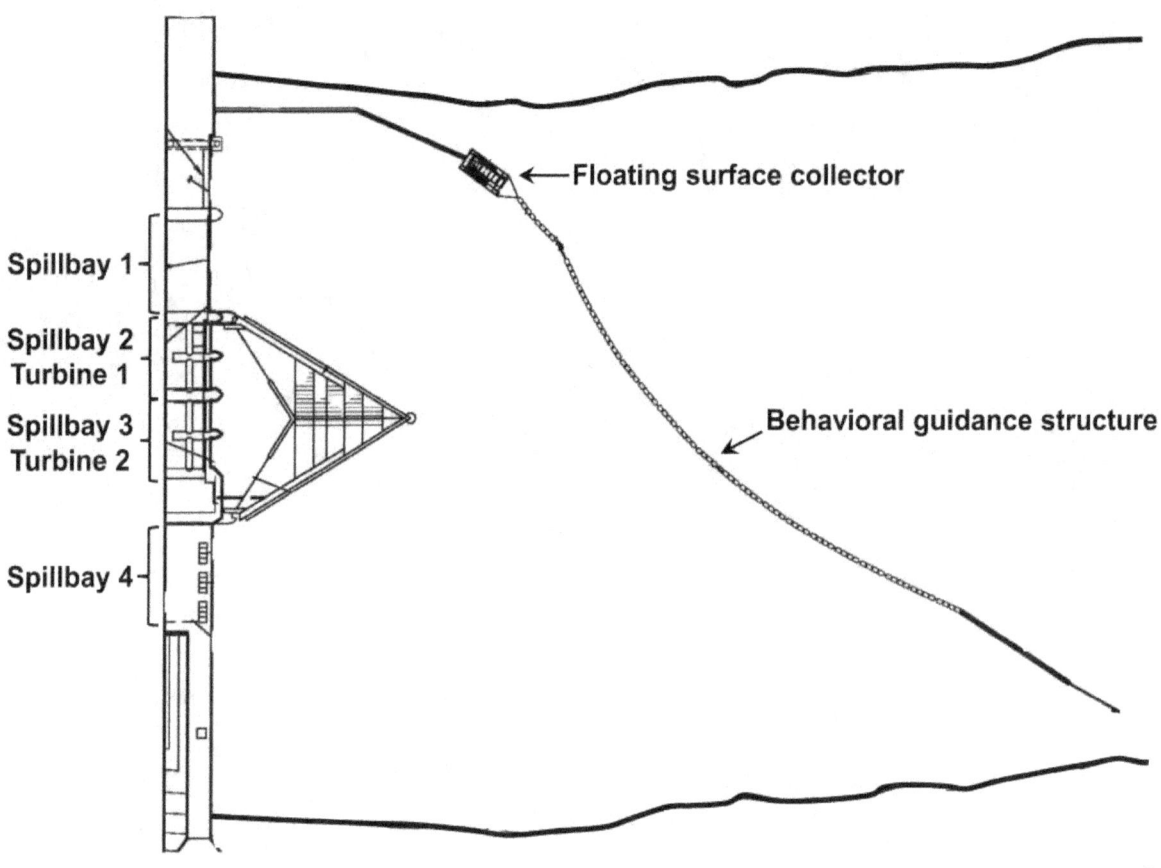

Figure 2. Diagram showing location of the behavioral guidance structure, floating surface collector, turbines, and spillbays at Cowlitz Falls Dam during 2011.

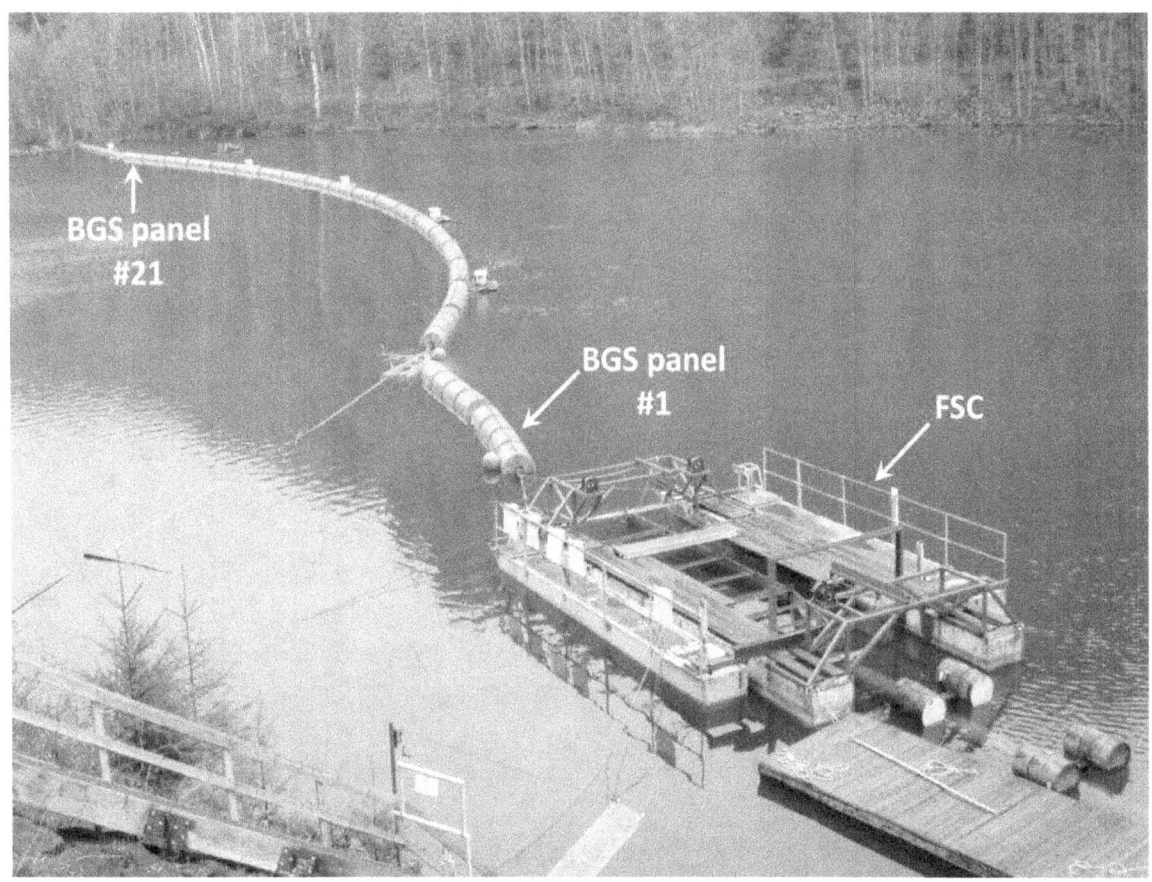

Figure 3. Photograph of the behavioral guidance structure (BGS) and floating surface collector (FSC) in the forebay of Cowlitz Falls Dam during 2011. BGS panels 1 and 21 also are shown to illustrate the panel numbering system referenced in this report. In the photograph, the river flows from left to right and Cowlitz Falls Dam is located approximately 60 meters downstream of the FSC.

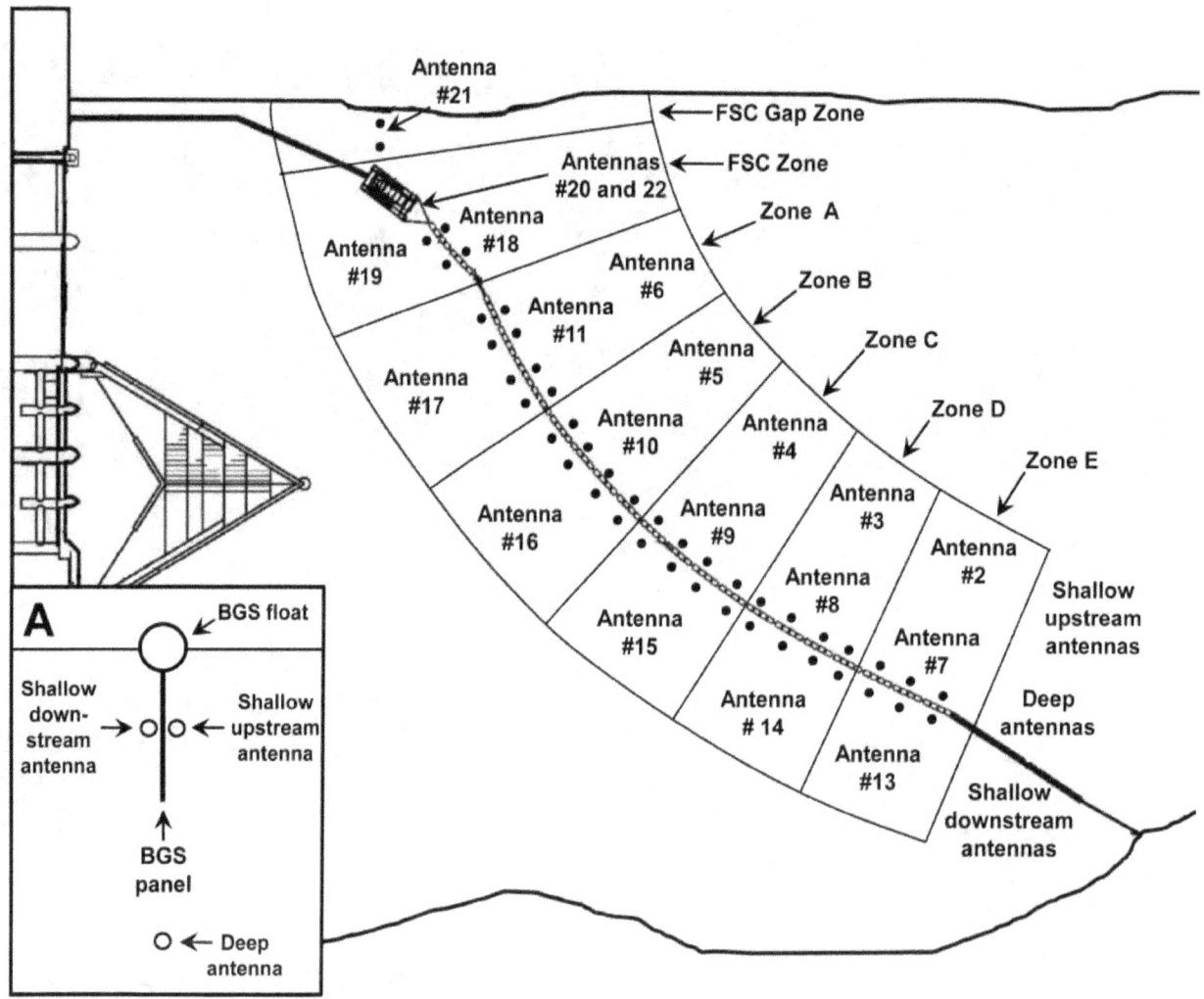

Figure 4. Diagram of the behavioral guidance structure (BGS) and floating surface collector (FSC) and location of underwater antennas that monitored movements of radio-tagged fish during 2011. Location of detection zones that were used during analysis of telemetry data also are shown. Inset A illustrates a side view of the BGS and the location of underwater antennas on the BGS (not to scale).

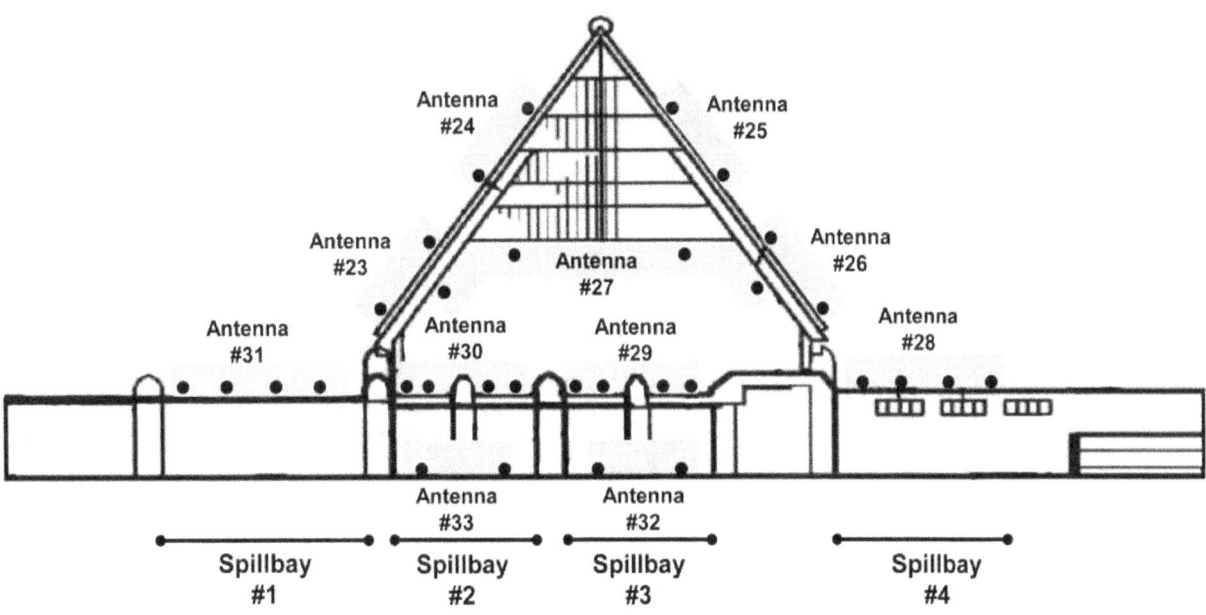

Figure 5. Diagram of Cowlitz Falls Dam and location of underwater antennas that monitored for movements of radio-tagged fish during 2011.

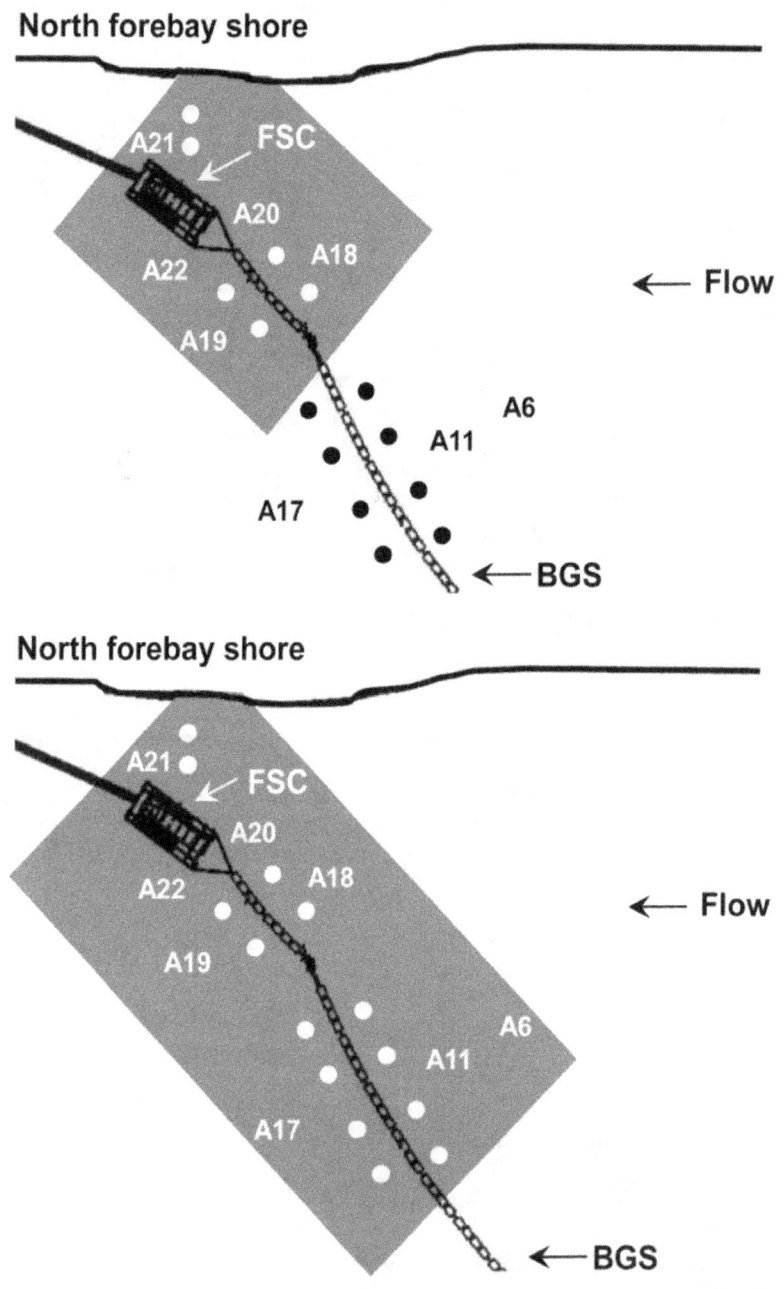

Figure 6. Diagram of the floating surface collector (FSC) and behavioral guidance structure (BGS) at Cowlitz Falls Dam during 2011 showing spatial boundaries that were used to define the FSC discovery area. The top panel shows the spatial boundaries of the small FSC discovery area and the bottom panel shows the spatial boundaries of the large FSC discovery area.

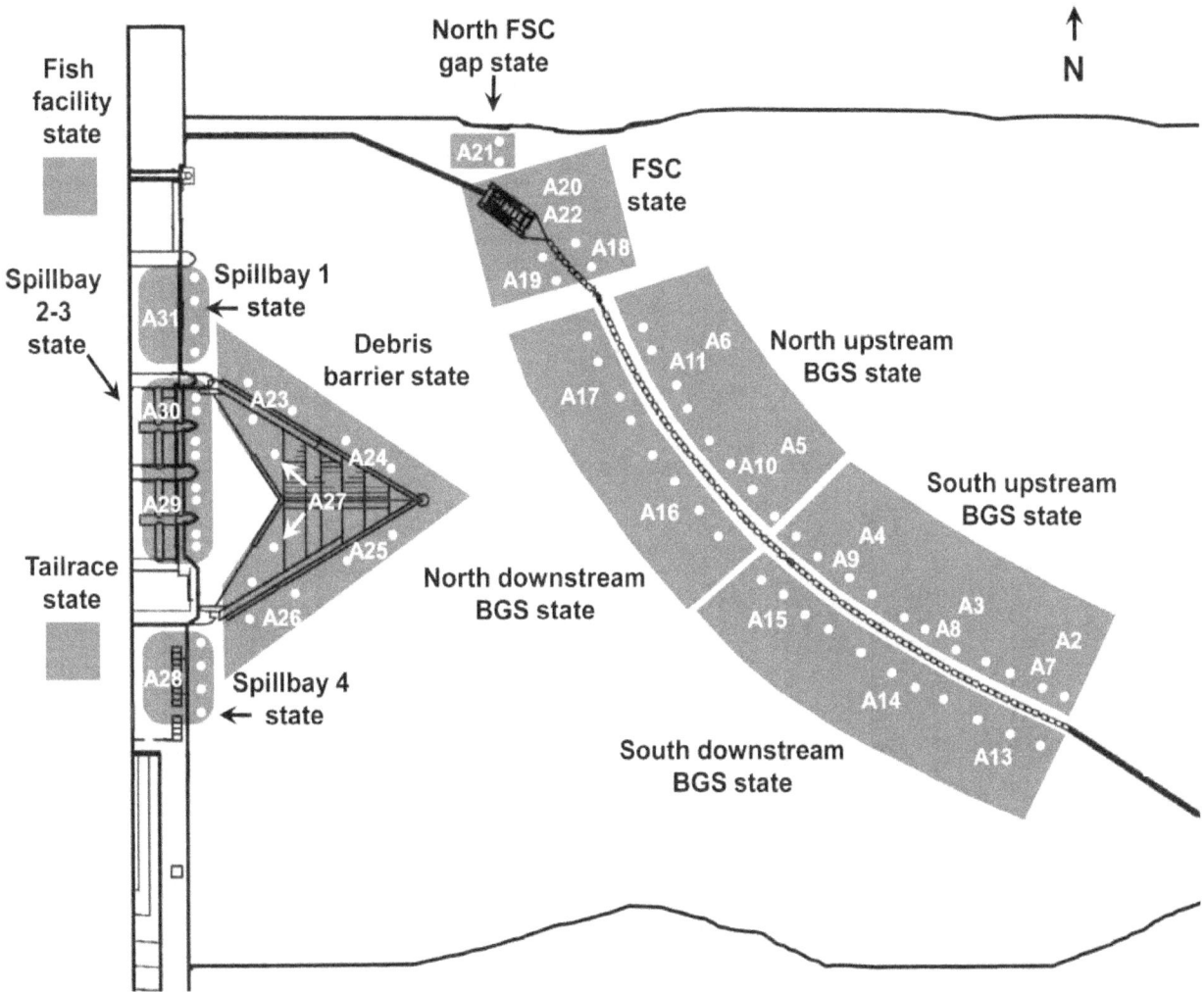

Figure 7. Diagram of antenna groupings used in a Markov chain analysis to describe movement patterns of radio-tagged juvenile steelhead, coho salmon, and Chinook salmon at Cowlitz Falls Dam during 2011.

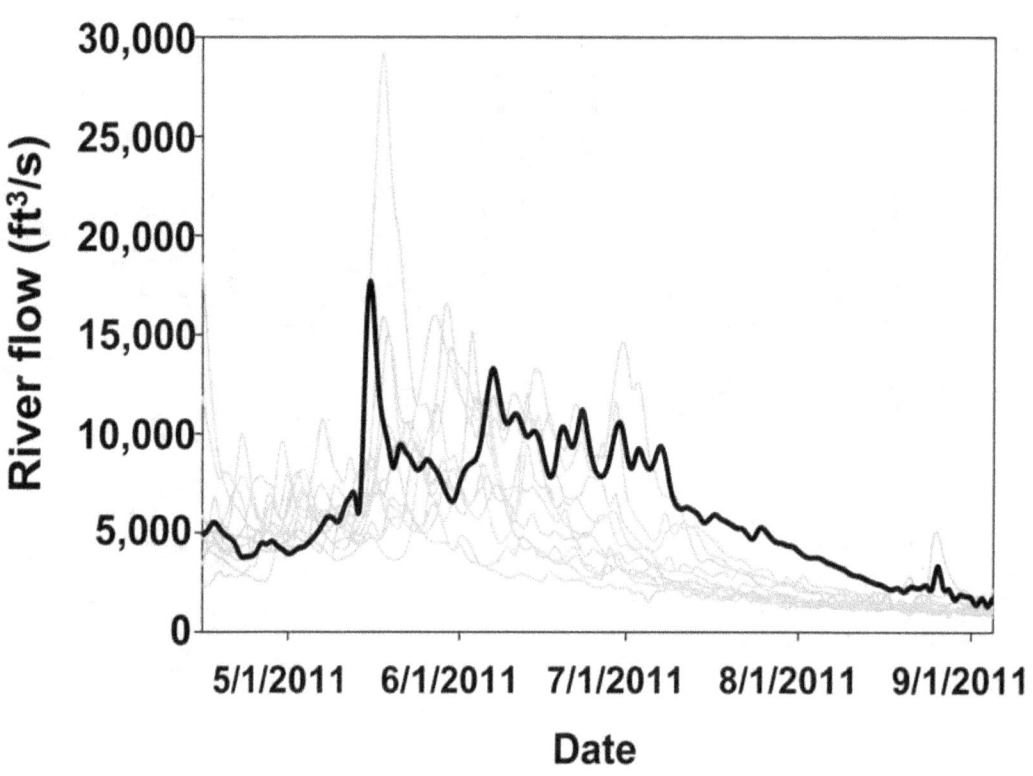

Figure 8. Mean daily river flow data (cubic feet per second) from 2011 (black line) and 2000–2010 (gray lines) on the Cowlitz River, Washington, as measured on the USGS Kosmos gage (#14233500).

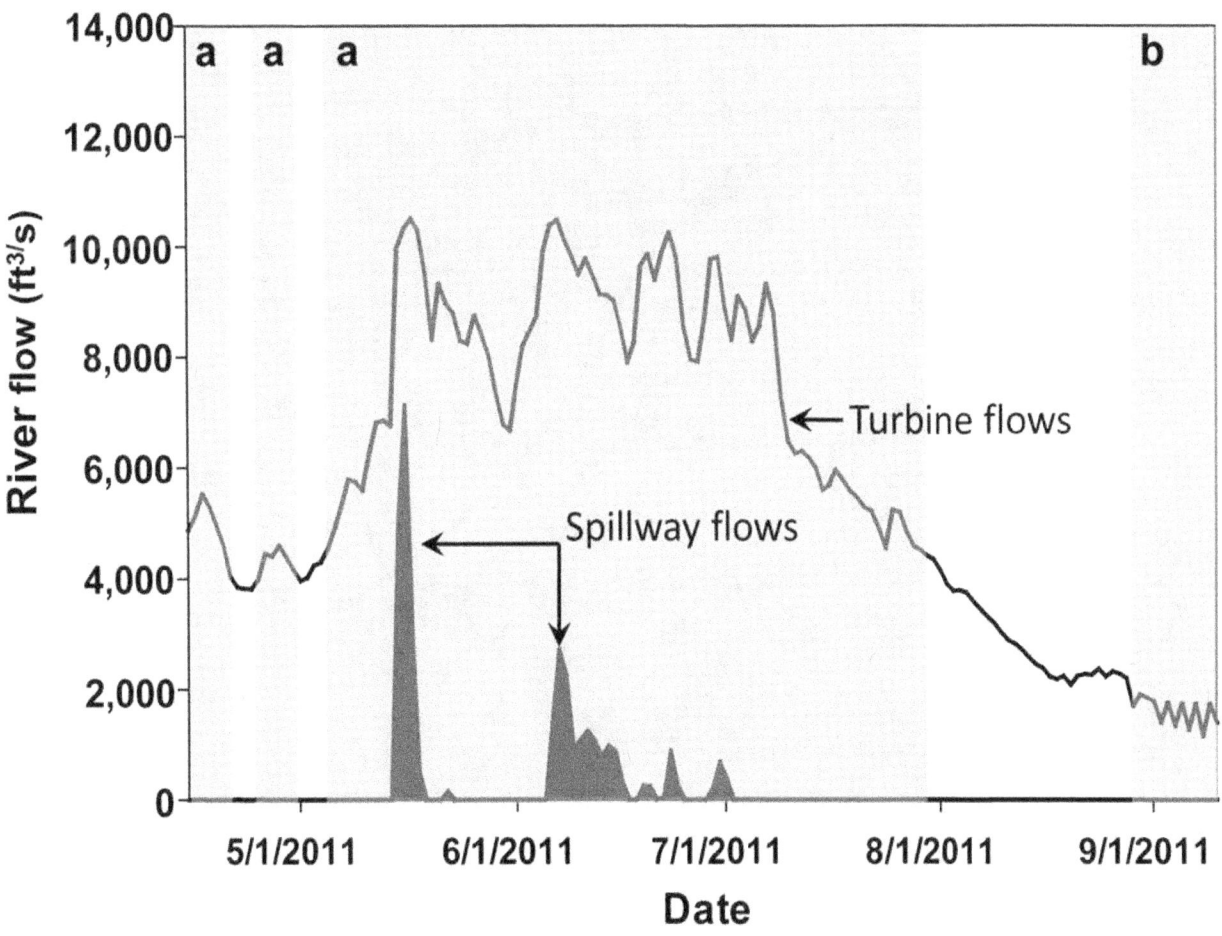

Figure 9. Spillway and turbine flows (cubic feet per second) at Cowlitz Falls Dam during the 2011 fish collection season. Turbine operating periods which included two-turbine operations (grey boxes identified by the letter a), one-turbine operations (unshaded boxes), and intermittent one-turbine operations (grey box identified by the letter b), also are shown.

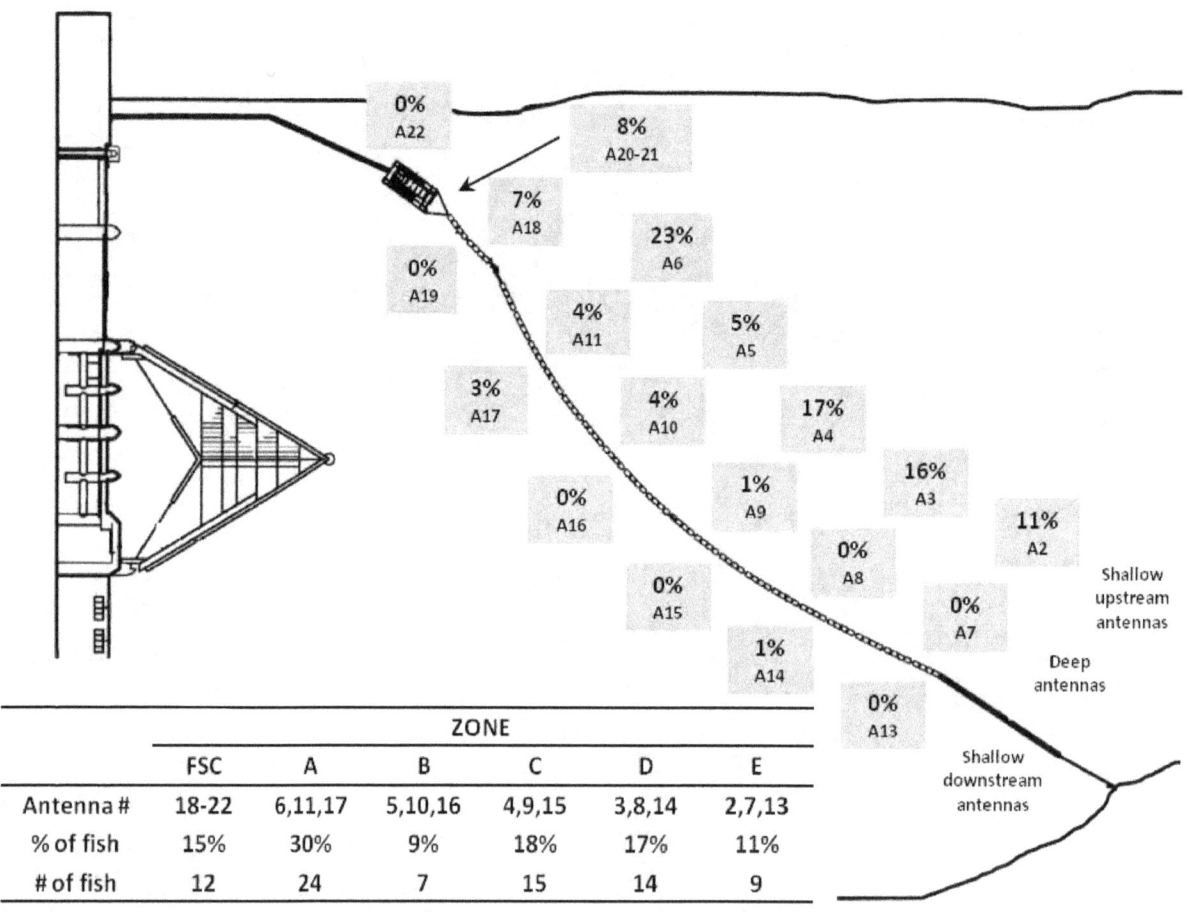

	ZONE					
	FSC	A	B	C	D	E
Antenna #	18-22	6,11,17	5,10,16	4,9,15	3,8,14	2,7,13
% of fish	15%	30%	9%	18%	17%	11%
# of fish	12	24	7	15	14	9

Figure 10. Proportion of radio-tagged juvenile steelhead that were first detected at specific detection sites along the behavioral guidance structure (BGS) and floating surface collector (FSC) in the forebay of Cowlitz Falls Dam during 2011. Individual fish were assigned a single location for the first detection.

28

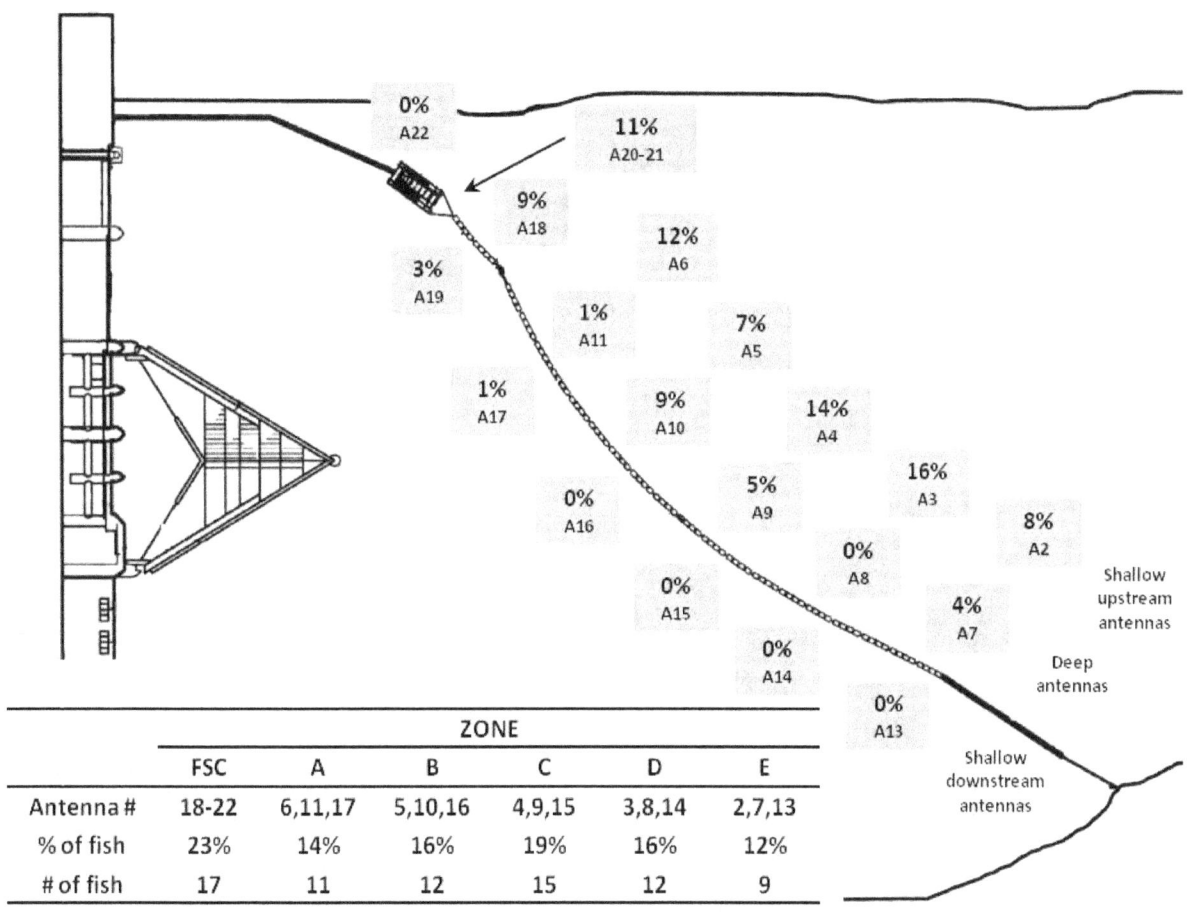

	ZONE					
	FSC	A	B	C	D	E
Antenna #	18-22	6,11,17	5,10,16	4,9,15	3,8,14	2,7,13
% of fish	23%	14%	16%	19%	16%	12%
# of fish	17	11	12	15	12	9

Figure 11. Proportion of radio-tagged juvenile coho salmon that were first detected at specific detection sites along the behavioral guidance structure (BGS) and floating surface collector (FSC) in the forebay of Cowlitz Falls Dam during 2011. Individual fish were assigned a single location for the first detection.

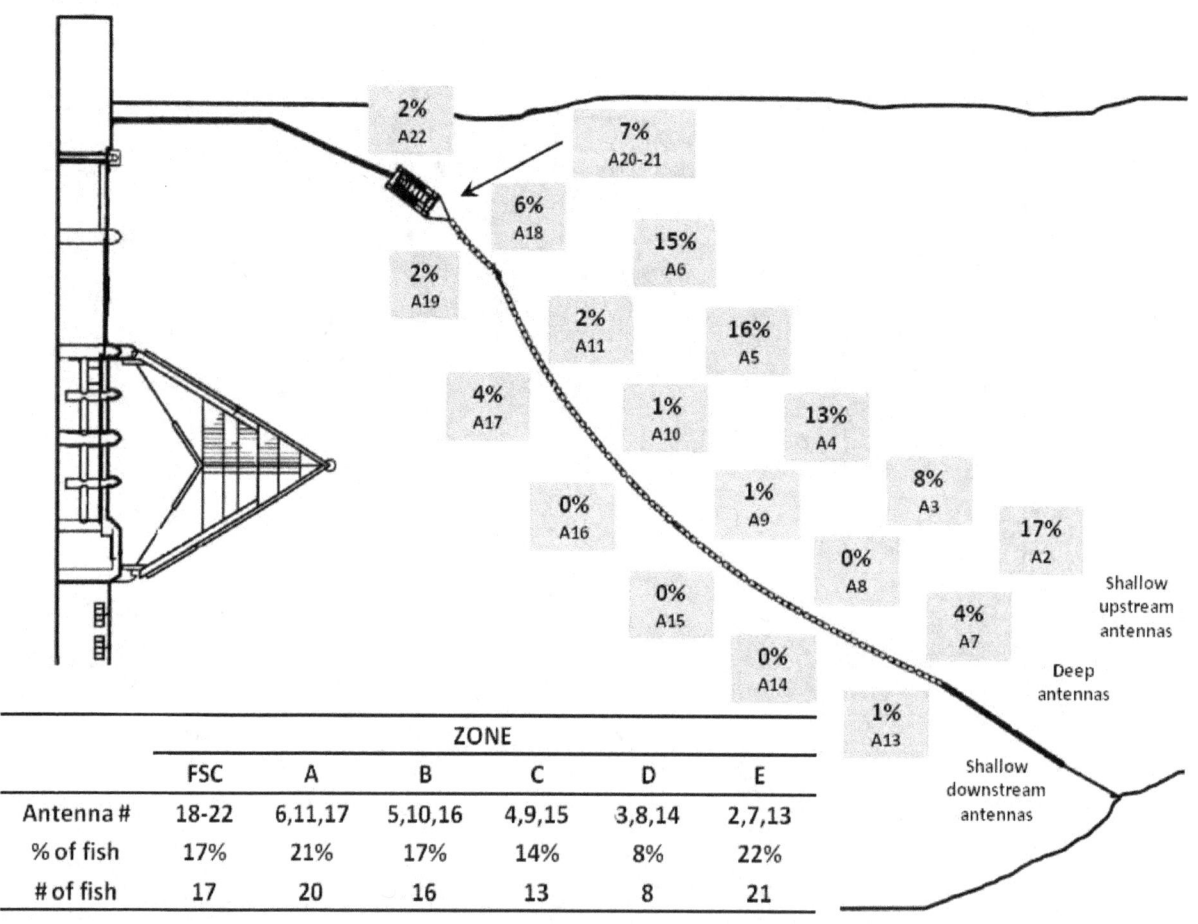

	ZONE					
	FSC	A	B	C	D	E
Antenna #	18-22	6,11,17	5,10,16	4,9,15	3,8,14	2,7,13
% of fish	17%	21%	17%	14%	8%	22%
# of fish	17	20	16	13	8	21

Figure 12. Proportion of radio-tagged juvenile Chinook salmon that were first detected at specific detection sites along the behavioral guidance structure (BGS) and floating surface collector (FSC) in the forebay of Cowlitz Falls Dam during 2011. Individual fish were assigned a single location for the first detection.

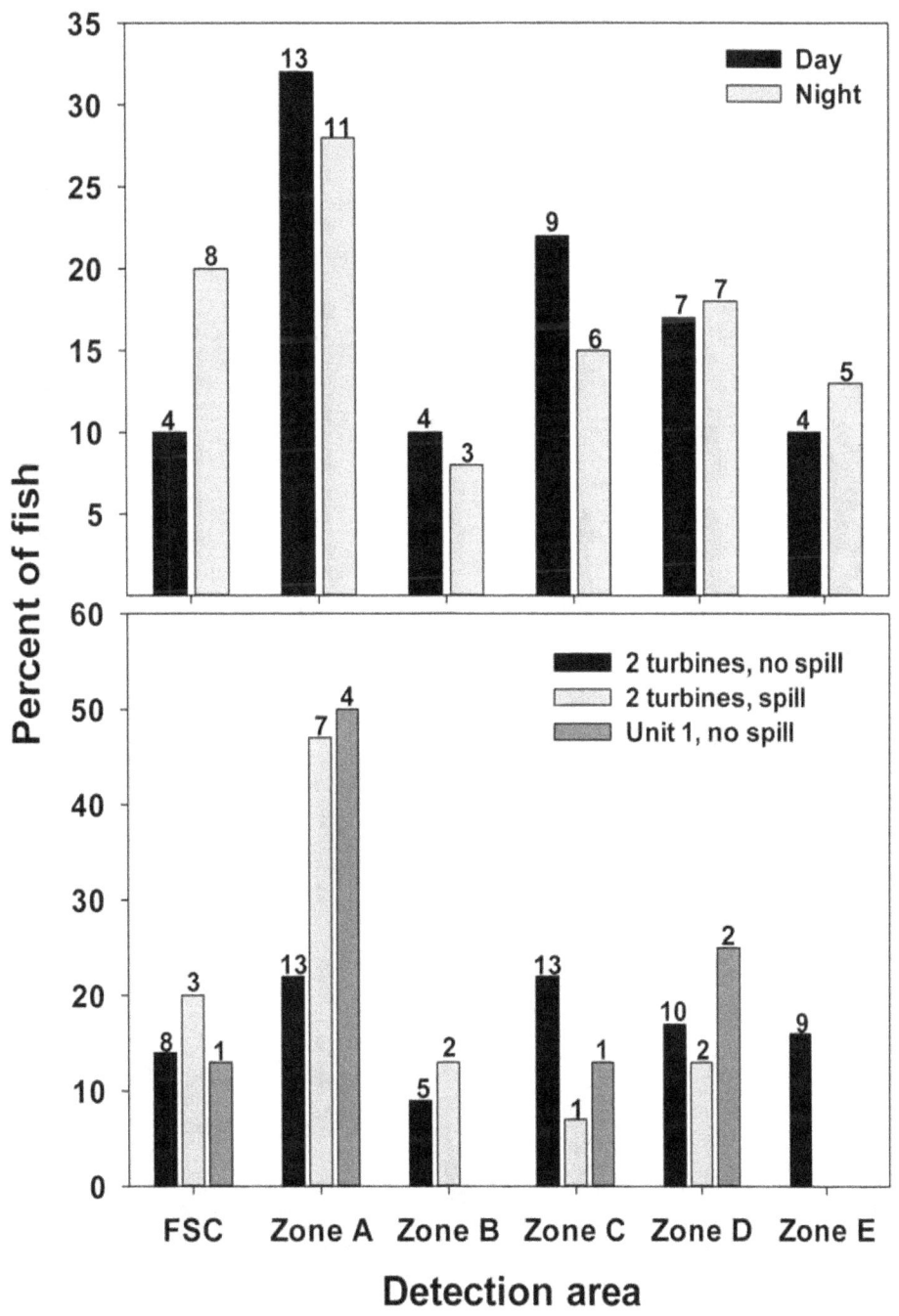

Figure 13. Detection zones for first detections of juvenile steelhead on the behavioral guidance structure (BGS) and floating surface collector (FSC) during day and night periods (top) and during various dam operating conditions (bottom) at Cowlitz Falls Dam in 2011. Numbers above bars are number of fish.

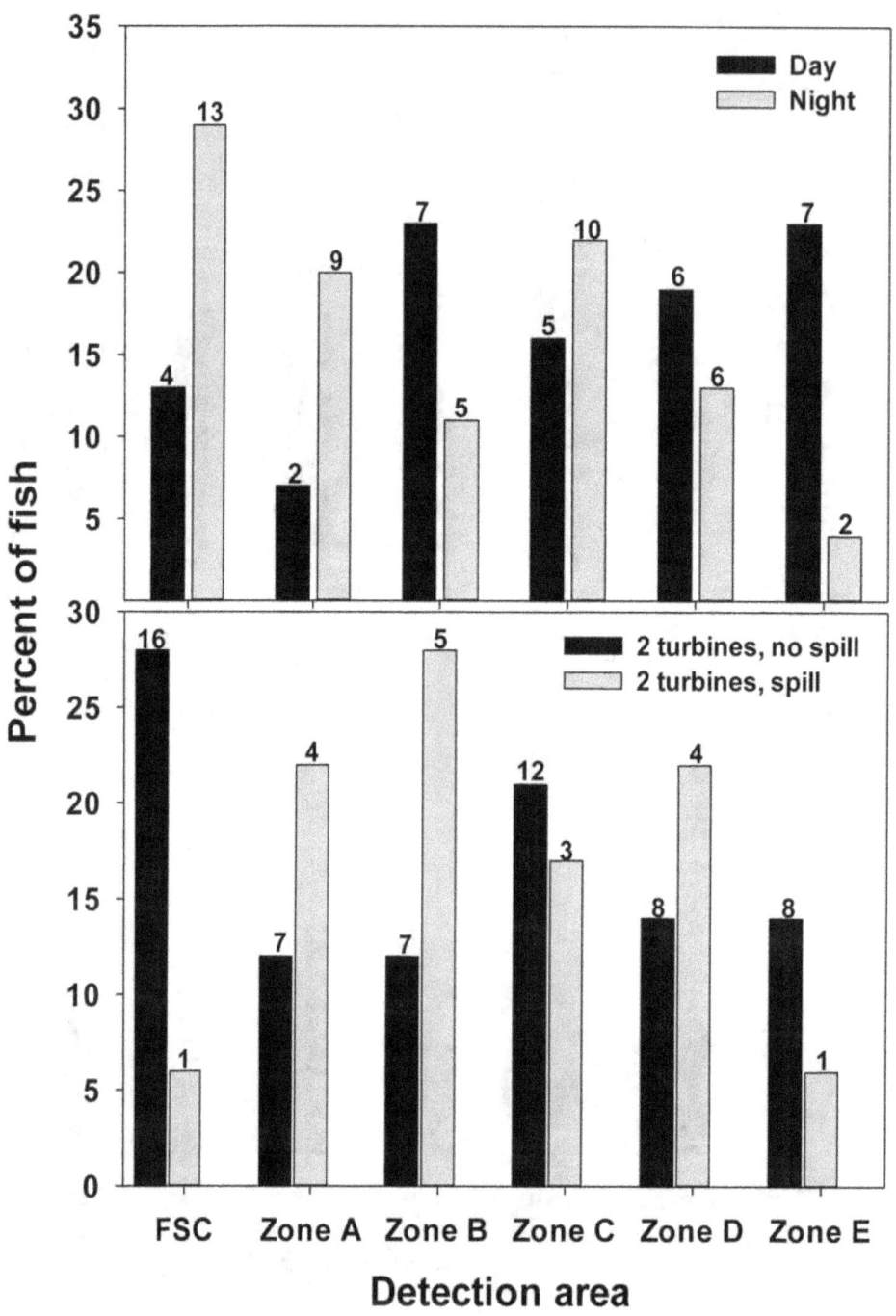

Figure 14. Detection zones for first detections of juvenile coho salmon on the BGS and FSC during day and night periods (top) and during various dam operating conditions (bottom) at Cowlitz Falls Dam in 2011. Numbers above bars are number of fish.

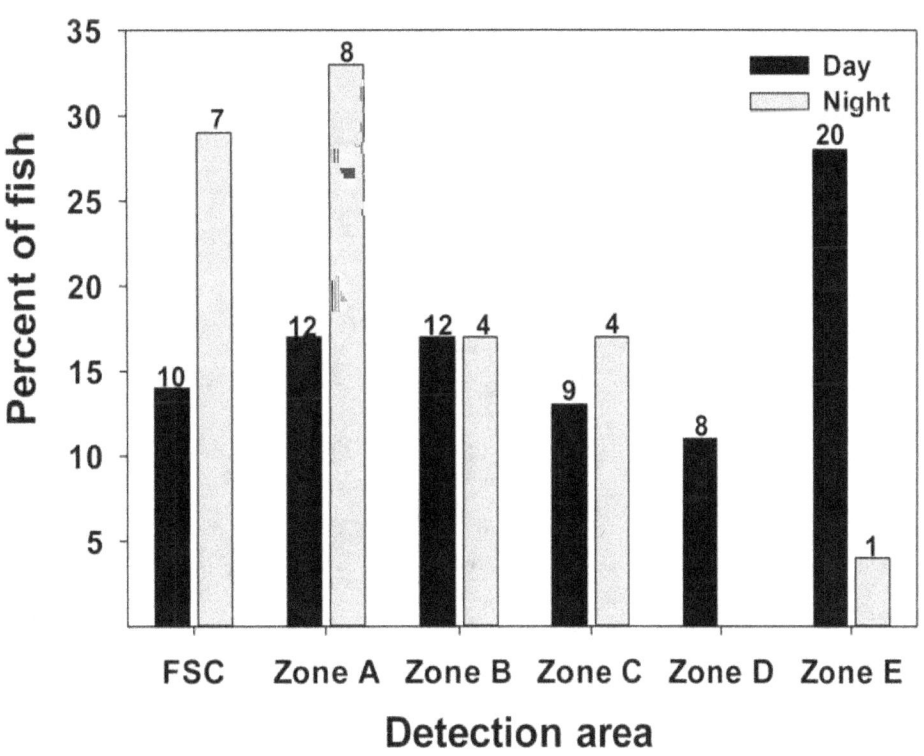

Figure 15. Detection zones for first detections of juvenile Chinook salmon on the BGS and FSC during day and night periods (top) at Cowlitz Falls Dam in 2011. Numbers above bars are number of fish.

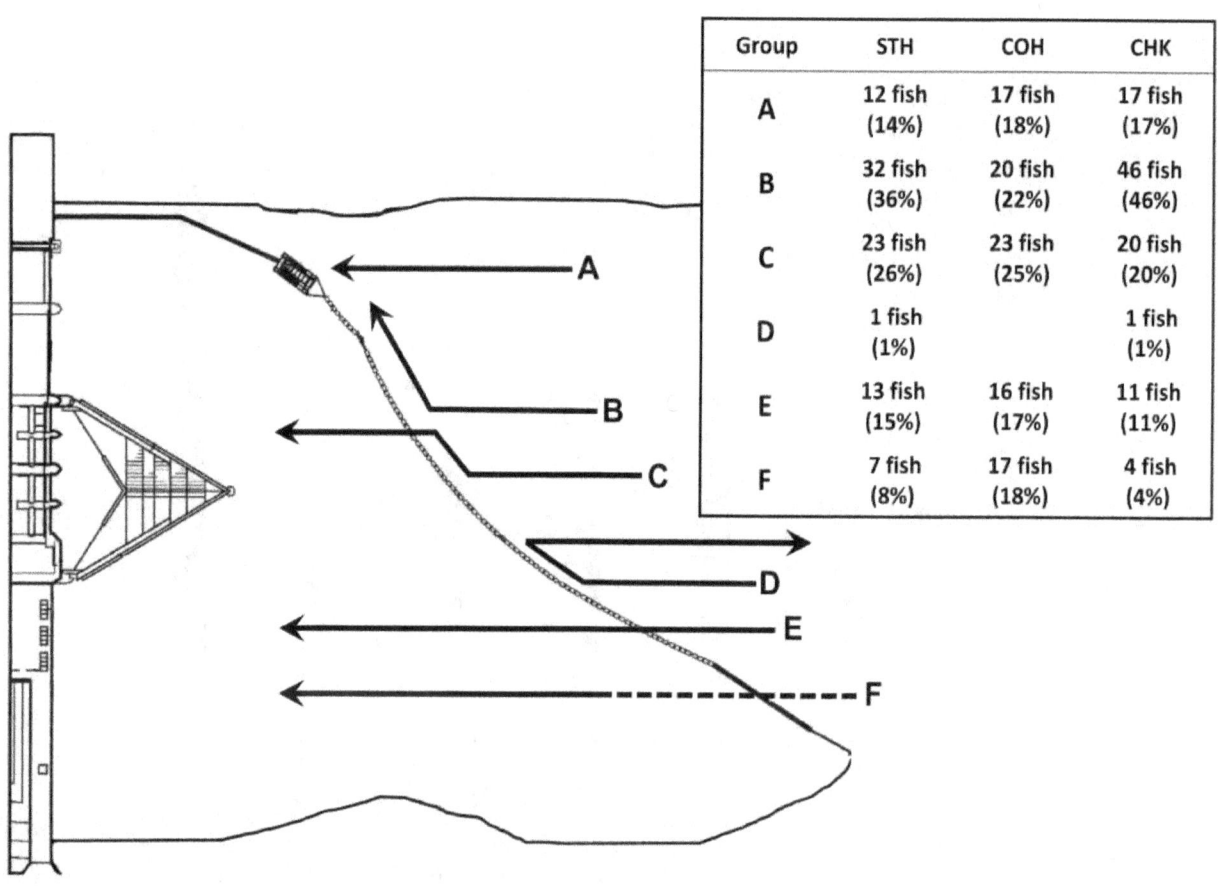

Group	STH	COH	CHK
A	12 fish (14%)	17 fish (18%)	17 fish (17%)
B	32 fish (36%)	20 fish (22%)	46 fish (46%)
C	23 fish (26%)	23 fish (25%)	20 fish (20%)
D	1 fish (1%)		1 fish (1%)
E	13 fish (15%)	16 fish (17%)	11 fish (11%)
F	7 fish (8%)	17 fish (18%)	4 fish (4%)

Figure 16. Guidance histories for juvenile steelhead, coho salmon, and Chinook salmon along the BGS at Cowlitz Falls Dam during 2011. Possible guidance histories include encountering the FSC without guidance (group A), guiding along the BGS to the FSC (group B), partial guidance along the BGS (group C), encountering the BGS and moving upstream (group D), no guidance along the BGS (group E), and no detections on the BGS prior to arriving at the dam (group F).

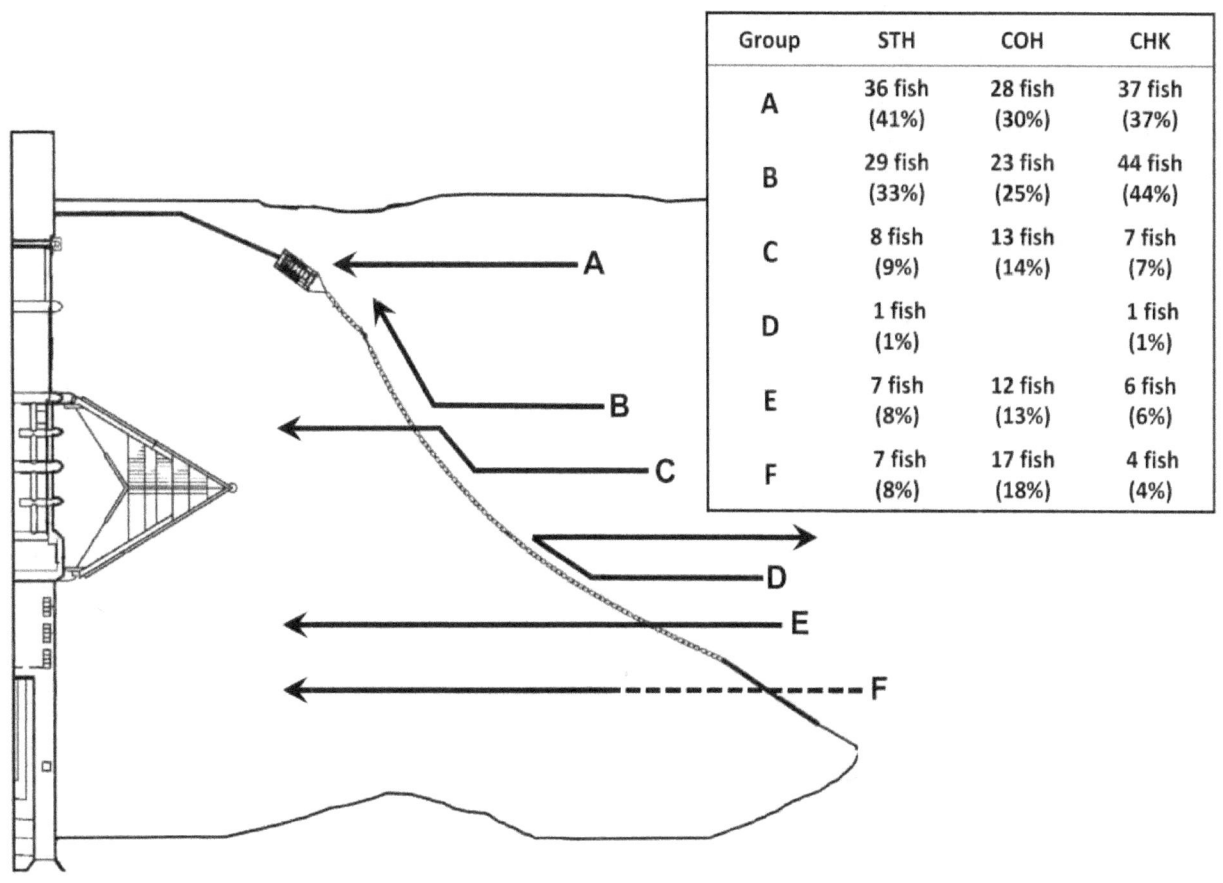

Group	STH	COH	CHK
A	36 fish (41%)	28 fish (30%)	37 fish (37%)
B	29 fish (33%)	23 fish (25%)	44 fish (44%)
C	8 fish (9%)	13 fish (14%)	7 fish (7%)
D	1 fish (1%)		1 fish (1%)
E	7 fish (8%)	12 fish (13%)	6 fish (6%)
F	7 fish (8%)	17 fish (18%)	4 fish (4%)

Figure 17. Guidance histories for juvenile steelhead, coho salmon, and Chinook salmon along the BGS at Cowlitz Falls Dam during 2011 using an liberal definition of the FSC. Antennas used for the alternative definition included the normal FSC antennas plus antennas 6, 11, and 17. Possible guidance histories include encountering the FSC without guidance (group A), guiding along the BGS to the FSC (group B), partial guidance along the BGS (group C), encountering the BGS and moving upstream (group D), no guidance along the BGS (group E), and no detections on the BGS prior to arriving at the dam (group F).

Table 1. Release date, number of fish released, mean weight, and mean fork length of juvenile steelhead monitored during a radiotelemetry evaluation at Cowlitz Falls Dam during 2011.

[Numbers in parentheses are one standard deviation from the mean. Asterisk (*) indicates release dates outside of the historical middle 95th percentile of the run timing for juvenile steelhead at Cowlitz Falls Dam]

Release date	Release site	Number of fish	Mean weight (g)	Mean fork length (mm)
27 April 2011	Cispus River	6	64.9 (18.5)	192.2 (14.4)
27 April 2011	Cowlitz River	5	67.2 (26.0)	194.6 (26.0)
1 May 2011	Cispus River	5	69.4 (18.1)	197.0 (17.2)
1 May 2011	Cowlitz River	5	85.6 (28.8)	209.4 (25.1)
6 May 2011	Cispus River	6	77.4 (16.1)	204.8 (17.4)
6 May 2011	Cowlitz River	6	75.3 (12.3)	205.5 (12.3)
11 May 2011	Cispus River	5	55.3 (10.8)	184.2 (13.8)
11 May 2011	Cowlitz River	6	66.7 (35.1)	193.0 (32.8)
16 May 2011	Cispus River	6	60.4 (17.8)	187.3 (18.3)
16 May 2011	Cowlitz River	5	52.6 (10.0)	182.2 (11.0)
25 May 2011	Cispus River	4	55.8 (10.1)	182.3 (13.6)
25 May 2011	Cowlitz River	6	61.3 (24.4)	187.7 (25.2)
26 May 2011	Cispus River	5	63.2 (13.4)	194.6 (14.0)
26 May 2011	Cowlitz River	6	76.2 (41.9)	200.7 (32.3)
1 June 2011	Cispus River	7	73.6 (19.2)	201.0 (20.4)
1 June 2011	Cowlitz River	5	56.5 (11.8)	187.0 (12.5)
6 June 2011	Cispus River	5	53.8 (17.0)	178.8 (18.4)
6 June 2011	Cowlitz River	6	49.7 (14.7)	176.2 (20.2)
16 June 2011*	Cispus River	1	50.1 (00.0)	175.0 (00.0)
16 June 2011*	Cowlitz River	1	36.7 (00.0)	155.0 (00.0)
18 June 2011*	Cispus River	2	59.2 (13.4)	184.0 (14.1)
18 June 2011*	Cowlitz River	3	69.9 (4.8)	199.0 (8.5)
19 June 2011*	Cispus River	3	63.6 (45.2)	180.7 (44.3)
19 June 2011*	Cowlitz River	1	42.3 (00.0)	168.0 (00.0)
Totals		110	64.5 (2.0)	191.5 (21.4)

Table 2. Release date, number of fish released, mean weight, and mean fork length of juvenile coho salmon monitored during a radiotelemetry evaluation at Cowlitz Falls Dam during 2011.

[Numbers in parentheses are one standard deviation from the mean. Asterisk (*) indicates release dates outside the historical middle 95th percentile of the run timing for juvenile coho salmon at Cowlitz Falls Dam]

Release date	Release site	Number of fish	Mean weight (g)	Mean fork length (mm)
11 May 2011	Cispus River	4	24.8 (3.6)	138.5 (6.6)
11 May 2011	Cowlitz River	5	24.4 (2.9)	137.4 (6.7)
16 May 2011	Cispus River	4	23.4 (5.3)	135.8 (8.8)
16 May 2011	Cowlitz River	5	20.6 (2.6)	131.0 (4.5)
25 May 2011	Cispus River	5	22.6 (3.1)	131.2 (6.3)
25 May 2011	Cowlitz River	4	23.3 (3.2)	131.3 (5.2)
26 May 2011	Cispus River	5	21.4 (2.4)	131.4 (4.7)
26 May 2011	Cowlitz River	4	21.8 (6.5)	130.5 (10.8)
1 June 2011	Cispus River	5	26.1 (2.9)	135.6 (5.7)
1 June 2011	Cowlitz River	5	27.6 (3.3)	138.4 (2.7)
6 June 2011	Cispus River	4	23.5 (4.2)	133.0 (5.7)
6 June 2011	Cowlitz River	5	24.7 (2.1)	135.8 (2.9)
11 June 2011	Cispus River	5	20.4 (3.5)	127.4 (7.8)
11 June 2011	Cowlitz River	5	17.2 (3.5)	119.8 (7.8)
16 June 2011	Cispus River	5	17.3 (2.7)	117.2 (5.0)
16 June 2011	Cowlitz River	4	17.2 (1.7)	117.8 (4.2)
21 June 2011	Cispus River	4	19.1 (4.2)	125.8 (8.7)
21 June 2011	Cowlitz River	5	17.8 (6.2)	118.8 (11.9)
26 June 2011	Cispus River	5	15.5 (3.6)	114.0 (9.3)
26 June 2011	Cowlitz River	4	19.3 (5.7)	119.8 (10.0)
1 July 2011	Cispus River	4	18.6 (2.9)	122.0 (8.4)
1 July 2011	Cowlitz River	5	17.3 (2.6)	118.6 (4.2)
6 July 2011	Cispus River	3	17.4 (1.0)	117.3 (5.5)
6 July 2011	Cowlitz River	3	18.3 (5.9)	121.3 (16.3)
16 July 2011*	Cispus River	2	18.0 (1.6)	124.5 (2.1)
16 July 2011*	Cowlitz River	1	16.2 (0.0)	119.0 (0.0)
Totals		110	20.8 (4.7)	127.1 (10.2)

Table 3. Release date, number of fish released, mean weight, and mean fork length of juvenile Chinook salmon monitored during a radiotelemetry evaluation at Cowlitz Falls Dam during 2011.

[Numbers in parentheses are one standard deviation from the mean]

Release date	Release site	Number of fish	Mean weight (g)	Mean fork length (mm)
31 July 2011	Cispus River	4	23.1 (2.8)	129.3 (5.7)
31 July 2011	Cowlitz River	3	23.9 (2.5)	130.3 (2.9)
3 August 2011	Cispus River	9	27.9 (5.5)	134.7 (8.7)
3 August 2011	Cowlitz River	9	25.5 (3.0)	133.3 (4.9)
6 August 2011	Cispus River	8	24.7 (3.2)	132.5 (4.3)
6 August 2011	Cowlitz River	11	21.4 (2.9)	126.5 (5.5)
9 August 2011	Cispus River	10	27.2 (3.9)	134.4 (6.3)
9 August 2011	Cowlitz River	9	24.2 (3.6)	129.7 (6.9)
12 August 2011	Cispus River	10	26.7 (5.3)	134.0 (7.5)
12 August 2011	Cowlitz River	9	25.1 (5.5)	131.0 (10.4)
15 August 2011	Cispus River	9	28.2 (3.3)	138.1 (5.3)
15 August 2011	Cowlitz River	9	25.0 (2.6)	133.4 (4.9)
17 August 2011	Cispus River	5	27.7 (7.3)	135.6 (12.0)
17 August 2011	Cowlitz River	5	24.6 (5.0)	130.2 (8.2)
Totals		110	25.4 (4.4)	132.5 (7.2)

Table 4. Summary of the number of radio-tagged steelhead, coho salmon, and Chinook salmon that made upstream trips during 2011.

[Upstream trips were defined by a minimum upstream movement by tagged fish from the forebay of Cowlitz Falls Dam to the fixed monitoring site located 1.3 river kilometers upstream of the dam]

Species	Number of upstream trips								Total
	0	1	2	3	4	5	6-10	10-12	
Steelhead	75 (77%)	12 (12%)	5 (5%)	1 (1%)	2 (2%)	3 (3%)	0	0	98
Coho salmon	95 (95%)	5 (5%)	0	0	0	0	0	0	100
Chinook salmon	19 (19%)	15 (15%)	12 (12%)	24 (24%)	5 (5%)	12 (12%)	7 (7%)	5 (5%)	99

Table 5. Number and percentage of radio-tagged juvenile steelhead, coho salmon and Chinook salmon that were first detected on underwater antennas on Cowlitz Falls Dam during 2011.

Species	Debris barrier					Spillbay 4	Spillbay 3	Spillbay 2	Spillbay 1	Total
	Antenna 23	Antenna 24	Antenna 25	Antenna 26	Antenna 27	Antenna 28	Antenna 29	Antenna 30	Antenna 31	
Steelhead	21 (22%)	16 (17%)	13 (14%)	2 (2%)	7 (7%)	8 (9%)	2 (2%)	3 (3%)	22 (23%)	94
Coho salmon	9 (10%)	17 (19%)	10 (11%)	5 (6%)	7 (8%)	11 (12%)	1 (1%)	3 (3%)	26 (29%)	89
Chinook salmon	13 (13%)	23 (24%)	11 (11%)	5 (5%)	9 (9%)	2 (2%)	1 (1%)	3 (3%)	30 (31%)	97

40

Table 6. Number and percentage of radio-tagged juvenile steelhead that were first detected on underwater antennas on Cowlitz Falls during day and night periods and under various dam operating conditions in 2011.

| Condition | Debris barrier | | | | | Spillbay 4 | Spillbay 3 | Spillbay 2 | Spillbay 1 | Total |
	Antenna 23	Antenna 24	Antenna 25	Antenna 26	Antenna 27	Antenna 28	Antenna 29	Antenna 30	Antenna 31	
Day	15 (26%)	14 (24%)	9 (16%)	1 (2%)	5 (9%)	4 (7%)	0	2 (3%)	8 (14%)	58
Night	6 (17%)	2 (6%)	4 (11%)	1 (3%)	2 (6%)	4 (11%)	2 (6%)	1 (3%)	14 (39%)	36
Two turbines, no spill	11 (18%)	14 (22%)	8 (13%)	2 (3%)	4 (6%)	6 (10%)	1 (2%)	2 (3%)	15 (24%)	63
Two turbines, spill	7 (32%)	2 (9%)	3 (14%)	0	3 (14%)	0	0	1 (5%)	6 (27%)	22
Unit 1, no spill	3 (33%)	0	2 (22%)	0	0	2 (22%)	1 (11%)	0	1 (11%)	9

Table 7. Number and percentage of radio-tagged juvenile coho salmon that were first detected on underwater antennas on Cowlitz Falls Dam during day and night periods and under various dam operating conditions in 2011.

Condition	Debris barrier					Spillbay 4	Spillbay 3	Spillbay 2	Spillbay 1	Total
	Antenna 23	Antenna 24	Antenna 25	Antenna 26	Antenna 27	Antenna 28	Antenna 29	Antenna 30	Antenna 31	
Day	7 (16%)	13 (30%)	4 (9%)	3 (7%)	4 (9%)	5 (12%)	0	0	7 (16%)	43
Night	2 (4%)	4 (9%)	6 (13%)	2 (4%)	3 (7%)	6 (13%)	1 (2%)	3 (7%)	19 (41%)	46
Two turbines, no spill	7 (11%)	6 (9%)	9 (14%)	4 (6%)	5 (8%)	10 (16%)	0	1 (2%)	22 (34%)	64
Two turbines, spill	2 (8%)	11 (44%)	1 (4%)	1 (4%)	2 (8%)	1 (4%)	1 (4%)	2 (8%)	4 (16%)	25

Table 8. Number and percentage of radio-tagged juvenile Chinook salmon that were detected on underwater antennas on Cowlitz Falls Dam during day and night periods and under various dam operating conditions in 2011.

| Condition | Debris barrier | | | | | Spillbay 4 | Spillbay 3 | Spillbay 2 | Spillbay 1 | |
	Antenna 23	Antenna 24	Antenna 25	Antenna 26	Antenna 27	Antenna 28	Antenna 29	Antenna 30	Antenna 31	Total
Day	12 (16%)	15 (21%)	7 (10%)	3 (4%)	9 (12%)	2 (3%)	1 (1%)	3 (4%)	21 (29%)	73
Night	1 (4%)	8 (33%)	4 (17%)	2 (8%)	0	0	0	0	9 (38%)	24
One turbine, no spill	13 (13%)	23 (24%)	11 (11%)	5 (5%)	9 (9%)	2 (2%)	1 (1%)	3 (3%)	30 (31%)	97

43

Table 9. Number and percentage of juvenile steelhead, coho salmon, and Chinook salmon detected near proposed collector entrances at Cowlitz Falls Dam during 2011.

Detection zone	Both locations	FSC only	Spillbays only	At least one location	Neither location
Steelhead					
FSC and spillbays 2-3	60 (61%)	11 (11%)	15 (15%)	86 (88%)	12 (12%)
FSC and spillbays 1-4	69 (70%)	2 (2%)	20 (20%)	91 (93%)	7 (7%)
Liberal FSC and spillbays 2-3	68 (69%)	13 (13%)	7 (7%)	88 (90%)	10 (10%)
Liberal FSC and spillbays 1-4	78 (80%)	3 (3%)	11 (11%)	92 (94%)	6 (6%)
Coho salmon					
FSC and spillbays 2-3	33 (33%)	15 (15%)	28 (28%)	76 (76%)	24 (24%)
FSC and spillbays 1-4	42 (42%)	6 (6%)	38 (38%)	86 (86%)	14 (14%)
Liberal FSC and spillbays 2-3	42 (42%)	23 (23%)	19 (19%)	84 (84%)	16 (16%)
Liberal FSC and spillbays 1-4	54 (54%)	11 (11%)	26 (26%)	91 (91%)	9 (9%)
Chinook salmon					
FSC and spillbays 2-3	87 (88%)	3 (3%)	4 (4%)	94 (95%)	5 (5%)
FSC and spillbays 1-4	90 (91%)	0	4 (4%)	94 (95%)	5 (5%)
Liberal FSC and spillbays 2-3	89 (90%)	3 (3%)	2 (2%)	94 (95%)	5 (5%)
Liberal FSC and spillbays 1-4	92 (93%)	0	2 (2%)	94 (95%)	5 (5%)

Table 10. Average elapsed time (min) spent by juvenile steelhead, coho salmon, and Chinook salmon in distinct areas of the forebay of Cowlitz Falls Dam as measured using radiotelemetry during 2011.

[Numbers in parentheses are one standard deviation from the mean]

Forebay area	Antennas	Steelhead		Coho salmon		Chinook salmon	
		n	mean (std)	*n*	mean (std)	*n*	mean (std)
BGS	2–11, 13–17	80	76.2 (815.9)	71	4.4 (118.6)	93	1725.4 (11726.6)
FSC	18–20, 22	71	20.3 (315.3)	49	2.8 (150.9)	91	34.4 (1836.6)
Debris barrier	23-27	90	69.7 (3046.1)	79	9.3 (113.0)	96	134.3 (4255.0)
Spillbay 1	31	65	79.0 (277.7)	41	21.3 (139.5)	84	46.9 (215.4)
Spillbay 2 entrances	30	66	64.6 (789.2)	47	9.3 (772.7)	91	225.1 (452.9)
Spillbay 3 entrances	29	45	472.2 (1676.4)	24	4.8 (1999.6)	86	9.5 (25.0)
Spillbay 4	28	58	25.4 (214.6)	30	6.8 (400.6)	85	46.1 (187.3)
Inside spillbay 2	33	59	22.4 (368.0)	35	11.3 (287.0)	87	43.1 (108.3)
Inside spillbay 3	33	41	91.6 (1739.0)	19	18.1 (1085.7)	54	5.5 (19.3)

Table 11. Assigned passage routes for radio-tagged juvenile steelhead, coho salmon, and Chinook salmon at Cowlitz Falls Dam during 2011.

[Fish that did not pass the dam prior to transmitter failure were assigned to the "did not pass" category. Numbers in parentheses are number of fish]

Species	Flumes	Floating surface collector	Turbines[1]	Turbines or spillbay[2]	Did not pass	Total
Steelhead	37% (36)	0	40% (39)	22% (22)	1% (1)	98
Coho salmon	14% (14)	0	53% (53)	32% (32)	1% (1)	100
Chinook salmon	22% (22)	1% (1)	33% (34)	0	43% (42)	99

[1]Known turbine passage, no spillways open.
[2]Unknown turbine or spillway passage, spillways open.

Table 12. Assigned passage routes using alternative detection criteria (compared to table 11) for radio-tagged juvenile steelhead, coho salmon, and Chinook salmon at Cowlitz Falls Dam during 2011.

[Detection data consisting of only one valid detection at a given site in the forebay were used in an attempt to distinguish between turbine and spillbay passage routes when both routes were available to tagged fish. Fish that did not pass the dam prior to transmitter failure were assigned to the "did not pass" category. The gray shaded area identifies the number of fish that were assigned turbine or spillbay passage during periods when both routes were available at the dam. Numbers in parentheses are number of fish]

Species	Flumes	Floating surface collector	Turbines[1]	Turbines	Spillbay	Did not pass	Total
Steelhead	37% (36)	0	40% (39)	16% (16)	6% (6)	1% (1)	98
Coho salmon	14% (14)	0	53% (53)	26% (26)	6% (6)	1% (1)	100
Chinook salmon	22% (22)	1% (1)	33% (34)	0	0	43% (42)	99

[1]Known turbine passage, no spillways open.

Table 13. Movement probabilities from the approach dataset for radio-tagged juvenile steelhead in the forebay of Cowlitz Falls Dam during 2011.

[Some state descriptions include BGS and FSC which stand for behavioral guidance structure and floating surface collector, respectively. Each cell contains five rows of data including the probability of movement (row 1), the 95-percent confidence interval for the probability estimate (row 2) the number of movements (row 3), the number of fish that made movements (row 4), and the average number of movements per fish (row 5)]

Current location	Next location										
	South upstream BGS state	South downstream BGS state	North upstream BGS state	North downstream BGS state	FSC state	North FSC gap state	Debris barrier state	Spillbay 1 state	Spillbay 2-3 state	Spillbay 4 state	Tailrace state
Forebay entry	0.378 0.156 37 37 1.0	0.010 0.195 1 1 1.0	0.296 0.166 29 29 1.0	0.020 0.194 2 2 1.0	0.102 0.188 10 10 1.0	0.020 0.194 2 2 1.0	0.122 0.185 12 12 1.0	0.000	0.010 0.195 1 1.0	0.010 0.195 1 1.0	0.031 0.196 3 3 1.0
South upstream BGS state	n/a	0.089 0.250 5 4 1.3	0.554 0.175 31 26 1.2	0.036 0.258 2 2 1.0	0.054 0.256 3 3 1.0	0.071 0.252 4 4 1.0	0.089 0.250 5 5 1.0	0.018 0.261 1 1 1.0	0.018 0.261 1 1 1.0	0.054 0.256 3 3 1.0	0.018 0.261 1 1 1.0
South downstream BGS state	0.444 0.487 4 3 1.3	n/a	0.111 0.616 1 1 1.0	0.111 0.616 1 1 1.0	0.000	0.111 0.616 1 1 1.0	0.111 0.616 1 1 1.0	0.000	0.000	0.111 0.616 1 1 1.0	0.000
North upstream BGS state	0.143 0.183 14 11 1.3	0.020 0.194 2 2 1.0	n/a	0.398 0.154 39 10 3.9	0.184 0.179 18 17 1.1	0.041 0.194 4 4 1.0	0.174 0.180 17 17 1.0	0.010 0.195 1 1 1.0	0.020 0.194 2 2 1.0	0.010 0.195 1 1 1.0	0.000
North downstream BGS state	0.000	0.017 0.253 1 1 1.0	0.542 0.173 32 7 4.6	n/a	0.288 0.215 17 4 4.3	0.017 0.253 1 1 1.0	0.085 0.244 5 5 1.0	0.034 0.251 2 2 1.0	0.000	0.017 0.253 1 1 1.0	0.000
FSC state	0.000	0.000	0.065 0.242 4 4 1.0	0.242 0.217 15 4 3.8	n/a	0.307 0.207 19 10 1.9	0.209 0.221 13 13 1.0	0.177 0.226 11 11 1.0	0.000	0.000	0.000
North FSC gap state	0.032 0.345 1 1 1.0	0.000	0.032 0.345 1 1 1.0	0.000	0.452 0.261 14 7 2.0	n/a	0.194 0.316 6 6 1.0	0.226 0.310 7 7 1.0	0.032 0.345 1 1 1.0	0.032 0.345 1 1 1.0	0.000

Table 14. Movement probabilities from the approach dataset for radio-tagged coho salmon in the forebay of Cowlitz Falls Dam during 2011.

[Some state descriptions include BGS and FSC which stand for behavioral guidance structure and floating surface collector, respectively. Each cell contains five rows of data including the probability of movement (row 1), the 95 percent confidence interval for the probability estimate (row 2) the number of movements (row 3), the number of fish that made movements (row 4), and the average number of movements per fish (row 5)]

Current location	Next location										
	South upstream BGS state	South downstream BGS state	North upstream BGS state	North downstream BGS state	FSC state	North FSC gap state	Debris barrier state	Spillbay 1 state	Spillbay 2-3 state	Spillbay 4 state	Tailrace state
Forebay entry	0.356 0.156 36 36 1.0	0.000	0.218 0.173 22 22 1.0	0.010 0.195 1 1 1.0	0.139 0.181 14 14 1.0	0.030 0.193 3 3 1.0	0.129 0.182 13 13 1.0	0.050 0.191 5 5 1.0	0.020 0.194 2 2 1.0	0.010 0.195 1 1 1.0	0.040 0.192 4 4 1.0
South upstream BGS state	n/a	0.196 0.259 9 8 1.1	0.522 0.200 24 22 1.1	0.065 0.279 3 3 1.0	0.065 0.279 3 3 1.0	0.000	0.087 0.276 4 4 1.0	0.000	0.000	0.022 0.287 1 1 1.0	0.044 0.284 2 2 1.0
South downstream BGS state	0.200 0.554 2 2 1.0	n/a	0.200 0.554 2 2 1.0	0.000	0.000	0.000	0.200 0.554 2 2 1.0	0.000	0.000	0.300 0.519 3 3 1.0	0.100 0.588 1 1 1.0
North upstream BGS state	0.085 0.244 5 4 1.3	0.017 0.253 1 1 1.0	n/a	0.322 0.210 19 14 1.4	0.254 0.220 15 15 1.0	0.051 0.249 3 3 1.0	0.136 0.238 8 8 1.0	0.034 0.251 2 2 1.0	0.000	0.068 0.247 4 4 1.0	0.034 0.251 2 2 1.0
North downstream BGS state	0.000	0.000	0.346 0.311 9 5 1.8	n/a	0.115 0.361 3 2 1.5	0.000	0.346 0.311 9 9 1.0	0.000	0.039 0.379 1 1 1.0	0.077 0.369 2 2 1.0	0.077 0.369 2 2 1.0
FSC state	0.033 0.248 2 2 1.0	0.000	0.033 0.248 2 2 1.0	0.050 0.247 3 3 1.0	n/a	0.550 0.170 33 12 2.8	0.117 0.238 7 7 1.0	0.183 0.229 11 11 1.0	0.017 0.253 1 1 1.0	0.000	0.017 0.253 1 1 1.0
North FSC gap state	0.026 0.312 1 1 1.0	0.000	0.000	0.000	0.641 0.188 25 6 4.2	n/a	0.128 0.293 5 5 1.0	0.205 0.280 8 8 1.0	0.000	0.000	0.000

48

Table 15. Movement probabilities from the approach dataset for radio-tagged Chinook salmon in the forebay of Cowlitz Falls Dam during 2011.

[Some state descriptions include BGS and FSC which stand for behavioral guidance structure and floating surface collector, respectively. Each cell contains five rows of data including the probability of movement (row 1), the 95 percent confidence interval for the probability estimate (row 2) the number of movements (row 3), the number of fish that made movements (row 4), and the average number of movements per fish (row 5)]

Current location	Next location										
	South upstream BGS state	South downstream BGS state	North upstream BGS state	North downstream BGS state	FSC state	North FSC gap state	Debris barrier state	Spillbay 1 state	Spillbay 2-3 state	Spillbay 4 state	Tailrace state
Forebay entry	0.414 0.151 41 41 1.0	0.010 0.195 1 1 1.0	0.323 0.162 32 32 1.0	0.040 0.192 4 4 1.0	0.152 0.182 15 15 1.0	0.020 0.194 2 2 1.0	0.030 0.193 3 3 1.0	0.000	0.000	0.000	0.010 0.195 1 1 1.0
South upstream BGS state	n/a	0.369 0.193 24 18 1.3	0.462 0.178 30 29 1.1	0.046 0.237 3 3 1.0	0.015 0.238 1 1 1.0	0.000	0.092 0.231 6 6 1.0	0.000	0.000	0.015 0.238 1 1 1.0	0.000
South downstream BGS state	0.556 0.251 15 11 1.4	n/a	0.000	0.148 0.348 4 4 1.0	0.037 0.370 1 1 1.0	0.000	0.222 0.333 6 6 1.0	0.000	0.000	0.037 0.370 1 1 1.0	0.000
North upstream BGS state	0.058 0.187 6 5 1.2	0.000	n/a	0.437 0.145 45 33 1.4	0.408 0.149 42 37 1.1	0.029 0.190 3 3 1.0	0.029 0.190 3 3 1.0	0.029 0.190 3 3 1.0	0.010 0.195 1 1 1.0	0.000	0.000
North downstream BGS state	0.016 0.246 1 1 1.0	0.016 0.246 1 1 1.0	0.468 0.182 29 19 1.5	n/a	0.161 0.228 10 9 1.1	0.000	0.226 0.219 14 14 1.0	0.097 0.237 6 6 1.0	0.016 0.246 1 1 1.0	0.000	0.000
FSC state	0.022 0.203 2 2 1.0	0.011 0.204 1 1 1.0	0.118 0.191 11 10 1.1	0.065 0.197 6 5 1.2	n/a	0.258 0.175 24 15 1.6	0.290 0.171 27 27 1.0	0.215 0.180 20 20 1.0	0.022 0.203 2 2 1.0	0.000	0.000
North FSC gap state	0.035 0.360 1 1 1.0	0.000	0.000	0.000	0.828 0.151 24 15 1.6	n/a	0.069 0.351 2 2 1.0	0.035 0.360 1 1 1.0	0.000	0.000	0.035 0.360 1 1 1.0

Table 16. Movement probabilities from the residence dataset for radio-tagged juvenile steelhead in the forebay of Cowlitz Falls Dam during 2011.

[Some state descriptions include BGS and FSC which stand for behavioral guidance structure and floating surface collector, respectively. Each cell contains five rows of data including the probability of movement (row 1), the 95 percent confidence interval for the probability estimate (row 2) the number of movements (row 3), the number of fish that made movements (row 4), and the average number of movements per fish (row 5)]

Current location	Next location											
	South upstream BGS state	South downstream BGS state	North upstream BGS state	North downstream BGS state	FSC state	North FSC gap state	Debris barrier state	Spillbay 1 state	Spillbay 2-3 state	Spillbay 4 state	Fish facility state	Tailrace state
South upstream BGS state	n/a	0.325 0.124 55 27 2.0	0.296 0.127 50 22 2.3	0.095 0.144 16 13 1.2	0.059 0.146 10 8 1.3	0.083 0.145 14 11 1.3	0.071 0.145 12 10 1.2	0.018 0.150 3 2 1.5	0.030 0.150 5 5 1.0	0.018 0.150 3 3 1.0	0.000	0.006 0.151 1 1 1.0
South downstream BGS state	0.395 0.097 98 33 3.0	n/a	0.057 0.121 14 11 1.3	0.327 0.102 81 34 2.4	0.028 0.122 7 5 1.4	0.020 0.123 5 5 1.0	0.109 0.118 27 18 1.5	0.020 0.123 5 4 1.3	0.004 0.124 1 1 1.0	0.036 0.122 9 8 1.1	0.000	0.004 0.124 1 1 1.0
North upstream BGS state	0.077 0.088 35 19 1.8	0.033 0.090 15 9 1.7	n/a	0.661 0.053 302 43 7.0	0.092 0.087 42 25 1.7	0.046 0.090 21 13 1.6	0.068 0.089 31 22 1.4	0.013 0.091 6 6 1.0	0.007 0.094 3 2 1.5	0.004 0.087 2 2 1.0	0.000	0.000
North downstream BGS state	0.008 0.071 6 5 1.2	0.082 0.067 64 31 2.1	0.435 0.053 341 46 7.4	n/a	0.276 0.060 216 40 5.4	0.001 0.062 1 1 1.0	0.153 0.064 120 40 3.0	0.022 0.070 17 15 1.1	0.001 0.062 1 1 1.0	0.023 0.069 18 12 1.5	0.000	0.000
FSC state	0.019 0.089 9 8 1.1	0.023 0.089 11 8 1.4	0.054 0.087 26 19 1.4	0.496 0.063 241 40 6.0	n/a	0.095 0.085 46 23 2.0	0.235 0.078 114 41 2.8	0.054 0.087 26 20 1.3	0.010 0.087 5 5 1.0	0.017 0.090 8 8 1.0	0.000	0.000
North FSC gap state	0.075 0.183 8 7 1.1	0.019 0.189 2 1 2.0	0.028 0.187 3 3 1.0	0.047 0.186 5 5 1.0	0.252 0.164 27 16 1.7	n/a	0.206 0.169 22 17 1.3	0.318 0.157 34 19 1.8	0.037 0.185 4 4 1.0	0.019 0.189 2 2 1.0	0.000	0.000

Table 16. Movement probabilities from the residence dataset for radio-tagged juvenile steelhead in the forebay of Cowlitz Falls Dam during 2011.—Continued

[Some state descriptions include BGS and FSC which stand for behavioral guidance structure and floating surface collector, respectively. Each cell contains five rows of data including the probability of movement (row 1), the 95 percent confidence interval for the probability estimate (row 2) the number of movements (row 3), the number of fish that made movements (row 4), and the average number of movements per fish (row 5)]

Current location		South upstream BGS state	South downstream BGS state	North upstream BGS state	North downstream BGS state	FSC state	North FSC gap state	Debris barrier state	Spillbay 1 state	Spillbay 2-3 state	Spillbay 4 state	Fish facility state	Tailrace state
Debris barrier state		0.008	0.066	0.016	0.110	0.150	0.011	n/a	0.191	0.167	0.265	0.000	0.016
		0.066	0.062	0.063	0.061	0.060	0.065		0.058	0.059	0.055		0.063
		7	61	15	101	138	10		175	153	243		15
		5	29	13	37	40	9		50	67	53		15
		1.4	2.1	1.2	2.7	3.5	1.1		3.5	2.3	4.6		1.0
Spillbay 1 state		0.003	0.027	0.007	0.050	0.097	0.020	0.710	n/a	0.060	0.013	0.003	0.010
		0.107	0.112	0.116	0.110	0.108	0.112	0.061		0.110	0.111	0.107	0.113
		1	8	2	15	29	6	213		18	4	1	3
		1	7	2	12	19	6	55		13	3	1	3
		1.0	1.1	1.0	1.3	1.5	1.0	3.9		1.4	1.3	1.0	1.0
Spillbays 2-3 state		0.000	0.010	0.005	0.010	0.005	0.010	0.555	0.055	n/a	0.030	0.175	0.145
			0.138	0.138	0.138	0.138	0.138	0.092	0.135		0.136	0.126	0.128
			2	1	2	1	2	111	11		6	35	29
			2	1	2	1	2	38	10		5	35	29
			1.0	1.0	1.0	1.0	1.0	2.9	1.1		1.2	1.0	1.0
Spillbay 4 state		0.017	0.099	0.017	0.069	0.053	0.007	0.690	0.003	0.020	n/a	0.000	0.026
		0.113	0.107	0.113	0.108	0.110	0.116	0.063	0.107	0.112			0.110
		5	30	5	21	16	2	209	1	6			8
		5	19	5	15	13	2	47	1	6			8
		1.0	1.6	1.0	1.4	1.2	1.0	4.4	1.0	1.0			1.0

51

Table 17. Movement probabilities from the residence dataset for radio-tagged juvenile coho salmon in the forebay of Cowlitz Falls Dam during 2011.

[Some state descriptions include BGS and FSC which stand for behavioral guidance structure and floating surface collector, respectively. Each cell contains five rows of data including the probability of movement (row 1), the 95 percent confidence interval for the probability estimate (row 2) the number of movements (row 3), the number of fish that made movements (row 4), and the average number of movements per fish (row 5)]

Current location	South upstream BGS state	South downstream BGS state	North upstream BGS state	North downstream BGS state	FSC state	North FSC gap state	Debris barrier state	Spillbay 1 state	Spillbay 2-3 state	Spillbay 4 state	Fish facility state	Tailrace state
South upstream BGS state	n/a	0.387 0.276 12 7 1.7	0.419 0.268 13 9 1.4	0.065 0.342 2 1 2.0	0.032 0.345 1 1 1.0	0.000	0.065 0.342 2 2 1.0	0.000	0.000	0.000	0.000	0.032 0.345 1 1 1.0
South downstream BGS state	0.439 0.229 18 10 1.8	n/a	0.073 0.294 3 2 1.5	0.293 0.258 12 6 2.0	0.024 0.300 1 1 1.0	0.000	0.171 0.279 7 6 1.2	0.000	0.000	0.000	0.000	0.000
North upstream BGS state	0.143 0.259 7 4 1.8	0.122 0.262 6 4 1.5	n/a	0.327 0.230 16 10 1.6	0.163 0.256 8 8 1.0	0.020 0.274 1 1 1.0	0.102 0.265 5 4 1.3	0.061 0.271 3 3 1.0	0.000	0.020 0.274 1 1 1.0	0.000	0.041 0.275 2 2 1.0
North downstream BGS state	0.031 0.240 2 2 1.0	0.031 0.240 2 2 1.0	0.369 0.193 24 11 2.2	n/a	0.200 0.217 13 8 1.6	0.015 0.238 1 1 1.0	0.293 0.205 19 13 1.5	0.031 0.240 2 2 1.0	0.000	0.031 0.240 2 2 1.0	0.000	0.000
FSC state	0.018 0.261 1 1 1.0	0.018 0.261 1 1 1.0	0.053 0.254 3 2 1.5	0.263 0.223 15 11 1.4	n/a	0.193 0.223 11 7 1.6	0.386 0.203 22 14 1.6	0.035 0.255 2 2 1.0	0.035 0.255 2 2 1.0	0.000	0.000	0.000
North FSC gap state	0.067 0.490 1 1 1.0	0.000	0.000	0.067 0.490 1 1 1.0	0.600 0.320 9 4 2.3	n/a	0.067 0.490 1 1 1.0	0.200 0.453 3 3 1.0	0.000	0.000	0.000	0.000

Table 17. Movement probabilities from the residence dataset for radio-tagged juvenile coho salmon in the forebay of Cowlitz Falls Dam during 2011.—Continued

[Some state descriptions include BGS and FSC which stand for behavioral guidance structure and floating surface collector, respectively. [Each cell contains five rows of data including the probability of movement (row 1), the 95 percent confidence interval for the probability estimate (row 2) the number of movements (row 3), the number of fish that made movements (row 4), and the average number of movements per fish (row 5)]

Current location	South upstream BGS state	South downstream BGS state	North upstream BGS state	North downstream BGS state	FSC state	North FSC gap state	Debris barrier state	Spillbay 1 state	Spillbay 2-3 state	Spillbay 4 state	Fish facility state	Tailrace state
Debris barrier state	0.006	0.030	0.012	0.039	0.045	0.003	n/a	0.192	0.258	0.362	0.000	0.054
	0.107	0.106	0.107	0.105	0.105	0.107		0.096	0.092	0.086		0.104
	2	10	4	13	15	1		64	86	121		18
	2	8	4	11	10	1		23	53	26		18
	1.0	1.3	1.0	1.2	1.5	1.0		2.8	1.6	4.7		1.0
Spillbay 1 state	0.000	0.000	0.000	0.000	0.088	0.010	0.794	n/a	0.069	0.000	0.000	0.039
					0.185	0.195	0.088		0.188			0.190
					9	1	81		7			4
					9	1	34		7			4
					1.0	1.0	2.4		1.0			1.0
Spillbays 2-3 state	0.000	0.010		0.000	0.000	0.000	0.398	0.020	n/a	0.000	0.122	0.449
		0.195					0.154	0.194			0.185	0.147
		1					39	2			12	44
		1					15	1			12	44
		1.0					2.6	2.0			1.0	1.0
Spillbay 4 state	0.000	0.067	0.015	0.044	0.007	0.000	0.815	0.000	0.007	n/a	0.000	0.044
		0.163	0.168	0.164	0.163		0.073		0.163			0.164
		9	2	6	1		110		1			6
		7	2	6	1		26		1			6
		1.3	1.0	1.0	1.0		4.2		1.0			1.0

53

Table 18. Movement probabilities from the residence dataset for radio-tagged juvenile Chinook salmon in the forebay of Cowlitz Falls Dam during 2011.

[Some state descriptions include BGS and FSC which stand for behavioral guidance structure and floating surface collector, respectively. Each cell contains five rows of data including the probability of movement (row 1), the 95 percent confidence interval for the probability estimate (row 2) the number of movements (row 3), the number of fish that made movements (row 4), and the average number of movements per fish (row 5)]

Current location	Next location											
	South upstream BGS state	South downstream BGS state	North upstream BGS state	North downstream BGS state	FSC state	North FSC gap state	Debris barrier state	Spillbay 1 state	Spillbay 2-3 state	Spillbay 4 state	Fish facility state	Tailrace state
South upstream BGS state	n/a	0.546 0.053 342 70 4.9	0.255 0.068 160 61 2.6	0.088 0.075 55 34 1.6	0.053 0.076 33 26 1.3	0.013 0.078 8 7 1.1	0.030 0.077 19 16 1.2	0.003 0.076 2 2 1.0	0.000	0.011 0.077 7 7 1.0	0.000	0.002 0.088 1 1 1.0
South downstream BGS state	0.694 0.044 418 10 41.8	n/a	0.015 0.079 9 8 1.1	0.128 0.075 77 44 1.8	0.015 0.079 9 9 1.0	0.000	0.078 0.077 47 32 1.5	0.003 0.076 2 2 1.0	0.000	0.063 0.077 38 32 1.2	0.000	0.003 0.076 2 2 1.0
North upstream BGS state	0.133 0.069 93 44 2.1	0.023 0.073 16 14 1.1	n/a	0.513 0.052 358 67 5.3	0.258 0.064 180 58 3.1	0.019 0.074 13 12 1.1	0.040 0.073 28 22 1.3	0.010 0.074 7 7 1.0	0.000	0.004 0.071 3 3 1.0	0.000	0.000
North downstream BGS state	0.044 0.067 36 28 1.3	0.106 0.065 86 48 1.8	0.452 0.051 367 67 5.5	n/a	0.181 0.062 147 59 2.5	0.003 0.076 2 2 1.0	0.153 0.063 124 51 2.4	0.027 0.068 22 21 1.1	0.003 0.076 2 2 1.0	0.031 0.068 25 19 1.3	0.000	0.001 0.062 1 1 1.0
FSC state	0.033 0.058 36 28 1.3	0.011 0.059 12 12 1.0	0.132 0.056 142 54 2.6	0.143 0.055 154 57 2.7	n/a	0.395 0.046 427 74 5.8	0.181 0.054 195 68 2.9	0.093 0.057 100 52 1.9	0.004 0.062 4 4 1.0	0.008 0.058 9 9 1.0	0.001 0.062 1 1 1.0	0.000
North FSC gap state	0.043 0.089 20 16 1.3	0.000	0.021 0.089 10 9 1.1	0.013 0.091 6 6 1.0	0.830 0.037 390 71 5.5	n/a	0.036 0.089 17 17 1.0	0.051 0.088 24 20 1.2	0.002 0.088 1 1 1.0	0.004 0.087 2 2 1.0	0.000	0.000

Table 18. Movement probabilities from the residence dataset for radio-tagged juvenile Chinook salmon in the forebay of Cowlitz Falls Dam during 2011.—Continued.

[Some state descriptions include BGS and FSC which stand for behavioral guidance structure and floating surface collector, respectively. Each cell contains five rows of data including the probability of movement (row 1), the 95 percent confidence interval for the probability estimate (row 2) the number of movements (row 3), the number of fish that made movements (row 4), and the average number of movements per fish (row 5)]

Current location	Next location											
	South upstream BGS state	South downstream BGS state	North upstream BGS state	North downstream BGS state	FSC state	North FSC gap state	Debris barrier state	Spillbay 1 state	Spillbay 2-3 state	Spillbay 4 state	Fish facility state	Tailrace state
Debris barrier state	0.006	0.022	0.004	0.032	0.051	0.003	n/a	0.186	0.444	0.247	0.000	0.005
	0.034	0.032	0.031	0.032	0.032	0.031		0.029	0.024	0.028		0.032
	20	79	16	116	184	12		671	1601	892		19
	18	49	14	49	64	10		76	90	84		19
	1.1	1.6	1.1	2.4	2.9	1.2		8.8	17.8	10.6		1.0
Spillbay 1 state	0.000	0.001	0.000	0.013	0.145	0.007	0.736	n/a	0.081	0.013	0.000	0.004
		0.062		0.064	0.059	0.062	0.033		0.061	0.064		0.062
		1		12	137	7	698		77	12		4
		1		9	55	6	81		45	12		4
		1.0		1.3	2.5	1.2	8.6		1.7	1.0		1.0
Spillbays 2-3 state	0.001	0.002	0.000	0.001	0.001	0.000	0.929	0.049	n/a	0.004	0.012	0.002
	0.062	0.051		0.044	0.062		0.013	0.046		0.051	0.048	0.051
	1	3		2	1		1580	84		6	20	3
	1	3		2	1		88	49		5	20	3
	1.0	1.0		1.0	1.0		18.0	1.7		1.2	1.0	1.0
Spillbay 4 state	0.014	0.068	0.003	0.033	0.008	0.001	0.849	0.008	0.012	n/a	0.000	0.003
	0.062	0.060	0.062	0.061	0.062	0.062	0.024	0.062	0.062			0.062
	14	68	3	33	8	1	846	8	12			3
	11	40	3	26	8	1	84	8	11			3
	1.3	1.7	1.0	1.3	1.0	1.0	10.1	1.0	1.1			1.0

55

Appendix A. Percentage of Detections Observed on Shallow Underwater Antennas on the Behavioral Guidance Structure in the Forebay of Cowlitz Falls Dam during Range-Testing Events in 2011.

Distance bands refer to the approximate distance between the test transmitter and the underwater antenna during testing.

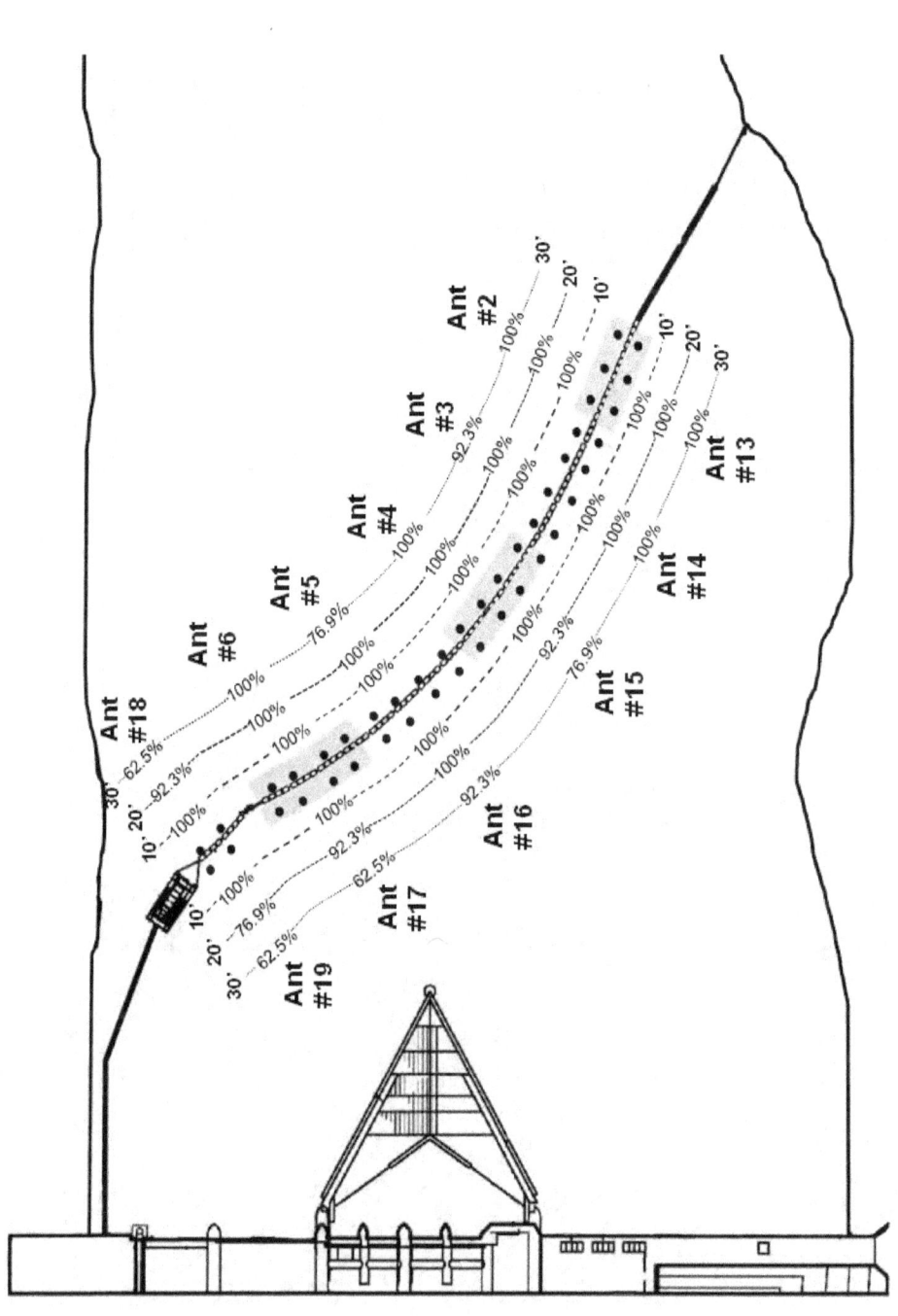

56

Appendix A. Percentage of Detections Observed on Shallow Underwater Antennas on the Behavioral Guidance Structure in the Forebay of Cowlitz Falls Dam during Range-Testing Events in 2011.—Continued

Distance bands refer to the approximate distance between the test transmitter and the underwater antenna during testing.

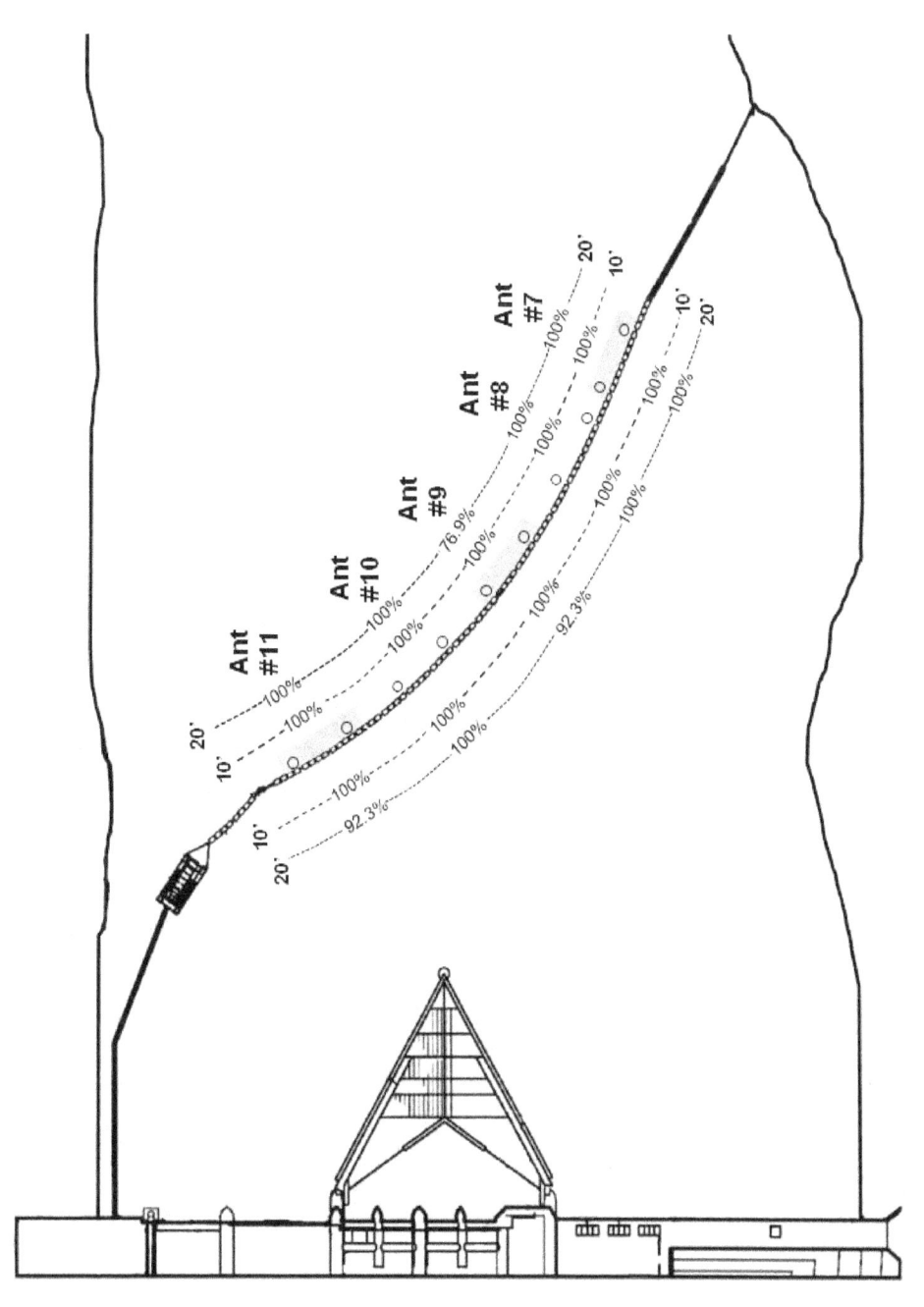

Appendix A. Percentage of Detections Observed on Shallow Underwater Antennas on the Behavioral Guidance Structure in the Forebay of Cowlitz Falls Dam during Range-Testing Events in 2011.—Continued

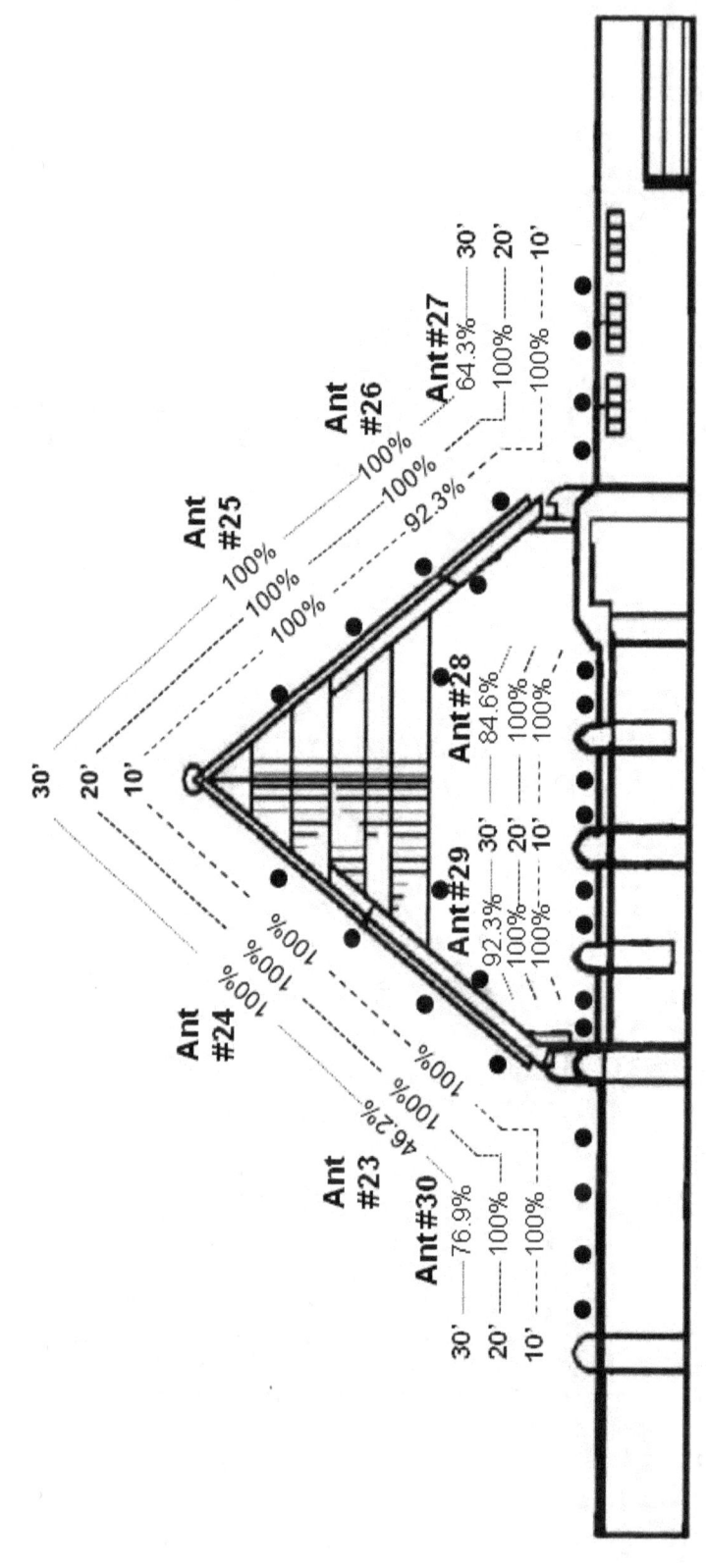

Appendix B. Summary of Juvenile Steelhead, Coho Salmon, and Chinook Salmon Release and Detection Numbers at Cowlitz Falls Dam during 2011.

[The term FSC refers to the floating surface collector]

Parameter	Descriptor	Number of steelhead (%)	Number of coho salmon (%)	Number of Chinook salmon (%)
Number of fish released	Total number of live tagged fish released during study at Cowlitz River and Cispus River release sites.	110 (100%)	110 (100%)	110 (100%)
Number of fish detected in forebay	Total number of tagged fish detected on aerial and underwater antennas in the forebay of Cowlitz Falls Dam.	98 (89%)	100 (91%)	99 (90%)
Discovery rate of small FSC zone	Total number of tagged fish detected on underwater antennas in the small FSC zone divided by the total number of tagged fish detected in the forebay of Cowlitz Falls Dam.	71 (72%)	48 (48%)	90 (91%)
Discovery rate of large FSC zone	Total number of tagged fish detected on underwater antennas in the large FSC zone divided by the total number of tagged fish detected in the forebay of Cowlitz Falls Dam.	81 (83%)	65 (65%)	90 (91%)
Discovery rate of the proposed weir box location	Total number of tagged fish detected on underwater antennas located near the entrances to spillbay 2 and 3 divided by the total number of tagged fish detected in the forebay of Cowlitz Falls Dam.	75 (77%)	61 (61%)	91 (92%)

Appendix C. Movement Probabilities for Radio-Tagged Steelhead between Individual Antennas from the Approach Dataset at Cowlitz Falls Dam during 2011.

[Each cell contains five rows of data including the probability of movement (row 1), the 95-percent confidence interval for the probability estimate (row 2) the number of movements (row 3), the number of fish that made movements (row 4), and the average number of movements per fish (row 5)]

Current location	stat	Antenna 2	3	4	5	6	8	9	10	11	13	14	15	16	17	18
Forebay entry	prob	0.092	0.133	0.143	0.041	0.194	0.000	0.010	0.031	0.031	0.000	0.010	0.000	0.000	0.020	0.061
	CI	0.189	0.185	0.183	0.194	0.178	0	0.195	0.196	0.196	0	0.195	0	0	0.194	0.192
	n mov	9	13	14	4	19	0	1	3	3	0	1	0	0	2	6
	n fish	9	13	14	4	19	0	1	3	3	0	1	0	0	2	6
	avg	1.0	1.0	1.0	1.0	1.0	0.0	1.0	1.0	1.0	0.0	1.0	0.0	0.0	1.0	1.0
2	prob	n/a	0.429	0.143	0.000	0.143	0.000	0.000	0.000	0.000	0.071	0.000	0.000	0.000	0.071	0.000
	CI		0.396	0.485	0	0.485	0	0	0	0	0.503	0	0	0	0.503	0
	n mov		6	2	0	2	0	0	0	0	1	0	0	0	1	0
	n fish		6	2	0	2	0	0	0	0	1	0	0	0	1	0
	avg		1.0	1.0	0.0	1.0	0.0	0.0	0.0	0.0	1.0	0.0	0.0	0.0	1.0	0.0
3	prob	0.143	n/a	0.429	0.000	0.107	0.000	0.000	0.000	0.000	0.036	0.000	0.036	0.000	0.036	0.036
	CI	0.343		0.280	0	0.350	0	0	0	0	0.365	0	0.365	0	0.365	0.365
	n mov	4		12	0	3	0	0	0	0	1	0	1	0	1	1
	n fish	3		12	0	3	0	0	0	0	1	0	1	0	1	1
	avg	1.3		1.0	0.0	1.0	0.0	0.0	0.0	0.0	1.0	0.0	1.0	0.0	1.0	1.0
4	prob	0.000	0.182	n/a	0.023	0.296	0.000	0.114	0.205	0.000	0.000	0.000	0.023	0.000	0.000	0.023
	CI	0	0.267		0.294	0.248	0	0.279	0.264	0	0	0	0.294	0	0	0.294
	n mov	0	8		1	13	0	5	9	0	0	0	1	0	0	1
	n fish	0	6		1	10	0	5	9	0	0	0	1	0	0	1
	avg	0.0	1.3		1.0	1.3	0.0	1.0	1.0	0.0	0.0	0.0	1.0	0.0	0.0	1.0
5	prob	0.000	0.000	0.125	n/a	0.125	0.000	0.000	0.375	0.125	0.000	0.000	0.000	0.125	0.125	0.000
	CI	0	0	0.648		0.648	0	0	0.548	0.648	0	0	0	0.648	0.648	0
	n mov	0	0	1		1	0	0	3	1	0	0	0	1	1	0
	n fish	0	0	1		1	0	0	3	1	0	0	0	1	1	0
	avg	0.0	0.0	1.0		1.0	0.0	0.0	1.1	1.0	0.0	0.0	0.0	1.0	1.0	0.0
6	prob	0.000	0.000	0.098	0.039	n/a	0.000	0.000	0.177	0.059	0.000	0.000	0.000	0.000	0.078	0.157
	CI	0	0	0.261	0.268		0	0	0.249	0.267	0	0	0	0	0.263	0.252
	n mov	0	0	5	2		0	0	9	3	0	0	0	0	4	8
	n fish	0	0	5	2		0	0	8	3	0	0	0	0	4	7
	avg	0.0	0.0	1.0	1.0		0.0	0.0	1.1	1.0	0.0	0.0	0.0	0.0	1.0	1.1
8	prob	0.000	0.000	0.000	0.000	1.000	n/a	0.000	0.000	0.000	0.000	0.000	0.000	0.000	0.000	0.000
	CI	0	0	0	0	0		0	0	0	0	0	0	0	0	0
	n mov	0	0	0	0	1		0	0	0	0	0	0	0	0	0
	n fish	0	0	0	0	1		0	0	0	0	0	0	0	0	0
	avg	0.0	0.0	0.0	0.0	1.0		0.0	0.0	0.0	0.0	0.0	0.0	0.0	0.0	0.0
9	prob	0.000	0.000	0.250	0.125	0.000	0.000	n/a	0.000	0.125	0.000	0.000	0.125	0.000	0.000	0.000
	CI	0	0	0.600	0.648	0	0		0	0.648	0	0	0.648	0	0	0
	n mov	0	0	2	1	0	0		0	1	0	0	1	0	0	0
	n fish	0	0	2	1	0	0		0	1	0	0	1	0	0	0
	avg	0.0	0.0	1.0	1.0	0.0	0.0		0.0	1.0	0.0	0.0	1.0	0.0	0.0	0.0
10	prob	0.000	0.000	0.259	0.000	0.148	0.000	0.037	n/a	0.000	0.000	0.000	0.037	0.037	0.148	0.000
	CI	0	0	0.325	0	0.348	0	0.370		0	0	0	0.370	0.370	0.348	0
	n mov	0	0	7	0	4	0	1		0	0	0	1	1	4	0
	n fish	0	0	5	0	4	0	1		0	0	0	1	1	4	0
	avg	0.0	0.0	1.4	0.0	1.0	0.0	1.0		0.0	0.0	0.0	1.0	1.0	1.0	0.0

Appendix C. Movement Probabilities for Radio-Tagged Steelhead between Individual Antennas from the Approach Dataset at Cowlitz Falls Dam during 2011. —Continued

[Each cell contains five rows of data including the probability of movement (row 1), the 95-percent confidence interval for the probability estimate (row 2) the number of movements (row 3), the number of fish that made movements (row 4), and the average number of movements per fish (row 5)]

Current location	Antenna													
	19	20	21	22	23	24	25	26	27	28	29	30	31	Tailrace
Forebay entry	0.000	0.041	0.020	0.000	0.051	0.010	0.041	0.010	0.010	0.010	0.000	0.010	0.000	0.031
	0	0.194	0.194	0	0.193	0.195	0.194	0.195	0.195	0.195	0	0.195	0	0.196
	0	4	2	0	5	1	4	1	1	1	0	1	0	3
	0	4	2	0	5	1	4	1	1	1	0	1	0	3
	0.0	1.0	1.0	0.0	1.0	1.0	1.0	1.0	1.0	1.0	0.0	1.0	0.0	1.0
2	0.000	0.000	0.143	0.000	0.000	0.000	0.000	0.000	0.000	0.000	0.000	0.000	0.000	0.000
	0	0	0.485	0	0	0	0	0	0	0	0	0	0	0
	0	0	2	0	0	0	0	0	0	0	0	0	0	0
	0	0	2	0	0	0	0	0	0	0	0	0	0	0
	0.0	0.0	1.0	0.0	0.0	0.0	0.0	0.0	0.0	0.0	0.0	0.0	0.0	0.0
3	0.000	0.000	0.071	0.000	0.000	0.000	0.036	0.000	0.000	0.000	0.000	0.036	0.000	0.036
	0	0	0.356	0	0	0	0.365	0	0	0	0	0.365	0	0.365
	0	0	2	0	0	0	1	0	0	0	0	1	0	1
	0	0	2	0	0	0	1	0	0	0	0	1	0	1
	0.0	0.0	1.0	0.0	0.0	0.0	1.0	0.0	0.0	0.0	0.0	1.0	0.0	1.0
4	0.023	0.000	0.000	0.000	0.000	0.023	0.000	0.000	0.023	0.046	0.000	0.000	0.023	0.000
	0.294	0	0	0	0	0.294	0	0	0.294	0.290	0	0	0.294	0
	1	0	0	0	0	1	0	0	1	2	0	0	1	0
	1	0	0	0	0	1	0	0	1	2	0	0	1	0
	1.0	0.0	0.0	0.0	0.0	1.0	0.0	0.0	1.0	1.0	0.0	0.0	1.0	0.0
5	0.000	0.000	0.000	0.000	0.000	0.000	0.000	0.000	0.000	0.000	0.000	0.000	0.000	0.000
	0	0	0	0	0	0	0	0	0	0	0	0	0	0
	0	0	0	0	0	0	0	0	0	0	0	0	0	0
	0	0	0	0	0	0	0	0	0	0	0	0	0	0
	0.0	0.0	0.0	0.0	0.0	0.0	0.0	0.0	0.0	0.0	0.0	0.0	0.0	0.0
6	0.098	0.059	0.039	0.000	0.059	0.059	0.000	0.000	0.039	0.000	0.020	0.020	0.000	0.000
	0.261	0.267	0.268	0	0.267	0.267	0	0	0.268	0	0.274	0.274	0	0
	5	3	2	0	3	3	0	0	2	0	1	1	0	0
	5	3	2	0	3	3	0	0	2	0	1	1	0	0
	1.0	1.0	1.0	0.0	1.0	1.0	0.0	0.0	1.0	0.0	1.0	1.0	0.0	0.0
8	0.000	0.000	0.000	0.000	0.000	0.000	0.000	0.000	0.000	0.000	0.000	0.000	0.000	0.000
	0	0	0	0	0	0	0	0	0	0	0	0	0	0
	0	0	0	0	0	0	0	0	0	0	0	0	0	0
	0	0	0	0	0	0	0	0	0	0	0	0	0	0
	0.0	0.0	0.0	0.0	0.0	0.0	0.0	0.0	0.0	0.0	0.0	0.0	0.0	0.0
9	0.000	0.000	0.000	0.000	0.000	0.000	0.125	0.125	0.000	0.125	0.000	0.000	0.000	0.000
	0	0	0	0	0	0	0.648	0.648	0	0.648	0	0	0	0
	0	0	0	0	0	0	1	1	0	1	0	0	0	0
	0	0	0	0	0	0	1	1	0	1	0	0	0	0
	0.0	0.0	0.0	0.0	0.0	0.0	1.0	1.0	0.0	1.0	0.0	0.0	0.0	0.0
10	0.000	0.000	0.074	0.037	0.037	0.000	0.111	0.000	0.037	0.037	0.000	0.000	0.000	0.000
	0	0	0.363	0.370	0.370	0	0.355	0	0.370	0.370	0	0	0	0
	0	0	2	1	1	0	3	0	1	1	0	0	0	0
	0	0	2	1	1	0	3	0	1	1	0	0	0	0
	0.0	0.0	1.0	1.0	1.0	0.0	1.0	0.0	1.0	1.0	0.0	0.0	0.0	0.0

Appendix C. Movement Probabilities for Radio-Tagged Steelhead between Individual Antennas from the Approach Dataset at Cowlitz Falls Dam during 2011. —Continued

[Each cell contains five rows of data including the probability of movement (row 1), the 95-percent confidence interval for the probability estimate (row 2) the number of movements (row 3), the number of fish that made movements (row 4), and the average number of movements per fish (row 5)]

Current location	2	3	4	5	6	8	9	10	11	13	14	15	16	17	18
11	0.000	0.000	0.000	0.000	0.079	0.000	0.000	0.000	n/a	0.000	0.000	0.026	0.000	0.737	0.000
	0	0	0	0	0.305	0	0	0		0	0	0.312	0	0.163	0
	0	0	0	0	3	0	0	0		0	0	1	0	28	0
	0	0	0	0	3	0	0	0		0	0	1	0	3	0
	0.0	0.0	0.0	0.0	1.0	0.0	0.0	0.0		0.0	0.0	1.0	0.0	9.3	0.0
13	0.167	0.000	0.000	0.000	0.000	0.000	0.000	0.000	0.000	n/a	0.833	0.000	0.000	0.000	0.000
	0.731	0	0	0	0	0	0	0	0		0.327	0	0	0	0
	1	0	0	0	0	0	0	0	0		5	0	0	0	0
	1	0	0	0	0	0	0	0	0		2	0	0	0	0
	1.0	0.0	0.0	0.0	0.0	0.0	0.0	0.0	0.0		2.5	0.0	0.0	0.0	0.0
14	0.000	0.143	0.000	0.000	0.000	0.000	0.000	0.000	0.000	0.571	n/a	0.143	0.000	0.000	0.000
	0	0.686	0	0	0	0	0	0	0	0.485		0.686	0	0	0
	0	1	0	0	0	0	0	0	0	4		1	0	0	0
	0	1	0	0	0	0	0	0	0	2		1	0	0	0
	0.0	1.0	0.0	0.0	0.0	0.0	0.0	0.0	0.0	2.0		1.0	0.0	0.0	0.0
15	0.000	0.000	0.000	0.000	0.000	0.143	0.143	0.143	0.000	0.000	0.143	n/a	0.143	0.000	0.000
	0	0	0	0	0	0.686	0.686	0.686	0	0	0.686		0.686	0	0
	0	0	0	0	0	1	1	1	0	0	1		1	0	0
	0	0	0	0	0	1	1	1	0	0	1		1	0	0
	0.0	0.0	0.0	0.0	0.0	1.0	1.0	1.0	0.0	0.0	1.0		1.0	0.0	0.0
16	0.000	0.000	0.000	0.000	0.333	0.000	0.000	0.000	0.000	0.000	0.000	0.000	n/a	0.333	0.000
	0	0	0	0	0.924	0	0	0	0	0	0	0		0.924	0
	0	0	0	0	1	0	0	0	0	0	0	0		1	0
	0	0	0	0	1	0	0	0	0	0	0	0		1	0
	0.0	0.0	0.0	0.0	1.0	0.0	0.0	0.0	0.0	0.0	0.0	0.0		1.0	0.0
17	0.000	0.000	0.000	0.000	0.018	0.000	0.000	0.018	0.509	0.000	0.000	0.018	0.000	n/a	0.018
	0	0	0	0	0.261	0	0	0.261	0.182	0	0	0.261	0		0.261
	0	0	0	0	1	0	0	1	29	0	0	1	0		1
	0	0	0	0	1	0	0	1	4	0	0	1	0		1
	0.0	0.0	0.0	0.0	1.0	0.0	0.0	1.0	7.3	0.0	0.0	1.0	0.0		1.0
18	0.000	0.000	0.000	0.000	0.100	0.000	0.000	0.000	0.000	0.000	0.000	0.000	0.000	0.000	n/a
	0	0	0	0	0.416	0	0	0	0	0	0	0	0	0	
	0	0	0	0	2	0	0	0	0	0	0	0	0	0	
	0	0	0	0	2	0	0	0	0	0	0	0	0	0	
	0.0	0.0	0.0	0.0	1.0	0.0	0.0	0.0	0.0	0.0	0.0	0.0	0.0	0.0	
19	0.000	0.000	0.000	0.000	0.000	0.000	0.000	0.000	0.036	0.000	0.000	0.000	0.000	0.536	0.036
	0	0	0	0	0	0	0	0	0.365	0	0	0	0	0.252	0.365
	0	0	0	0	0	0	0	0	1	0	0	0	0	15	1
	0	0	0	0	0	0	0	0	1	0	0	0	0	4	1
	0.0	0.0	0.0	0.0	0.0	0.0	0.0	0.0	1.0	0.0	0.0	0.0	0.0	3.8	1.0
20	0.000	0.000	0.000	0.000	0.039	0.000	0.000	0.000	0.000	0.000	0.000	0.000	0.000	0.000	0.077
	0	0	0	0	0.379	0	0	0	0	0	0	0	0	0	0.369
	0	0	0	0	1	0	0	0	0	0	0	0	0	0	2
	0	0	0	0	1	0	0	0	0	0	0	0	0	0	2
	0.0	0.0	0.0	0.0	1.0	0.0	0.0	0.0	0.0	0.0	0.0	0.0	0.0	0.0	1.0

Appendix C. Movement Probabilities for Radio-Tagged Steelhead between Individual Antennas from the Approach Dataset at Cowlitz Falls Dam during 2011. —Continued

[Each cell contains five rows of data including the probability of movement (row 1), the 95-percent confidence interval for the probability estimate (row 2) the number of movements (row 3), the number of fish that made movements (row 4), and the average number of movements per fish (row 5)]

Current location	Antenna													
	19	20	21	22	23	24	25	26	27	28	29	30	31	Tailrace
11	0.000 0 0 0.0	0.026 0.312 1 1 1.0	0.000 0 0 0.0	0.000 0 0 0.0	0.053 0.310 2 2 1.0	0.026 0.312 1 1 1.0	0.026 0.312 1 1 1.0	0.000 0 0 0.0	0.000 0 0 0.0	0.000 0 0 0.0	0.000 0 0 0.0	0.000 0 0 0.0	0.026 0.312 1 1 1.0	0.000 0 0 0.0
13	0.000 0 0 0.0	0.000 0 0 0.0	0.000 0 0 0.0	0.000 0 0 0.0	0.000 0 0 0.0	0.000 0 0 0.0	0.000 0 0 0.0	0.000 0 0 0.0	0.000 0 0 0.0	0.000 0 0 0.0	0.000 0 0 0.0	0.000 0 0 0.0	0.000 0 0 0.0	0.000 0 0 0.0
14	0.000 0 0 0.0	0.000 0 0 0.0	0.000 0 0 0.0	0.000 0 0 0.0	0.000 0 0 0.0	0.000 0 0 0.0	0.000 0 0 0.0	0.000 0 0 0.0	0.000 0 0 0.0	0.143 0.686 1 1 1.0	0.000 0 0 0.0	0.000 0 0 0.0	0.000 0 0 0.0	0.000 0 0 0.0
15	0.000 0 0 0.0	0.000 0 0 0.0	0.143 0.686 1 1 1.0	0.000 0 0 0.0	0.000 0 0 0.0	0.000 0 0 0.0	0.143 0.686 1 1 1.0	0.000 0 0 0.0	0.000 0 0 0.0	0.000 0 0 0.0	0.000 0 0 0.0	0.000 0 0 0.0	0.000 0 0 0.0	0.000 0 0 0.0
16	0.000 0 0 0.0	0.000 0 0 0.0	0.000 0 0 0.0	0.000 0 0 0.0	0.000 0 0 0.0	0.000 0 0 0.0	0.333 0.924 1 1 1.0	0.000 0 0 0.0	0.000 0 0 0.0	0.000 0 0 0.0	0.000 0 0 0.0	0.000 0 0 0.0	0.000 0 0 0.0	0.000 0 0 0.0
17	0.228 0.228 13 3 4.3	0.053 0.254 3 3 1.0	0.018 0.261 1 1 1.0	0.000 0 0 0.0	0.000 0 0 0.0	0.070 0.250 4 4 1.0	0.000 0 0 0.0	0.000 0 0 0.0	0.000 0 0 0.0	0.018 0.261 1 1 1.0	0.000 0 0 0.0	0.000 0 0 0.0	0.035 0.255 2 2 1.0	0.000 0 0 0.0
18	0.150 0.404 3 2 1.5	0.350 0.353 7 7 1.0	0.200 0.392 4 4 1.0	0.000 0 0 0.0	0.100 0.416 2 2 1.0	0.050 0.427 1 1 1.0	0.000 0 0 0.0	0.000 0 0 0.0	0.000 0 0 0.0	0.000 0 0 0.0	0.000 0 0 0.0	0.000 0 0 0.0	0.050 0.427 1 1 1.0	0.000 0 0 0.0
19	n/a	0.143 0.343 4 4 1.0	0.000 0 0 0.0	0.000 0 0 0.0	0.036 0.365 1 1 1.0	0.107 0.350 3 3 1.0	0.000 0 0 0.0	0.000 0 0 0.0	0.000 0 0 0.0	0.000 0 0 0.0	0.000 0 0 0.0	0.000 0 0 0.0	0.107 0.350 3 3 1.0	0.000 0 0 0.0
20	0.192 0.345 5 3 1.7	n/a	0.231 0.337 6 5 1.2	0.077 0.369 2 2 1.0	0.077 0.369 2 2 1.0	0.000 0 0 0.0	0.039 0.379 1 1 1.0	0.000 0 0 0.0	0.077 0.369 2 2 1.0	0.000 0 0 0.0	0.000 0 0 0.0	0.000 0 0 0.0	0.192 0.345 5 5 1.0	0.000 0 0 0.0

Appendix C. Movement Probabilities for Radio-Tagged Steelhead between Individual Antennas from the Approach Dataset at Cowlitz Falls Dam during 2011. —Continued

[Each cell contains five rows of data including the probability of movement (row 1), the 95-percent confidence interval for the probability estimate (row 2) the number of movements (row 3), the number of fish that made movements (row 4), and the average number of movements per fish (row 5)]

Current location		Antenna													
	2	3	4	5	6	8	9	10	11	13	14	15	16	17	18
21	0.000	0.000	0.032	0.000	0.000	0.000	0.000	0.032	0.000	0.000	0.000	0.000	0.000	0.000	0.000
			0.345					0.345							
	0	0	1	0	0	0	0	1	0	0	0	0	0	0	0
	0	0	1	0	0	0	0	1	0	0	0	0	0	0	0
	0.0	0.0	1.0	0.0	0.0	0.0	0.0	1.0	0.0	0.0	0.0	0.0	0.0	0.0	0.0
22	0.000	0.000	0.000	0.000	0.000	0.000	0.000	0.000	0.000	0.000	0.000	0.000	0.000	0.000	0.000
	0	0	0	0	0	0	0	0	0	0	0	0	0	0	0
	0	0	0	0	0	0	0	0	0	0	0	0	0	0	0
	0.0	0.0	0.0	0.0	0.0	0.0	0.0	0.0	0.0	0.0	0.0	0.0	0.0	0.0	0.0

Current location		Antenna													
	19	20	21	22	23	24	25	26	27	28	29	30	31	Tailrace
21	0.000	0.129	n/a	0.323	0.129	0.065	0.000	0.000	0.000	0.032	0.032	0.000	0.226	0.000
		0.328		0.290	0.328	0.342				0.345	0.345		0.310	
	0	4		10	4	2	0	0	0	1	1	0	7	0
	0	3		5	4	2	0	0	0	1	1	0	7	0
	0.0	1.3		2.0	1.0	1.0	0.0	0.0	0.0	1.0	1.0	0.0	1.0	0.0
22	0.077	0.000	0.692	n/a	0.077	0.000	0.000	0.000	0.000	0.000	0.000	0.000	0.154	0.000
	0.523		0.302		0.523								0.500	
	1	0	9		1	0	0	0	0	0	0	0	2	0
	1	0	3		1	0	0	0	0	0	0	0	2	0
	1.0	0.0	3.0		1.0	0.0	0.0	0.0	0.0	0.0	0.0	0.0	1.0	0.0

64

Appendix D. Movement Probabilities for Radio-Tagged Coho Salmon between Individual Antennas from the Approach Dataset at Cowlitz Falls Dam during 2011.

[Each cell contains five rows of data including the probability of movement (row 1), the 95-percent confidence interval for the probability estimate (row 2) the number of movements (row 3), the number of fish that made movements (row 4), and the average number of movements per fish (row 5)]

Current location	Antenna														
	2	3	4	5	6	7	9	10	11	13	14	15	16	17	18
Forebay entry	0.059 0.189 6 6 1.0	0.119 0.183 12 12 1.0	0.109 0.184 11 11 1.0	0.050 0.191 5 5 1.0	0.089 0.186 9 9 1.0	0.030 0.193 3 3 1.0	0.040 0.192 4 4 1.0	0.069 0.188 7 7 1.0	0.010 0.195 1 1 1.0	0.000 0 0 0.0	0.000 0 0 0.0	0.000 0 0 0.0	0.000 0 0 0.0	0.010 0.195 1 1 1.0	0.069 0.188 7 7 1.0
2	n/a	0.000 0 0 0.0	0.100 0.588 1 1 1.0	0.200 0.554 2 2 1.0	0.100 0.588 1 1 1.0	0.300 0.519 3 3 1.0	0.000 0 0 0.0	0.000 0 0 0.0	0.000 0 0 0.0	0.000 0 0 0.0	0.100 0.588 1 1 1.0	0.000 0 0 0.0	0.000 0 0 0.0	0.000 0 0 0.0	0.100 0.588 1 1 1.0
3	0.000 0 0 0.0	n/a	0.478 0.295 11 10 1.1	0.000 0 0 0.0	0.044 0.402 1 1 1.0	0.087 0.391 2 2 1.0	0.087 0.391 2 2 1.0	0.000 0 0 0.0	0.000 0 0 0.0	0.000 0 0 0.0	0.087 0.391 2 2 1.0	0.130 0.381 3 3 1.0	0.044 0.402 1 1 1.0	0.000 0 0 0.0	0.000 0 0 0.0
4	0.000 0 0 0.0	0.133 0.333 4 4 1.0	n/a	0.200 0.320 6 6 1.0	0.100 0.339 3 3 1.0	0.000 0 0 0.0	0.100 0.339 3 3 1.0	0.233 0.313 7 7 1.0	0.000 0 0 0.0	0.000 0 0 0.0	0.000 0 0 0.0	0.033 0.350 1 1 1.0	0.033 0.350 1 1 1.0	0.000 0 0 0.0	0.033 0.350 1 1 1.0
5	0.000 0 0 0.0	0.044 0.402 1 1 1.0	0.130 0.381 3 3 1.0	n/a	0.391 0.319 9 8 1.1	0.000 0 0 0.0	0.000 0 0 0.0	0.304 0.341 7 6 1.2	0.000 0 0 0.0	0.000 0 0 0.0	0.044 0.402 1 1 1.0	0.000 0 0 0.0	0.000 0 0 0.0	0.000 0 0 0.0	0.000 0 0 0.0
6	0.000 0 0 0.0	0.000 0 0 0.0	0.026 0.312 1 1 1.0	0.051 0.305 2 2 1.0	n/a	0.000 0 0 0.0	0.000 0 0 0.0	0.077 0.302 3 3 1.0	0.077 0.302 3 3 1.0	0.000 0 0 0.0	0.000 0 0 0.0	0.000 0 0 0.0	0.000 0 0 0.0	0.205 0.280 8 5 1.6	0.231 0.275 9 9 1.0
7	0.250 0.600 2 2 1.0	0.375 0.548 3 3 1.0	0.000 0 0 0.0	0.125 0.648 1 1 1.0	0.000 0 0 0.0	n/a	0.000 0 0 0.0	0.000 0 0 0.0	0.000 0 0 0.0	0.125 0.648 1 1 1.0	0.000 0 0 0.0	0.000 0 0 0.0	0.000 0 0 0.0	0.000 0 0 0.0	0.000 0 0 0.0
9	0.000 0 0 0.0	0.111 0.616 1 1 1.0	0.222 0.576 2 2 1.0	0.111 0.616 1 1 1.0	0.222 0.333 6 6 1.0	0.000 0 0 0.0	n/a	0.222 0.576 2 2 1.0	0.000 0 0 0.0	0.000 0 0 0.0	0.000 0 0 0.0	0.111 0.616 1 1 1.0	0.111 0.616 1 1 1.0	0.000 0 0 0.0	0.000 0 0 0.0
10	0.000 0 0 0.0	0.000 0 0 0.0	0.000 0 0 0.0	0.111 0.355 3 3 1.0	0.000 0 0 0.0	0.000 0 0 0.0	0.000 0 0 0.0	n/a	0.037 0.370 1 1 1.0	0.000 0 0 0.0	0.000 0 0 0.0	0.000 0 0 0.0	0.222 0.333 6 6 1.0	0.111 0.355 3 3 1.0	0.000 0 0 0.0

65

Appendix D. Movement Probabilities for Radio-Tagged Coho Salmon between Individual Antennas from the Approach Dataset at Cowlitz Falls Dam during 2011. —Continued

[Each cell contains five rows of data including the probability of movement (row 1), the 95-percent confidence interval for the probability estimate (row 2) the number of movements (row 3), the number of fish that made movements (row 4), and the average number of movements per fish (row 5)]

Current location		19	20	21	22	23	24	25	26	27	28	29	30	31	Tailrace
Antenna															
Forebay entry		0.020	0.050	0.030	0.000	0.030	0.020	0.020	0.030	0.030	0.010	0.000	0.020	0.050	0.040
		0.194	0.191	0.193	0	0.193	0.194	0.194	0.193	0.193	0.195	0	0.194	0.191	0.192
		2	5	3	0	3	2	2	3	3	1	0	2	5	4
		2	5	3	0.0	3	2	2	3	3	1	0.0	2	5	4
		1.0	1.0	1.0		1.0	1.0	1.0	1.0	1.0	1.0		1.0	1.0	1.0
2		0.000	0.100	0.000	0.000	0.000	0.000	0.000	0.000	0.000	0.000	0.000	0.000	0.000	0.000
		0	0.588	0	0	0	0	0	0	0	0	0	0	0	0
		0	1	0	0	0	0	0	0	0	0	0	0	0	0
		0.0	1	0.0	0.0	0.0	0.0	0.0	0.0	0.0	0.0	0.0	0.0	0.0	0.0
			1.0												
3		0.000	0.000	0.000	0.000	0.000	0.000	0.000	0.000	0.000	0.000	0.000	0.000	0.000	0.044
		0	0	0	0	0	0	0	0	0	0	0	0	0	0.402
		0	0	0	0	0	0	0	0	0	0	0	0	0	1
		0.0	0.0	0.0	0.0	0.0	0.0	0.0	0.0	0.0	0.0	0.0	0.0	0.0	1
															1.0
4		0.000	0.000	0.000	0.000	0.000	0.033	0.067	0.033	0.000	0.000	0.000	0.000	0.000	0.000
		0	0	0	0	0	0.350	0.347	0.350	0	0	0	0	0	0
		0	0	0	0	0	1	2	1	0	0	0	0	0	0
		0.0	0.0	0.0	0.0	0.0	1	2	1	0.0	0.0	0.0	0.0	0.0	0.0
							1.0	1.0	1.0						
5		0.000	0.000	0.000	0.000	0.000	0.044	0.000	0.000	0.000	0.044	0.000	0.000	0.000	0.000
		0	0	0	0	0	0.402	0	0	0	0.402	0	0	0	0
		0	0	0	0	0	1	0	0	0	1	0	0	0	0
		0.0	0.0	0.0	0.0	0.0	1	0.0	0.0	0.0	1	0.0	0.0	0.0	0.0
							1.0				1.0				
6		0.128	0.026	0.077	0.000	0.026	0.000	0.000	0.026	0.026	0.000	0.000	0.000	0.026	0.000
		0.293	0.312	0.302	0	0.312	0	0	0.312	0.312	0	0	0	0.312	0
		5	1	3	0	1	0	0	1	1	0	0	0	1	0
		5	1	3	0.0	1	0.0	0.0	1	1	0.0	0.0	0.0	1	0.0
		1.0	1.0	1.0		1.0			1.0	1.0				1.0	
7		0.000	0.000	0.000	0.000	0.000	0.000	0.000	0.000	0.000	0.111	0.000	0.000	0.000	0.125
		0	0	0	0	0	0	0	0	0	0.616	0	0	0	0.648
		0	0	0	0	0	0	0	0	0	1	0	0	0	1
		0.0	0.0	0.0	0.0	0.0	0.0	0.0	0.0	0.0	1	0.0	0.0	0.0	1
											1.0				1.0
9		0.000	0.000	0.000	0.000	0.000	0.000	0.111	0.000	0.000	0.111	0.000	0.000	0.000	0.000
		0	0	0	0	0	0	0.355	0	0	0.355	0	0	0	0
		0	0	0	0	0	0	3	0	0	3	0	0	0	0
		0.0	0.0	0.0	0.0	0.0	0.0	3	0.0	0.0	3	0.0	0.0	0.0	0.0
								1.0			1.0				
10		0.000	0.000	0.000	0.000	0.000	0.000	0.111	0.000	0.000	0.111	0.000	0.000	0.037	0.037
		0	0	0	0	0	0	0.355	0	0	0.355	0	0	0.370	0.370
		0	0	0	0	0	0	3	0	0	3	0	0	1	1
		0.0	0.0	0.0	0.0	0.0	0.0	3	0.0	0.0	3	0.0	0.0	1	1
								1.0			1.0			1.0	1.0

Appendix D. Movement Probabilities for Radio-Tagged Coho Salmon between Individual Antennas from the Approach Dataset at Cowlitz Falls Dam during 2011. —Continued

[Each cell contains five rows of data including the probability of movement (row 1), the 95-percent confidence interval for the probability estimate (row 2) the number of movements (row 3), the number of fish that made movements (row 4), and the average number of movements per fish (row 5)]

Current location	Antenna														
	2	3	4	5	6	7	9	10	11	13	14	15	16	17	18
11	0.000	0.000	0.000	0.000	0.429	0.000	0.000	0.000	n/a	0.000	0.000	0.000	0.000	0.286	0.000
	0	0	0	0	0.560	0	0	0		0	0	0	0	0.626	0
	0	0	0	0	3	0	0	0		0	0	0	0	2	0
	0	0	0	0	3	0	0	0		0	0	0	0	2	0
	0.0	0.0	0.0	0.0	1.0	0.0	0.0	0.0		0.0	0.0	0.0	0.0	1.0	0.0
13	0.000	0.500	0.000	0.000	0.000	0.000	0.000	0.000	0.000	n/a	0.500	0.000	0.000	0.000	0.000
	0	0.980	0	0	0	0	0	0	0		0.980	0	0	0	0
	0	1	0	0	0	0	0	0	0		1	0	0	0	0
	0	1	0	0	0	0	0	0	0		1	0	0	0	0
	0.0	1.0	0.0	0.0	0.0	0.0	0.0	0.0	0.0		1.0	0.0	0.0	0.0	0.0
14	0.000	0.000	0.000	0.000	0.000	0.000	0.000	0.000	0.200	0.200	n/a	0.000	0.000	0.000	0.000
	0	0	0	0	0	0	0	0	0.784	0.784		0	0	0	0
	0	0	0	0	0	0	0	0	1	1		0	0	0	0
	0	0	0	0	0	0	0	0	1	1		0	0	0	0
	0.0	0.0	0.0	0.0	0.0	0.0	0.0	0.0	1.0	1.0		0.0	0.0	0.0	0.0
15	0.000	0.000	0.200	0.200	0.100	0.000	0.000	0.200	0.000	0.000	0.000	n/a	0.000	0.000	0.000
	0	0	0.784	0.554	0.588	0	0	0.784	0	0	0		0	0	0
	0	0	1	2	1	0	0	1	0	0	0		0	0	0
	0	0	1	2	1	0	0	1	0	0	0		0	0	0
	0.0	0.0	1.0	1.0	1.0	0.0	0.0	1.0	0.0	0.0	0.0		0.0	0.0	0.0
16	0.000	0.000	0.000	0.000	0.263	0.000	0.000	0.000	0.053	0.000	0.000	0.000	n/a	0.300	0.000
	0	0	0	0	0.386	0	0	0	0.439	0	0	0		0.519	0
	0	0	0	0	5	0	0	0	1	0	0	0		3	0
	0	0	0	0	2	0	0	0	1	0	0	0		3	0
	0.0	0.0	0.0	0.0	2.5	0.0	0.0	0.0	1.0	0.0	0.0	0.0		1.0	0.0
17	0.000	0.000	0.000	0.040	0.040	0.000	0.000	0.000	0.000	0.000	0.000	0.000	0.040	n/a	0.000
	0	0	0	0.384	0.384	0	0	0	0	0	0	0	0.384		0
	0	0	0	1	1	0	0	0	0	0	0	0	1		0
	0	0	0	1	1	0	0	0	0	0	0	0	1		0
	0.0	0.0	0.0	1.0	1.0	0.0	0.0	0.0	0.0	0.0	0.0	0.0	1.0		0.0
18	0.040	0.000	0.000	0.000	0.000	0.000	0.000	0.000	0.000	0.000	0.000	0.000	0.000	0.000	n/a
	0.384	0	0	0	0	0	0	0	0	0	0	0	0	0	
	1	0	0	0	0	0	0	0	0	0	0	0	0	0	
	1	0	0	0	0	0	0	0	0	0	0	0	0	0	
	1.0	0.0	0.0	0.0	0.0	0.0	0.0	0.0	0.0	0.0	0.0	0.0	0.0	0.0	
19	0.000	0.071	0.000	0.000	0.000	0.000	0.000	0.000	0.000	0.000	0.000	0.000	0.000	0.143	0.214
	0	0.503	0	0	0	0	0	0	0	0	0	0	0	0.485	0.464
	0	1	0	0	0	0	0	0	0	0	0	0	0	2	3
	0	1	0	0	0	0	0	0	0	0	0	0	0	2	3
	0.0	1.0	0.0	0.0	0.0	0.0	0.0	0.0	0.0	0.0	0.0	0.0	0.0	1.0	1.0
20	0.000	0.000	0.000	0.000	0.000	0.000	0.000	0.000	0.000	0.000	0.000	0.000	0.000	0.000	0.071
	0	0	0	0	0	0	0	0	0	0	0	0	0	0	0.356
	0	0	0	0	0	0	0	0	0	0	0	0	0	0	2
	0	0	0	0	0	0	0	0	0	0	0	0	0	0	2
	0.0	0.0	0.0	0.0	0.0	0.0	0.0	0.0	0.0	0.0	0.0	0.0	0.0	0.0	1.0

Appendix D. Movement Probabilities for Radio-Tagged Coho Salmon between Individual Antennas from the Approach Dataset at Cowlitz Falls Dam during 2011. —Continued

[Each cell contains five rows of data including the probability of movement (row 1), the 95-percent confidence interval for the probability estimate (row 2) the number of movements (row 3), the number of fish that made movements (row 4), and the average number of movements per fish (row 5)]

Current location	Antenna													
	19	20	21	22	23	24	25	26	27	28	29	30	31	Tailrace
11	0.000	0.000	0.000	0.000	0.143	0.000	0.000	0.000	0.000	0.000	0.000	0.000	0.000	0.143
					0.686									0.686
	0	0	0	0	1	0	0	0	0	0	0	0	0	1
	0	0	0	0	1	0	0	0	0	0	0	0	0	1
	0.0	0.0	0.0	0.0	1.0	0.0	0.0	0.0	0.0	0.0	0.0	0.0	0.0	1.0
13	0.000	0.000	0.000	0.000	0.000	0.000	0.000	0.000	0.000	0.000	0.000	0.000	0.000	0.000
	0	0	0	0	0	0	0	0	0	0	0	0	0	0
	0	0	0	0	0	0	0	0	0	0	0	0	0	0
	0.0	0.0	0.0	0.0	0.0	0.0	0.0	0.0	0.0	0.0	0.0	0.0	0.0	0.0
14	0.000	0.000	0.000	0.000	0.000	0.000	0.000	0.000	0.000	0.200	0.000	0.000	0.000	0.000
										0.784				
	0	0	0	0	0	0	0	0	0	1	0	0	0	0
	0	0	0	0	0	0	0	0	0	1	0	0	0	0
	0.0	0.0	0.0	0.0	0.0	0.0	0.0	0.0	0.0	1.0	0.0	0.0	0.0	0.0
15	0.000	0.000	0.000	0.000	0.000	0.200	0.400	0.000	0.000	0.400	0.000	0.000	0.000	0.200
						0.554	0.679			0.679				0.784
	0	0	0	0	0	2	2	0	0	2	0	0	0	1
	0	0	0	0	0	2	2	0	0	2	0	0	0	1
	0.0	0.0	0.0	0.0	0.0	1.0	1.0	0.0	0.0	1.0	0.0	0.0	0.0	1.0
16	0.000	0.000	0.000	0.000	0.000	0.000	0.100	0.000	0.000	0.000	0.000	0.000	0.000	0.100
							0.588							0.588
	0	0	0	0	0	0	1	0	0	0	0	0	0	1
	0	0	0	0	0	0	1	0	0	0	0	0	0	1
	0.0	0.0	0.0	0.0	0.0	0.0	1.0	0.0	0.0	0.0	0.0	0.0	0.0	1.0
17	0.158	0.000	0.000	0.000	0.000	0.263	0.000	0.000	0.053	0.105	0.053	0.000	0.000	0.053
	0.413					0.386			0.439	0.425	0.439			0.439
	3	0	0	0	0	5	0	0	1	2	1	0	0	1
	2	0	0	0	0	5	0	0	1	2	1	0	0	1
	1.5	0.0	0.0	0.0	0.0	1.0	0.0	0.0	1.0	1.0	1.0	0.0	0.0	1.0
18	0.080	0.600	0.040	0.000	0.000	0.040	0.000	0.000	0.040	0.000	0.000	0.000	0.040	0.000
	0.376	0.248	0.384			0.384			0.384				0.384	
	2	15	1	0	0	1	0	0	1	0	0	0	1	0
	2	14	1	0	0	1	0	0	1	0	0	0	1	0
	1.0	1.1	1.0	0.0	0.0	1.0	0.0	0.0	1.0	0.0	0.0	0.0	1.0	0.0
19	n/a	0.214	0.000	0.000	0.000	0.143	0.000	0.000	0.000	0.000	0.000	0.000	0.214	0.000
		0.464				0.485							0.464	
		3	0	0	0	2	0	0	0	0	0	0	3	0
		2	0	0	0	2	0	0	0	0	0	0	3	0
		1.5	0.0	0.0	0.0	1.0	0.0	0.0	0.0	0.0	0.0	0.0	1.0	0.0
20	0.071	n/a	0.429	0.036	0.107	0.000	0.000	0.000	0.000	0.000	0.000	0.036	0.214	0.036
	0.356		0.280	0.365	0.350							0.365	0.328	0.365
	2		12	1	3	0	0	0	0	0	0	1	6	1
	2		9	1	3	0	0	0	0	0	0	1	6	1
	1.0		1.3	1.0	1.0	0.0	0.0	0.0	0.0	0.0	0.0	1.0	1.0	1.0

68

Appendix D. Movement Probabilities for Radio-Tagged Coho Salmon between Individual Antennas from the Approach Dataset at Cowlitz Falls Dam during 2011. —Continued

[Each cell contains five rows of data including the probability of movement (row 1), the 95-percent confidence interval for the probability estimate (row 2) the number of movements (row 3), the number of fish that made movements (row 4), and the average number of movements per fish (row 5)]

Current location		Antenna														
		2	3	4	5	6	7	9	10	11	13	14	15	16	17	18
21		0.026	0.000	0.000	0.000	0.000	0.000	0.000	0.000	0.000	0.000	0.000	0.000	0.000	0.000	0.051
		0.312	0	0	0	0	0	0	0	0	0	0	0	0	0	0.305
		1	0	0	0	0	0	0	0	0	0	0	0	0	0	2
		1	0	0	0	0	0	0	0	0	0	0	0	0	0	1
		1.0	0.0	0.0	0.0	0.0	0.0	0.0	0.0	0.0	0.0	0.0	0.0	0.0	0.0	2.0
22		0.000	0.000	0.000	0.000	0.000	0.000	0.000	0.000	0.000	0.000	0.000	0.000	0.000	0.000	0.000
		0	0	0	0	0	0	0	0	0	0	0	0	0	0	0
		0	0	0	0	0	0	0	0	0	0	0	0	0	0	0
		0.0	0.0	0.0	0.0	0.0	0.0	0.0	0.0	0.0	0.0	0.0	0.0	0.0	0.0	0.0

Current location		Antenna													
		19	20	21	22	23	24	25	26	27	28	29	30	31	Tailrace
21		0.000	0.077	n/a	0.513	0.026	0.077	0.000	0.000	0.026	0.000	0.000	0.000	0.205	0.000
		0	0.302		0.219	0.312	0.302	0	0	0.312	0	0	0	0.280	0
		0	3		20	1	3	0	0	1	0	0	0	8	0
		0	2		4	1	3	0	0	1	0	0	0	8	0
		0.0	1.5		5.0	1.0	1.0	0.0	0.0	1.0	0.0	0.0	0.0	1.0	0.0
22		0.000	0.000	0.952	n/a	0.000	0.000	0.000	0.000	0.000	0.000	0.000	0.000	0.048	0.000
		0	0	0.094		0	0	0	0	0	0	0	0	0.419	0
		0	0	20		0	0	0	0	0	0	0	0	1	0
		0	0	4		0	0	0	0	0	0	0	0	1	0
		0.0	0.0	5.0		0.0	0.0	0.0	0.0	0.0	0.0	0.0	0.0	1.0	0.0

Appendix E. Movement Probabilities for Radio-Tagged Chinook Salmon between Individual Antennas from the Approach Dataset at Cowlitz Falls Dam during 2011.

[Each cell contains five rows of data including the probability of movement (row 1), the 95-percent confidence interval for the probability estimate (row 2) the number of movements (row 3), the number of fish that made movements (row 4), and the average number of movements per fish (row 5)]

Current location	2	3	4	5	6	7	8	9	10	11	13	14	15	16	17
Forebay entry	0.162	0.081	0.121	0.152	0.141	0.040	0.000	0.010	0.010	0.020	0.010	0.000	0.000	0.000	0.040
	0.181	0.189	0.185	0.182	0.182	0.192		0.195	0.195	0.194	0.195				0.192
	16	8	12	15	14	4	0	1	1	2	1	0	0	0	4
	16	8	12	15	14	4	0	1	1	2	1	0	0	0	4
	1.0	1.0	1.0	1.0	1.0	1.0	0.0	1.0	1.0	1.0	1.0	0.0	0.0	0.0	1.0
2	n/a	0.600	0.040	0.040	0.040	0.080	0.000	0.000	0.000	0.000	0.080	0.000	0.000	0.000	0.040
		0.248	0.384	0.384	0.384	0.376					0.376				0.384
		15	1	1	1	2	0	0	0	0	2	0	0	0	1
		14	1	1	1	2	0	0	0	0	2	0	0	0	1
		1.1	1.0	1.0	1.0	1.0	0.0	0.0	0.0	0.0	1.0	0.0	0.0	0.0	1.0
3	0.073	n/a	0.342	0.024	0.073	0.000	0.171	0.049	0.000	0.000	0.049	0.122	0.073	0.000	0.000
	0.294		0.248	0.300	0.294		0.279	0.299			0.299	0.287	0.294		
	3		14	1	3	0	7	2	0	0	2	5	3	0	0
	2		14	1	3	0	7	2	0	0	2	5	3	0	0
	1.5		1.0	1.0	1.0	0.0	1.0	1.0	0.0	0.0	1.0	1.0	1.0	0.0	0.0
4	0.026	0.132	n/a	0.553	0.079	0.000	0.000	0.158	0.000	0.000	0.000	0.000	0.026	0.000	0.000
	0.312	0.297		0.213	0.305			0.292					0.312		
	1	5		21	3	0	0	6	0	0	0	0	1	0	0
	1	4		21	3	0	0	6	0	0	0	0	1	0	0
	1.0	1.3		1.0	1.0	0.0	0.0	1.0	0.0	0.0	0.0	0.0	1.0	0.0	0.0
5	0.000	0.000	0.063	n/a	0.500	0.000	0.000	0.016	0.156	0.000	0.000	0.000	0.000	0.063	0.141
			0.238		0.173			0.246	0.225					0.238	0.227
	0	0	4		32	0	0	1	10	0	0	0	0	4	9
	0	0	4		29	0	0	1	7	0	0	0	0	4	9
	0.0	0.0	1.0		1.1	0.0	0.0	1.0	1.4	0.0	0.0	0.0	0.0	1.0	1.0
6	0.000	0.000	0.011	0.148	n/a	0.000	0.000	0.000	0.034	0.080	0.000	0.000	0.000	0.023	0.216
			0.204	0.193					0.205	0.201				0.208	0.185
	0	0	1	13		0	0	0	3	7	0	0	0	2	19
	0	0	1	12		0	0	0	3	7	0	0	0	2	16
	0.0	0.0	1.0	1.1		0.0	0.0	0.0	1.0	1.0	0.0	0.0	0.0	1.0	1.2
7	0.286	0.286	0.000	0.000	0.000	n/a	0.000	0.000	0.000	0.000	0.429	0.000	0.000	0.000	0.000
	0.626	0.626									0.560				
	2	2	0	0	0		0	0	0	0	3	0	0	0	0
	2	2	0	0	0		0	0	0	0	3	0	0	0	0
	1.0	1.0	0.0	0.0	0.0		0.0	0.0	0.0	0.0	1.0	0.0	0.0	0.0	0.0
8	0.000	0.222	0.111	0.000	0.000	0.000	n/a	0.222	0.000	0.000	0.000	0.111	0.111	0.000	0.000
		0.576	0.616					0.576				0.616	0.616		
	0	2	1	0	0	0		2	0	0	0	1	1	0	0
	0	2	1	0	0	0		2	0	0	0	1	1	0	0
	0.0	1.0	1.0	0.0	0.0	0.0		1.0	0.0	0.0	0.0	1.0	1.0	0.0	0.0
9	0.063	0.125	0.188	0.000	0.000	0.000	0.000	n/a	0.000	0.000	0.063	0.063	0.250	0.125	0.000
	0.476	0.458	0.442								0.476	0.476	0.424	0.458	
	1	2	3	0	0	0	0		0	0	1	1	4	2	0
	1	2	3	0	0	0	0		0	0	1	1	4	2	0
	1.0	1.0	1.0	0.0	0.0	0.0	0.0		0.0	0.0	1.0	1.0	1.0	1.0	0.0

Appendix E. Movement Probabilities for Radio-Tagged Chinook Salmon between Individual Antennas from the Approach Dataset at Cowlitz Falls Dam during 2011.—Continued

[Each cell contains five rows of data including the probability of movement (row 1), the 95-percent confidence interval for the probability estimate (row 2) the number of movements (row 3), the number of fish that made movements (row 4), and the average number of movements per fish (row 5)]

Current location	Antenna														
	18	19	20	21	22	23	24	25	26	27	28	29	30	31	Tailrace
Forebay entry	0.061	0.020	0.051	0.020	0.020	0.000	0.000	0.000	0.000	0.030	0.000	0.000	0.000	0.000	0.010
	0.192	0.194	0.193	0.194	0.194	0	0	0	0	0.193	0	0	0	0	0.195
	6	2	5	2	2	0	0	0	0	3	0	0	0	0	1
	6	2	5	2	2	0	0	0	0	3	0	0	0	0	1
	1.0	1.0	1.0	1.0	1.0	0.0	0.0	0.0	0.0	1.0	0.0	0.0	0.0	0.0	1.0
2	0.040	0.000	0.000	0.000	0.000	0.000	0.000	0.000	0.000	0.000	0.040	0.000	0.000	0.000	0.000
	0.384	0	0	0	0	0	0	0	0	0	0.384	0	0	0	0
	1	0	0	0	0	0	0	0	0	0	1	0	0	0	0
	1	0	0	0	0	0	0	0	0	0	1	0	0	0	0
	1.0	0.0	0.0	0.0	0.0	0.0	0.0	0.0	0.0	0.0	1.0	0.0	0.0	0.0	0.0
3	0.000	0.000	0.000	0.000	0.000	0.000	0.000	0.000	0.000	0.000	0.000	0.000	0.000	0.000	0.000
	0	0	0	0	0	0	0	0	0	0	0	0	0	0	0
	0	0	0	0	0	0	0	0	0	0	0	0	0	0	0
	0	0	0	0	0	0	0	0	0	0	0	0	0	0	0
	0.0	0.0	0.0	0.0	0.0	0.0	0.0	0.0	0.0	0.0	0.0	0.0	0.0	0.0	0.0
4	0.000	0.000	0.000	0.000	0.000	0.000	0.024	0.000	0.026	0.000	0.000	0.000	0.000	0.000	0.000
	0	0	0	0	0	0	0.300	0	0.312	0	0	0	0	0	0
	0	0	0	0	0	0	1	0	1	0	0	0	0	0	0
	0	0	0	0	0	0	1	0	1	0	0	0	0	0	0
	0.0	0.0	0.0	0.0	0.0	0.0	1.0	0.0	1.0	0.0	0.0	0.0	0.0	0.0	0.0
5	0.000	0.016	0.000	0.000	0.000	0.000	0.000	0.011	0.000	0.000	0.000	0.016	0.000	0.000	0.000
	0	0.246	0	0	0	0	0	0.204	0	0	0	0.246	0	0	0
	0	1	0	0	0	0	0	1	0	0	0	1	0	0	0
	0	1	0	0	0	0	0	1	0	0	0	1	0	0	0
	0.0	1.0	0.0	0.0	0.0	0.0	0.0	1.0	0.0	0.0	0.0	1.0	0.0	0.0	0.0
6	0.341	0.046	0.023	0.034	0.000	0.000	0.011	0.000	0.000	0.000	0.000	0.000	0.000	0.023	0.000
	0.170	0.205	0.208	0.205	0	0	0.204	0	0	0	0	0	0	0.208	0
	30	4	2	3	0	0	1	0	0	0	0	0	0	2	0
	27	4	2	3	0	0	1	0	0	0	0	0	0	2	0
	1.1	1.0	1.0	1.0	0.0	0.0	1.0	0.0	0.0	0.0	0.0	0.0	0.0	1.0	0.0
7	0.000	0.000	0.000	0.000	0.000	0.000	0.000	0.000	0.000	0.000	0.000	0.000	0.000	0.000	0.000
	0	0	0	0	0	0	0	0	0	0	0	0	0	0	0
	0	0	0	0	0	0	0	0	0	0	0	0	0	0	0
	0	0	0	0	0	0	0	0	0	0	0	0	0	0	0
	0.0	0.0	0.0	0.0	0.0	0.0	0.0	0.0	0.0	0.0	0.0	0.0	0.0	0.0	0.0
8	0.000	0.000	0.000	0.000	0.000	0.111	0.111	0.000	0.000	0.000	0.000	0.000	0.000	0.000	0.000
	0	0	0	0	0	0.616	0.616	0	0	0	0	0	0	0	0
	0	0	0	0	0	1	1	0	0	0	0	0	0	0	0
	0	0	0	0	0	1	1	0	0	0	0	0	0	0	0
	0.0	0.0	0.0	0.0	0.0	1.0	1.0	0.0	0.0	0.0	0.0	0.0	0.0	0.0	0.0
9	0.000	0.000	0.000	0.000	0.000	0.063	0.000	0.000	0.063	0.000	0.000	0.000	0.000	0.000	0.000
	0	0	0	0	0	0.476	0	0	0.476	0	0	0	0	0	0
	0	0	0	0	0	1	0	0	1	0	0	0	0	0	0
	0	0	0	0	0	1	0	0	1	0	0	0	0	0	0
	0.0	0.0	0.0	0.0	0.0	1.0	0.0	0.0	1.0	0.0	0.0	0.0	0.0	0.0	0.0

Appendix E. Movement Probabilities for Radio-Tagged Chinook Salmon between Individual Antennas from the Approach Dataset at Cowlitz Falls Dam during 2011.—Continued

[Each cell contains five rows of data including the probability of movement (row 1), the 95-percent confidence interval for the probability estimate (row 2) the number of movements (row 3), the number of fish that made movements (row 4), and the average number of movements per fish (row 5)]

Current location	row	Antenna														
		2	3	4	5	6	7	8	9	10	11	13	14	15	16	17
10	1	0.000	0.000	0.000	0.600	0.200	0.000	0.000	0.000	n/a	0.000	0.000	0.000	0.000	0.133	0.000
	2	0	0	0	0.320	0.453	0	0	0		0	0	0	0	0.471	0
	3	0	0	0	9	3	0	0	0		0	0	0	0	2	0
	4	0	0	0	6	3	0	0	0		0	0	0	0	2	0
	5	0.0	0.0	0.0	1.5	1.0	0.0	0.0	0.0		0.0	0.0	0.0	0.0	1.0	0.0
11	1	0.000	0.000	0.000	0.000	0.188	0.000	0.000	0.000	0.000	n/a	0.000	0.000	0.000	0.000	0.563
	2	0	0	0	0	0.442	0	0	0	0		0	0	0	0	0.324
	3	0	0	0	0	3	0	0	0	0		0	0	0	0	9
	4	0	0	0	0	3	0	0	0	0		0	0	0	0	8
	5	0.0	0.0	0.0	0.0	1.0	0.0	0.0	0.0	0.0		0.0	0.0	0.0	0.0	1.1
13	1	0.167	0.250	0.000	0.000	0.000	0.083	0.000	0.000	0.000	0.000	n/a	0.500	0.000	0.000	0.000
	2	0.517	0.490	0	0	0	0.541	0	0	0	0		0.400	0	0	0
	3	2	3	0	0	0	1	0	0	0	0		6	0	0	0
	4	2	3	0	0	0	1	0	0	0	0		6	0	0	0
	5	1.0	1.0	0.0	0.0	0.0	1.0	0.0	0.0	0.0	0.0		1.0	0.0	0.0	0.0
14	1	0.000	0.143	0.000	0.000	0.000	0.000	0.143	0.071	0.000	0.000	0.143	n/a	0.214	0.071	0.000
	2	0	0.485	0	0	0	0	0.485	0.503	0	0	0.485		0.464	0.503	0
	3	0	2	0	0	0	0	2	1	0	0	2		3	1	0
	4	0	2	0	0	0	0	2	1	0	0	2		3	1	0
	5	0.0	1.0	0.0	0.0	0.0	0.0	1.0	1.0	0.0	0.0	1.0		1.0	1.0	0.0
15	1	0.000	0.077	0.077	0.000	0.000	0.000	0.000	0.154	0.000	0.000	0.000	0.077	n/a	0.231	0.000
	2	0	0.523	0.523	0	0	0	0	0.500	0	0	0	0.523		0.477	0
	3	0	1	1	0	0	0	0	2	0	0	0	1		3	0
	4	0	1	1	0	0	0	0	2	0	0	0	1		3	0
	5	0.0	1.0	1.0	0.0	0.0	0.0	0.0	1.0	0.0	0.0	0.0	1.0		1.0	0.0
16	1	0.000	0.000	0.000	0.067	0.000	0.000	0.000	0.000	0.067	0.000	0.000	0.000	0.067	n/a	0.467
	2	0	0	0	0.490	0	0	0	0	0.490	0	0	0	0.490		0.370
	3	0	0	0	1	0	0	0	0	1	0	0	0	1		7
	4	0	0	0	1	0	0	0	0	1	0	0	0	1		7
	5	0.0	0.0	0.0	1.0	0.0	0.0	0.0	0.0	1.0	0.0	0.0	0.0	1.0		1.0
17	1	0.000	0.000	0.000	0.036	0.327	0.000	0.000	0.018	0.000	0.127	0.000	0.000	0.000	0.018	n/a
	2	0	0	0	0.258	0.217	0	0	0.261	0	0.247	0	0	0	0.261	
	3	0	0	0	2	18	0	0	1	0	7	0	0	0	1	
	4	0	0	0	2	13	0	0	1	0	6	0	0	0	1	
	5	0.0	0.0	0.0	1.0	1.4	0.0	0.0	1.0	0.0	1.2	0.0	0.0	0.0	1.0	
18	1	0.000	0.015	0.015	0.000	0.167	0.000	0.000	0.000	0.000	0.000	0.000	0.000	0.000	0.000	0.015
	2	0	0.238	0.238	0	0.220	0	0	0	0	0	0	0	0	0	0.238
	3	0	1	1	0	11	0	0	0	0	0	0	0	0	0	1
	4	0	1	1	0	10	0	0	0	0	0	0	0	0	0	1
	5	0.0	1.0	1.0	0.0	1.1	0.0	0.0	0.0	0.0	0.0	0.0	0.0	0.0	0.0	1.0
19	1	0.000	0.000	0.000	0.000	0.000	0.000	0.000	0.000	0.000	0.000	0.000	0.000	0.000	0.000	0.079
	2	0	0	0	0	0	0	0	0	0	0	0	0	0	0	0.305
	3	0	0	0	0	0	0	0	0	0	0	0	0	0	0	3
	4	0	0	0	0	0	0	0	0	0	0	0	0	0	0	3
	5	0.0	0.0	0.0	0.0	0.0	0.0	0.0	0.0	0.0	0.0	0.0	0.0	0.0	0.0	1.0

Appendix E. Movement Probabilities for Radio-Tagged Chinook Salmon between Individual Antennas from the Approach Dataset at Cowlitz Falls Dam during 2011.—Continued

[Each cell contains five rows of data including the probability of movement (row 1), the 95-percent confidence interval for the probability estimate (row 2) the number of movements (row 3), the number of fish that made movements (row 4), and the average number of movements per fish (row 5)]

Current location	18	19	20	21	22	23	24	25	26	27	28	29	30	31	Tailrace
10	0.000 0 0 0.0	0.000 0 0 0.0	0.067 0.490 1 1 1.0	0.000 0 0 0.0	0.000 0 0 0.0	0.000 0 0 0.0	0.000 0 0 0.0	0.000 0 0 0.0	0.000 0 0 0.0	0.000 0 0 0.0	0.000 0 0 0.0	0.000 0 0 0.0	0.000 0 0 0.0	0.000 0 0 0.0	0.000 0 0 0.0
11	0.000 0 0 0.0	0.063 0.476 1 1 1.0	0.000 0 0 0.0	0.000 0 0 0.0	0.063 0.476 1 1 1.0	0.000 0 0 0.0	0.000 0 0 0.0	0.063 0.476 1 1 1.0	0.000 0 0 0.0	0.000 0 0 0.0	0.000 0 0 0.0	0.000 0 0 0.0	0.000 0 0 0.0	0.063 0.476 1 1 1.0	0.000 0 0 0.0
13	0.000 0 0 0.0	0.000 0 0 0.0	0.000 0 0 0.0	0.000 0 0 0.0	0.000 0 0 0.0	0.000 0 0 0.0	0.000 0 0 0.0	0.000 0 0 0.0	0.000 0 0 0.0	0.000 0 0 0.0	0.000 0 0 0.0	0.000 0 0 0.0	0.000 0 0 0.0	0.000 0 0 0.0	0.000 0 0 0.0
14	0.000 0 0 0.0	0.000 0 0 0.0	0.000 0 0 0.0	0.000 0 0 0.0	0.071 0.503 1 1 1.0	0.000 0 0 0.0	0.071 0.503 1 1 1.0	0.000 0 0 0.0	0.000 0 0 0.0	0.000 0 0 0.0	0.071 0.503 1 1 1.0	0.000 0 0 0.0	0.000 0 0 0.0	0.000 0 0 0.0	0.000 0 0 0.0
15	0.000 0 0 0.0	0.000 0 0 0.0	0.000 0 0 0.0	0.000 0 0 0.0	0.000 0 0 0.0	0.000 0 0 0.0	0.000 0 0 0.0	0.154 0.500 2 2 1.0	0.077 0.523 1 1 1.0	0.154 0.500 2 2 1.0	0.000 0 0 0.0	0.0 0 0 0.0	0.000 0 0 0.0	0.000 0 0 0.0	0.0 0 0 0.0
16	0.000 0 0 0.0	0.000 0 0 0.0	0.000 0 0 0.0	0.000 0 0 0.0	0.000 0 0 0.0	0.000 0 0 0.0	0.067 0.490 1 1 1.0	0.133 0.471 2 2 1.0	0.067 0.490 1 1 1.0	0.067 0.490 1 1 1.0	0.000 0 0 0.0	0.000 0 0 0.0	0.000 0 0 0.0	0.000 0 0 0.0	0.000 0 0 0.0
17	0.036 0.258 2 2 1.0	0.091 0.252 5 5 1.0	0.036 0.258 2 2 1.0	0.000 0 0 0.0	0.018 0.261 1 1 1.0	0.000 0 0 0.0	0.091 0.252 5 5 1.0	0.055 0.258 3 3 1.0	0.018 0.261 1 1 1.0	0.000 0 0 0.0	0.000 0 0 0.0	0.000 0 0 0.0	0.018 0.261 1 1 1.0	0.109 0.249 6 6 1.0	0.000 0 0 0.0
18	n/a	0.273 0.206 18 15 1.2	0.379 0.190 25 21 1.2	0.061 0.235 4 4 1.0	0.015 0.238 1 1 1.0	0.000 0 0 0.0	0.015 0.238 1 1 1.0	0.000 0 0 0.0	0.000 0 0 0.0	0.000 0 0 0.0	0.000 0 0 0.0	0.000 0 0 0.0	0.000 0 0 0.0	0.046 0.237 3 3 1.0	0.000 0 0 0.0
19	0.263 0.273 10 8 1.3	n/a	0.263 0.273 10 9 1.1	0.000 0 0 0.0	0.026 0.312 1 1 1.0	0.079 0.305 3 3 1.0	0.132 0.297 5 5 1.0	0.000 0 0 0.0	0.000 0 0 0.0	0.026 0.312 1 1 1.0	0.000 0 0 0.0	0.000 0 0 0.0	0.026 0.312 1 1 1.0	0.105 0.300 4 4 1.0	0.000 0 0 0.0

Appendix E. Movement Probabilities for Radio-Tagged Chinook Salmon between Individual Antennas from the Approach Dataset at Cowlitz Falls Dam during 2011.—Continued

[Each cell contains five rows of data including the probability of movement (row 1), the 95-percent confidence interval for the probability estimate (row 2) the number of movements (row 3), the number of fish that made movements (row 4), and the average number of movements per fish (row 5)]

Current location	Antenna														
	2	3	4	5	6	7	8	9	10	11	13	14	15	16	17
20	0.000 0 0 0.0	0.000 0 0 0.0	0.000 0 0 0.0	0.000 0 0 0.0	0.000 0 0 0.0	0.000 0 0 0.0	0.000 0 0 0.0	0.000 0 0 0.0	0.000 0 0 0.0	0.000 0 0 0.0	0.000 0 0 0.0	0.000 0 0 0.0	0.000 0 0 0.0	0.000 0 0 0.0	0.000 0 0 0.0
21	0.000 0 0 0.0	0.000 0 0 0.0	0.000 0 0 0.0	0.035 0.360 1 1 1.0	0.000 0 0 0.0	0.000 0 0 0.0	0.000 0 0 0.0	0.000 0 0 0.0	0.000 0 0 0.0	0.000 0 0 0.0	0.000 0 0 0.0	0.000 0 0 0.0	0.000 0 0 0.0	0.000 0 0 0.0	0.000 0 0 0.0
22	0.000 0 0 0.0	0.000 0 0 0.0	0.000 0 0 0.0	0.000 0 0 0.0	0.000 0 0 0.0	0.000 0 0 0.0	0.000 0 0 0.0	0.000 0 0 0.0	0.000 0 0 0.0	0.000 0 0 0.0	0.037 0.370 1 1 1.0	0.000 0 0 0.0	0.000 0 0 0.0	0.000 0 0 0.0	0.074 0.363 2 2 1.0

Current location	Antenna														
	18	19	20	21	22	23	24	25	26	27	28	29	30	31	Tailrace
20	0.254 0.220 15 12 1.3	0.102 0.242 6 5 1.2	n/a	0.271 0.218 16 9 1.8	0.153 0.235 9 9 1.0	0.068 0.247 4 4 1.0	0.034 0.251 2 2 1.0	0.034 0.251 2 2 1.0	0.000 0 0 0.0	0.017 0.253 1 1 1.0	0.000 0 0 0.0	0.000 0 0 0.0	0.017 0.253 1 1 1.0	0.051 0.249 3 3 1.0	0.000 0 0 0.0
21	0.000 0 0 0.0	0.000 0 0 0.0	0.448 0.270 13 7 1.9	n/a	0.379 0.287 11 9 1.2	0.000 0 0 0.0	0.035 0.360 1 1 1.0	0.000 0 0 0.0	0.000 0 0 0.0	0.035 0.360 1 1 1.0	0.000 0 0 0.0	0.000 0 0 0.0	0.000 0 0 0.0	0.035 0.360 1 1 1.0	0.035 0.360 1 1 1.0
22	0.000 0 0 0.0	0.037 0.370 1 1 1.0	0.037 0.370 1 1 1.0	0.148 0.348 4 3 1.3	n/a	0.148 0.348 4 4 1.0	0.148 0.348 4 4 1.0	0.000 0 0 0.0	0.000 0 0 0.0	0.000 0 0 0.0	0.000 0 0 0.0	0.000 0 0 0.0	0.000 0 0 0.0	0.370 0.299 10 10 1.0	0.000 0 0 0.0

Appendix F. Movement Probabilities for Radio-Tagged Steelhead between Individual Antennas from the Residence Dataset at Cowlitz Falls Dam during 2011.

[Each cell contains five rows of data including the probability of movement (row 1), the 95-percent confidence interval for the probability estimate (row 2) the number of movements (row 3), the number of fish that made movements (row 4), and the average number of movements per fish (row 5)]

Current location	Antenna 2	3	4	5	6	7	8	9	10	11	13	14	15	16	17	18	19
2	n/a	0.308 0.261 12 10 1.2	0.103 0.297 4 4 1.0	0.000 0 0 0.0	0.103 0.297 4 4 1.0	0.103 0.297 4 3 1.3	0.000 0 0 0.0	0.000 0 0 0.0	0.026 0.310 1 1 1.0	0.000 0 0 0.0	0.128 0.293 5 4 1.3	0.026 0.310 1 1 1.0	0.026 0.312 1 1 1.0	0.000 0 0 0.0	0.000 0 0 0.0	0.026 0.310 1 1 1.0	0.000 0 0 0.0
3	0.148 0.232 9 9 1.0	n/a	0.213 0.223 13 10 1.3	0.000 0 0 0.0	0.098 0.238 6 6 1.0	0.000 0 0 0.0	0.049 0.245 3 3 1.0	0.033 0.247 2 2 1.0	0.016 0.249 1 1 1.0	0.016 0.249 1 1 1.0	0.033 0.247 2 2 1.0	0.115 0.236 7 5 1.4	0.049 0.245 3 3 1.0	0.000 0 0 0.0	0.000 0 0 0.0	0.000 0 0 0.0	0.016 0.249 1 1 1.0
4	0.041 0.225 3 3 1.0	0.206 0.204 15 10 1.5	n/a	0.041 0.225 3 3 1.0	0.123 0.215 9 6 1.5	0.000 0 0 0.0	0.000 0 0 0.0	0.082 0.220 6 5 1.2	0.206 0.204 15 9 1.7	0.000 0 0 0.0	0.000 0 0 0.0	0.014 0.228 1 1 1.0	0.069 0.221 5 5 1.0	0.014 0.228 1 1 1.0	0.000 0 0 0.0	0.000 0 0 0.0	0.014 0.228 1 1 1.0
5	0.118 0.446 2 1 2.0	0.000 0 0 0.0	0.118 0.446 2 2 1.0	n/a	0.118 0.446 2 2 1.0	0.000 0 0 0.0	0.000 0 0 0.0	0.059 0.461 1 1 1.0	0.235 0.416 4 4 1.0	0.000 0 0 0.0	0.000 0 0 0.0	0.000 0 0 0.0	0.000 0 0 0.0	0.059 0.461 1 1 1.0	0.000 0 0 0.0	0.000 0 0 0.0	0.000 0 0 0.0
6	0.010 0.198 1 1 1.0	0.021 0.197 2 2 1.0	0.031 0.196 3 3 1.0	0.021 0.197 2 2 1.0	n/a	0.000 0 0 0.0	n/a	0.000 0 0 0.0	0.124 0.186 12 7 1.7	0.134 0.185 13 11 1.2	0.000 0 0 0.0	0.010 0.198 1 1 1.0	0.000 0 0 0.0	0.000 0 0 0.0	0.237 0.174 23 14 1.6	0.062 0.193 6 5 1.2	0.031 0.196 3 3 1.0
7	0.750 0.490 3 2 1.5	0.000 0 0 0.0	0.250 0.849 1 1 1.0	0.000 0 0 0.0	0.000 0 0 0.0	n/a	0.000 0 0 0.0	0.000 0 0 0.0	0.000 0 0 0.0	0.000 0 0 0.0	0.000 0 0 0.0	0.000 0 0 0.0	0.000 0 0 0.0	0.000 0 0 0.0	0.000 0 0 0.0	0.000 0 0 0.0	0.000 0 0 0.0
8	0.118 0.446 2 2 1.0	0.118 0.446 2 2 1.0	0.000 0 0 0.0	0.000 0 0 0.0	0.000 0 0 0.0	0.000 0 0 0.0	n/a	0.000 0 0 0.0	0.059 0.461 1 1 1.0	0.000 0 0 0.0	0.059 0.462 1 1 1.0	0.529 0.326 9 7 1.3	0.000 0 0 0.0	0.000 0 0 0.0	0.000 0 0 0.0	0.000 0 0 0.0	0.000 0 0 0.0
9	0.016 0.249 1 1 1.0	0.000 0 0 0.0	0.098 0.238 6 4 1.5	0.000 0 0 0.0	0.049 0.245 3 3 1.0	0.000 0 0 0.0	0.000 0 0 0.0	n/a	0.098 0.238 6 6 1.0	0.000 0 0 0.0	0.000 0 0 0.0	0.016 0.249 1 1 1.0	0.312 0.208 19 10 1.9	0.246 0.218 15 12 1.3	0.000 0 0 0.0	0.000 0 0 0.0	0.016 0.249 1 1 1.0
10	0.005 0.144 1 1 1.0	0.005 0.144 1 1 1.0	0.091 0.137 17 10 1.7	0.048 0.140 9 7 1.3	0.091 0.137 17 15 1.1	0.000 0 0 0.0	0.000 0 0 0.0	0.022 0.142 4 4 1.0	n/a	0.032 0.141 6 6 1.0	0.000 0 0 0.0	0.005 0.144 1 1 1.0	0.059 0.139 11 7 1.6	0.350 0.116 65 20 3.3	0.129 0.134 24 15 1.6	0.011 0.143 2 2 1.0	0.016 0.142 3 3 1.0

Appendix F. Movement Probabilities for Radio-Tagged Steelhead between Individual Antennas from the Residence Dataset at Cowlitz Falls Dam during 2011. —Continued

[Each cell contains five rows of data including the probability of movement (row 1), the 95-percent confidence interval for the probability estimate (row 2) the number of movements (row 3), the number of fish that made movements (row 4), and the average number of movements per fish (row 5)]

Current location	20	21	22	23	24	25	26	27	28	29	30	31	32	33	Facility	Tailrace
2	0.000	0.077	0.000	0.000	0.000	0.026	0.000	0.000	0.000	0.026	0.000	0.000	0.000	0.026	0.000	0.000
	0	0.301	0	0	0	0.310	0	0	0	0.310	0	0	0	0.310	0	0
	0	3	0	0	0	1	0	0	0	1	0	0	0	1	0	0
	0	3	0	0	0	1	0	0	0	1	0	0	0	1	0	0
	0.0	1.0	0.0	0.0	0.0	1.0	0.0	0.0	0.0	1.0	0.0	0.0	0.0	1.0	0.0	0.0
3	0.066	0.049	0.000	0.016	0.000	0.000	0.000	0.016	0.000	0.033	0.000	0.033	0.000	0.000	0.000	0.000
	0.243	0.245	0	0.249	0	0	0	0.249	0	0.247	0	0.247	0	0	0	0
	4	3	0	1	0	0	0	1	0	2	0	2	0	0	0	0
	4	3	0	1	0	0	0	1	0	2	0	2	0	0	0	0
	1.0	1.0	0.0	1.0	0.0	0.0	0.0	1.0	0.0	1.0	0.0	1.0	0.0	0.0	0.0	0.0
4	0.027	0.082	0.000	0.000	0.000	0.014	0.014	0.014	0.014	0.000	0.000	0.000	0.000	0.014	0.000	0.014
	0.226	0.220	0	0	0	0.228	0.228	0.228	0.228	0	0	0	0	0.228	0	0.228
	2	6	0	0	0	1	1	1	1	0	0	0	0	1	0	1
	2	5	0	0	0	1	1	1	1	0	0	0	0	1	0	1
	1.0	1.2	0.0	0.0	0.0	1.0	1.0	1.0	1.0	0.0	0.0	0.0	0.0	1.0	0.0	1.0
5	0.000	0.059	0.000	0.000	0.059	0.059	0.059	0.000	0.000	0.059	0.000	0.000	0.000	0.000	0.000	0.000
	0	0.461	0	0	0.461	0.461	0.461	0	0	0.461	0	0	0	0	0	0
	0	1	0	0	1	1	1	0	0	1	0	0	0	0	0	0
	0	1	0	0	1	1	1	0	0	1	0	0	0	0	0	0
	0.0	1.0	0.0	0.0	1.0	1.0	1.0	0.0	0.0	1.0	0.0	0.0	0.0	0.0	0.0	0.0
6	0.062	0.103	0.031	0.021	0.031	0.021	0.010	0.000	0.000	0.010	0.000	0.031	0.000	0.000	0.000	0.000
	0.193	0.188	0.196	0.197	0.196	0.197	0.198	0	0	0.198	0	0.196	0	0	0	0
	6	10	3	2	3	2	1	0	0	1	0	3	0	0	0	0
	5	7	3	2	3	2	1	0	0	1	0	3	0	0	0	0
	1.2	1.4	1.0	1.0	1.0	1.0	1.0	0.0	0.0	1.0	0.0	1.0	0.0	0.0	0.0	0.0
7	0.000	0.000	0.000	0.000	0.000	0.000	0.000	0.000	0.000	0.000	0.000	0.000	0.000	0.000	0.000	0.000
	0	0	0	0	0	0	0	0	0	0	0	0	0	0	0	0
	0	0	0	0	0	0	0	0	0	0	0	0	0	0	0	0
	0	0	0	0	0	0	0	0	0	0	0	0	0	0	0	0
	0.0	0.0	0.0	0.0	0.0	0.0	0.0	0.0	0.0	0.0	0.0	0.0	0.0	0.0	0.0	0.0
8	0.000	0.059	0.000	0.000	0.000	0.000	0.000	0.059	0.000	0.000	0.000	0.000	0.000	0.000	0.000	0.000
	0	0.461	0	0	0	0	0	0.461	0	0	0	0	0	0	0	0
	0	1	0	0	0	0	0	1	0	0	0	0	0	0	0	0
	0	1	0	0	0	0	0	1	0	0	0	0	0	0	0	0
	0.0	1.0	0.0	0.0	0.0	0.0	0.0	1.0	0.0	0.0	0.0	0.0	0.0	0.0	0.0	0.0
9	0.000	0.016	0.000	0.016	0.000	0.049	0.016	0.000	0.033	0.000	0.000	0.016	0.000	0.000	0.000	0.000
	0	0.249	0	0.249	0	0.245	0.249	0	0.247	0	0	0.249	0	0	0	0
	0	1	0	1	0	3	1	0	2	0	0	1	0	0	0	0
	0	1	0	1	0	3	1	0	2	0	0	1	0	0	0	0
	0.0	1.0	0.0	1.0	0.0	1.0	1.0	0.0	1.0	0.0	0.0	1.0	0.0	0.0	0.0	0.0
10	0.000	0.027	0.005	0.022	0.016	0.005	0.032	0.005	0.011	0.005	0.000	0.005	0.000	0.000	0.000	0.000
	0	0.142	0.144	0.142	0.142	0.144	0.141	0.144	0.143	0.144	0	0.144	0	0	0	0
	0	5	1	4	3	1	6	1	2	1	0	1	0	0	0	0
	0	5	1	3	3	1	6	1	2	1	0	1	0	0	0	0
	0.0	1.0	1.0	1.3	1.0	1.0	1.0	1.0	1.0	1.0	0.0	1.0	0.0	0.0	0.0	0.0

Appendix F. Movement Probabilities for Radio-Tagged Steelhead between Individual Antennas from the Residence Dataset at Cowlitz Falls Dam during 2011.—Continued

[Each cell contains five rows of data including the probability of movement (row 1), the 95-percent confidence interval for the probability estimate (row 2) the number of movements (row 3), the number of fish that made movements (row 4), and the average number of movements per fish (row 5)]

Current location		Antenna																
		2	3	4	5	6	7	8	9	10	11	13	14	15	16	17	18	19
11		0.000	0.004	0.000	0.004	0.051	0.000	0.000	0.000	0.008	n/a	0.000	0.008	0.000	0.004	0.793	0.004	0.051
		0	0.127	0	0.127	0.124	0	0	0	0.126		0	0.126	0	0.127	0.058	0.127	0.124
		0	1	0	1	12	0	0	0	2		0	2	0	1	188	1	12
		0	1	0	1	10	0	0	0	2		0	2	0	1	35	1	10
		0.0	1.0	0.0	1.0	1.2	0.0	0.0	0.0	1.0		0.0	1.0	0.0	1.0	5.4	1.0	1.2
13		0.169	0.046	0.015	0.000	0.031	0.000	0.000	0.015	0.000	0.000	n/a	0.415	0.108	0.031	0.000	0.000	0.031
		0.222	0.238	0.241	0	0.239	0	0	0.241	0	0		0.186	0.230	0.239	0	0	0.239
		11	3	1	0	2	0	0	1	0	0		27	7	2	0	0	2
		8	3	1	0	2	0	0	1	0	0		15	6	2	0	0	2
		1.4	1.0	1.0	0.0	1.0	0.0	0.0	1.0	0.0	0.0		1.8	1.2	1.0	0.0	0.0	1.0
14		0.008	0.129	0.008	0.000	0.000	0.000	0.081	0.008	0.024	0.000	0.234	n/a	0.315	0.032	0.024	0.000	0.008
		0.176	0.164	0.176	0	0	0	0.169	0.176	0.174	0	0.154		0.146	0.173	0.174	0	0.176
		1	16	1	0	0	0	10	1	3	0	29		39	4	3	0	1
		1	14	1	0	0	0	8	1	3	0	18		22	4	3	0	1
		1.0	1.1	1.0	0.0	0.0	0.0	1.3	1.0	1.0	0.0	1.6		1.8	1.0	1.0	0.0	1.0
15		0.000	0.011	0.069	0.000	0.000	0.000	0.005	0.197	0.037	0.011	0.011	0.128	n/a	0.325	0.059	0.005	0.011
		0	0.142	0.138	0	0	0	0.142	0.128	0.140	0.142	0.142	0.134		0.117	0.139	0.142	0.142
		0	2	13	0	0	0	1	37	7	2	2	24		61	11	1	2
		0	2	9	0	0	0	1	19	5	2	2	15		30	9	1	2
		0.0	1.0	1.4	0.0	0.0	0.0	1.0	1.9	1.4	1.0	1.0	1.6		2.0	1.2	1.0	1.0
16		0.000	0.000	0.003	0.000	0.007	0.000	0.000	0.010	0.307	0.003	0.007	0.007	0.137	n/a	0.355	0.000	0.024
		0	0	0.114	0	0.114	0	0	0.114	0.095	0.114	0.114	0.114	0.106		0.092	0	0.113
		0	0	1	0	2	0	0	3	90	1	2	2	40		104	0	7
		0	0	1	0	2	0	0	2	27	1	2	2	22		35	0	6
		0.0	0.0	1.0	0.0	1.0	0.0	0.0	1.5	3.3	1.0	1.0	1.0	1.8		3.0	0.0	1.2
17		0.000	0.000	0.001	0.000	0.036	0.000	0.000	0.001	0.044	0.274	0.004	0.010	0.014	0.151	n/a	0.013	0.265
		0	0	0.073	0	0.073	0	0	0.073	0.072	0.063	0.074	0.074	0.074	0.068		0.073	0.063
		0	0	1	0	25	0	0	1	31	192	3	7	10	106		9	186
		0	0	1	0	13	0	0	1	15	36	3	7	10	33		8	36
		0.0	0.0	1.0	0.0	1.9	0.0	0.0	1.0	2.1	5.3	1.0	1.0	1.0	3.2		1.1	5.2
18		0.000	0.000	0.012	0.000	0.036	0.000	0.000	0.006	0.018	0.000	0.000	0.006	0.000	0.000	0.012	n/a	0.824
		0	0	0.152	0	0.150	0	0	0.153	0.151	0	0	0.153	0	0	0.152		0.064
		0	0	2	0	6	0	0	1	3	0	0	1	0	0	2		136
		0	0	2	0	5	0	0	1	3	0	0	1	0	0	2		21
		0.0	0.0	1.0	0.0	1.2	0.0	0.0	1.0	1.0	0.0	0.0	1.0	0.0	0.0	1.0		6.5
19		0.000	0.002	0.000	0.000	0.005	0.000	0.002	0.000	0.002	0.016	0.003	0.003	0.005	0.006	0.364	0.215	n/a
		0	0.078	0	0	0.078	0	0.078	0	0.078	0.078	0.078	0.078	0.078	0.078	0.063	0.070	
		0	1	0	0	3	0	1	0	1	10	2	2	3	4	227	134	
		0	1	0	0	3	0	1	0	1	10	2	2	3	4	39	22	
		0.0	1.0	0.0	0.0	1.0	0.0	1.0	0.0	1.0	1.0	1.0	1.0	1.0	1.0	5.8	6.1	
20		0.009	0.000	0.004	0.000	0.004	0.000	0.000	0.000	0.004	0.000	0.000	0.004	0.009	0.000	0.017	0.038	0.592
		0.127	0	0.128	0	0.128	0	0	0	0.128	0	0	0.124	0.127	0	0.127	0.125	0.082
		2	0	1	0	1	0	0	0	1	0	0	1	2	0	4	9	139
		2	0	1	0	1	0	0	0	1	0	0	1	2	0	4	8	28
		1.0	0.0	1.0	0.0	1.0	0.0	0.0	0.0	1.0	0.0	0.0	1.0	1.0	0.0	1.0	1.1	5.0

Appendix F. Movement Probabilities for Radio-Tagged Steelhead between Individual Antennas from the Residence Dataset at Cowlitz Falls Dam during 2011.—Continued

[Each cell contains five rows of data including the probability of movement (row 1), the 95-percent confidence interval for the probability estimate (row 2) the number of movements (row 3), the number of fish that made movements (row 4), and the average number of movements per fish (row 5)]

Current location	Antenna															
	20	21	22	23	24	25	26	27	28	29	30	31	32	33	Facility	Tailrace
11	0.017	0.021	0.004	0.008	0.004	0.000	0.004	0.004	0.000	0.000	0.000	0.008	0.000	0.000	0.000	0.000
	0.126	0.126	0.127	0.126	0.127	0	0.127	0.127	0	0	0	0.126	0	0	0	0
	4	5	1	2	1	0	1	1	0	0	0	2	0	0	0	0
	3	5	1	2	1	0	1	1	0	0	0	2	0	0	0	0
	1.3	1.0	1.0	1.0	1.0	0.0	1.0	1.0	0.0	0.0	0.0	1.0	0.0	0.0	0.0	0.0
13	0.000	0.000	0.000	0.000	0.046	0.031	0.015	0.000	0.015	0.000	0.015	0.015	0.000	0.000	0.000	0.000
	0	0	0	0	0.238	0.239	0.241	0	0.241	0	0.241	0.241	0	0	0	0
	0	0	0	0	3	2	1	0	1	0	1	1	0	0	0	0
	0	0	0	0	2	2	1	0	1	0	1	1	0	0	0	0
	0.0	0.0	0.0	0.0	1.5	1.0	1.0	0.0	1.0	0.0	1.0	1.0	0.0	0.0	0.0	0.0
14	0.000	0.008	0.000	0.000	0.016	0.040	0.016	0.008	0.024	0.000	0.000	0.008	0.000	0.000	0.000	0.008
	0	0.176	0	0	0.174	0.172	0.174	0.176	0.174	0	0	0.176	0	0	0	0.176
	0	1	0	0	2	5	2	1	3	0	0	1	0	0	0	1
	0	1	0	0	2	5	2	1	3	0	0	1	0	0	0	1
	0.0	1.0	0.0	0.0	1.0	1.0	1.0	1.0	1.0	0.0	0.0	1.0	0.0	0.0	0.0	1.0
15	0.005	0.021	0.000	0.016	0.016	0.021	0.005	0.005	0.027	0.000	0.000	0.016	0.001	0.000	0.000	0.000
	0.142	0.141	0	0.142	0.142	0.141	0.142	0.138	0.141	0	0	0.142	0.073	0	0	0
	1	4	0	3	3	4	1	1	5	0	0	3	1	0	0	0
	1	4	0	3	3	4	1	1	4	0	0	2	1	0	0	0
	1.0	1.0	0.0	1.0	1.0	1.0	1.0	1.0	1.3	0.0	0.0	1.5	1.0	0.0	0.0	0.0
16	0.007	0.003	0.000	0.007	0.041	0.038	0.017	0.007	0.014	0.000	0.000	0.007	0.000	0.000	0.000	0.000
	0.114	0.114	0	0.114	0.112	0.112	0.114	0.114	0.114	0	0	0.114	0	0	0	0
	2	1	0	2	12	11	5	2	4	0	0	2	0	0	0	0
	2	1	0	2	11	10	5	2	4	0	0	2	0	0	0	0
	1.0	1.0	0.0	1.0	1.1	1.1	1.0	1.0	1.0	0.0	0.0	1.0	0.0	0.0	0.0	0.0
17	0.010	0.000	0.007	0.024	0.059	0.026	0.011	0.006	0.020	0.000	0.000	0.021	0.001	0.000	0.000	0.000
	0.074	0	0.074	0.073	0.072	0.073	0.074	0.074	0.073	0	0	0.073	0.073	0	0	0
	7	0	5	17	41	18	8	4	14	0	0	15	1	0	0	0
	7	0	4	10	26	15	8	4	8	0	0	13	1	0	0	0
	1.0	0.0	1.3	1.7	1.6	1.2	1.0	1.0	1.8	0.0	0.0	1.2	1.0	0.0	0.0	0.0
18	0.061	0.000	0.000	0.000	0.006	0.000	0.000	0.006	0.000	0.006	0.000	0.006	0.000	0.000	0.000	0.000
	0.148	0	0	0	0.153	0	0	0.153	0	0.153	0	0.153	0	0	0	0
	10	0	0	0	1	0	0	1	0	1	0	1	0	0	0	0
	7	0	0	0	1	0	0	1	0	1	0	1	0	0	0	0
	1.4	0.0	0.0	0.0	1.0	0.0	0.0	1.0	0.0	1.0	0.0	1.0	0.0	0.0	0.0	0.0
19	0.215	0.008	0.011	0.024	0.069	0.006	0.011	0.003	0.005	0.000	0.003	0.021	0.000	0.000	0.000	0.000
	0.070	0.078	0.078	0.078	0.076	0.078	0.078	0.078	0.078	0	0.078	0.078	0	0	0	0
	134	5	7	15	43	4	7	2	3	0	2	13	0	0	0	0
	26	4	5	10	26	4	7	2	3	0	2	12	0	0	0	0
	5.2	1.3	1.4	1.5	1.7	1.0	1.0	1.0	1.0	0.0	1.0	1.1	0.0	0.0	0.0	0.0
20	n/a	0.128	0.030	0.030	0.047	0.004	0.013	0.009	0.021	0.004	0.000	0.034	0.000	0.000	0.000	0.000
		0.119	0.126	0.126	0.125	0.128	0.127	0.127	0.127	0.128	0	0.126	0	0	0	0
		30	7	7	11	1	3	2	5	1	0	8	0	0	0	0
		17	5	6	11	1	3	1	5	1	0	7	0	0	0	0
		1.8	1.4	1.2	1.0	1.0	1.0	2.0	1.0	1.0	0.0	1.1	0.0	0.0	0.0	0.0

Appendix F. Movement Probabilities for Radio-Tagged Steelhead between Individual Antennas from the Residence Dataset at Cowlitz Falls Dam during 2011.—Continued

[Each cell contains five rows of data including the probability of movement (row 1), the 95-percent confidence interval for the probability estimate (row 2) the number of movements (row 3), the number of fish that made movements (row 4), and the average number of movements per fish (row 5)]

Current location	Antenna																
	2	3	4	5	6	7	8	9	10	11	13	14	15	16	17	18	19
21	0.019	0.019	0.028	0.000	0.009	0.000	0.009	0.000	0.019	0.000	0.000	0.009	0.009	0.009	0.037	0.000	0.009
	0.188	0.188	0.187	0	0.188	0	0.188	0	0.188	0	0	0.188	0.185	0.185	0.186	0	0.188
	2	2	3	0	1	0	1	0	2	0	0	1	1	1	4	0	1
	2	2	3	0	1	0	1	0	2	0	0	1	1	1	4	0	1
	1.0	1.0	1.0	0.0	1.0	0.0	1.0	0.0	1.0	0.0	0.0	1.0	1.0	1.0	1.0	0.0	1.0
22	0.000	0.015	0.002	0.000	0.000	0.000	0.000	0.000	0.000	0.015	0.000	0.000	0.000	0.015	0.044	0.000	0.265
	0	0.236	0.085	0	0	0	0	0	0	0.236	0	0	0	0.236	0.232	0	0.204
	0	1	1	0	0	0	0	0	0	1	0	0	0	1	3	0	18
	0	1	1	0	0	0	0	0	0	1	0	0	0	1	3	0	13
	0.0	1.0	1.0	0.0	0.0	0.0	0.0	0.0	0.0	1.0	0.0	0.0	0.0	1.0	1.0	0.0	1.4
23	0.000	0.000	0.000	0.000	0.002	0.000	0.000	0.000	0.000	0.000	0.000	0.004	0.004	0.000	0.021	0.000	0.028
	0	0	0	0	0.085	0	0	0	0	0	0	0.084	0.087	0	0.084	0	0.084
	0	0	1	0	1	0	0	0	0	0	0	2	2	0	11	0	15
	0	0	1	0	1	0	0	0	0	0	0	2	2	0	9	0	11
	0.0	0.0	1.0	0.0	1.0	0.0	0.0	0.0	0.0	0.0	0.0	1.0	1.0	0.0	1.2	0.0	1.4
24	0.000	0.000	0.003	0.003	0.000	0.000	0.000	0.003	0.000	0.017	0.013	0.017	0.017	0.030	0.124	0.003	0.114
	0	0	0.112	0.112	0	0	0	0.112	0	0.112	0.113	0.112	0.112	0.112	0.106	0.112	0.107
	0	0	1	1	0	0	0	1	0	5	4	5	5	9	37	1	34
	0	0	1	1	0	0	0	1	0	4	4	5	4	6	23	1	24
	0.0	0.0	1.0	1.0	0.0	0.0	0.0	1.0	0.0	1.3	1.0	1.0	1.3	1.5	1.6	1.0	1.4
25	0.000	0.003	0.000	0.000	0.000	0.000	0.000	0.003	0.003	0.007	0.007	0.010	0.020	0.030	0.070	0.003	0.063
	0	0.112	0	0	0	0	0	0.112	0.112	0.112	0.112	0.113	0.112	0.111	0.109	0.112	0.109
	0	1	0	0	0	0	0	1	1	2	2	3	6	9	21	1	19
	0	1	0	0	0	0	0	1	1	2	2	3	6	6	12	1	15
	0.0	1.0	0.0	0.0	0.0	0.0	0.0	1.0	1.0	1.0	1.0	1.0	1.0	1.5	1.8	1.0	1.3
26	0.000	0.000	0.000	0.000	0.000	0.000	0.000	0.000	0.000	0.007	0.007	0.022	0.022	0.009	0.015	0.000	0.015
	0	0	0	0	0	0	0	0	0	0.092	0.092	0.091	0.091	0.091	0.091	0	0.091
	0	0	0	0	0	0	0	0	0	3	3	10	10	4	7	0	7
	0	0	0	0	0	0	0	0	0	3	3	7	8	4	6	0	6
	0.0	0.0	0.0	0.0	0.0	0.0	0.0	0.0	0.0	1.0	1.0	1.4	1.3	1.0	1.2	0.0	1.2
27	0.000	0.002	0.000	0.000	0.000	0.000	0.002	0.000	0.002	0.002	0.000	0.013	0.007	0.002	0.004	0.000	0.015
	0	0.092	0	0	0	0	0.092	0	0.092	0.092	0	0.090	0.091	0.092	0.091	0	0.090
	0	1	0	0	0	0	1	0	1	1	0	6	3	1	2	0	7
	0	1	0	0	0	0	1	0	1	1	0	5	3	1	2	0	5
	0.0	1.0	0.0	0.0	0.0	0.0	1.0	0.0	1.0	1.0	0.0	1.2	1.0	1.0	1.0	0.0	1.4
28	0.003	0.003	0.007	0.000	0.010	0.000	0.000	0.003	0.007	0.000	0.017	0.020	0.063	0.020	0.050	0.000	0.036
	0.112	0.112	0.112	0	0.112	0	0	0.112	0.112	0	0.112	0.111	0.109	0.111	0.110	0	0.111
	1	1	2	0	3	0	0	1	2	0	5	6	19	6	15	0	11
	1	1	2	0	3	0	0	1	2	0	4	6	14	5	11	0	8
	1.0	1.0	1.0	0.0	1.0	0.0	0.0	1.0	1.0	1.0	1.3	1.0	1.4	1.2	1.4	0.0	1.4
29	0.000	0.000	0.000	0.000	0.000	0.000	0.000	0.000	0.000	0.000	0.000	0.000	0.000	0.000	0.000	0.000	0.000
	0	0	0	0	0	0	0	0	0	0	0	0	0.020	0	0.020	0	0
	0	0	0	0	0	0	0	0	0	0	0	0	1	0	2	0	0
	0	0	0	0	0	0	0	0	0	0	0	0	1	0	2	0	0
	0.0	0.0	0.0	0.0	0.0	0.0	0.0	0.0	0.0	0.0	0.0	0.0	1.0	0.0	1.0	0.0	0.0

Appendix F. Movement Probabilities for Radio-Tagged Steelhead between Individual Antennas from the Residence Dataset at Cowlitz Falls Dam during 2011.—Continued

[Each cell contains five rows of data including the probability of movement (row 1), the 95-percent confidence interval for the probability estimate (row 2) the number of movements (row 3), the number of fish that made movements (row 4), and the average number of movements per fish (row 5)]

Current location	\<Antenna\> 20	21	22	23	24	25	26	27	28	29	30	31	32	33	Facility	Tailrace
21	0.094		0.150	0.112	0.056	0.000	0.009	0.028	0.019	0.009	0.028	0.318	0.000	0.000	0.000	0.000
	0.180	n/a	0.175	0.179	0.184		0.188	0.187	0.188	0.188	0.187	0.157				
	10		16	12	6	0	1	3	2	1	3	34	0	0	0	0
	9		8	10	6	0	1	3	2	1	3	19	0	0	0	0
	1.1		2.0	1.2	1.0	0.0	1.0	1.0	1.0	1.0	1.0	1.8	0.0	0.0	0.0	0.0
22	0.162	0.162		0.103	0.118	0.000	0.029	0.000	0.000	0.000	0.000	0.059	0.015	0.000	0.000	0.000
	0.218	0.218	n/a	0.225	0.223		0.234					0.231	0.236			
	11	11		7	8	0	2	0	0	0	0	4	1	0	0	0
	8	11		7	4	0	2	0	0	0	0	4	1	0	0	0
	1.4	1.0		1.0	2.0	0.0	1.0	0.0	0.0	0.0	0.0	1.0	1.0	0.0	0.0	0.0
23	0.009	0.004	0.009		0.163	0.017	0.013	0.408	0.013	0.013	0.039	0.236	0.006	0.004	0.000	0.006
	0.085	0.084	0.085	n/a	0.078	0.084	0.084	0.065	0.084	0.084	0.083	0.074	0.084	0.084		0.084
	5	2	5		87	9	7	218	7	7	21	126	3	2	0	3
	5	2	5		30	9	7	42	7	6	20	39	3	2	0	3
	1.0	1.0	1.0		2.9	1.0	1.0	5.2	1.0	1.2	1.1	3.2	1.0	1.0	0.0	1.0
24	0.050	0.007	0.033	0.241		0.094	0.054	0.044	0.027	0.013	0.007	0.077	0.000	0.003	0.000	0.007
	0.111	0.113	0.111	0.099	n/a	0.108	0.110	0.111	0.112	0.113	0.113	0.109		0.112		0.113
	15	2	10	72		28	16	13	8	4	2	23	0	1	0	2
	10	2	6	30		20	11	10	7	4	2	20	0	1	0	2
	1.5	1.0	1.7	2.4		1.4	1.5	1.3	1.1	1.0	1.0	1.2	0.0	1.0	0.0	1.0
25	0.037	0.010	0.003	0.007	0.060		0.412	0.076	0.126	0.010	0.007	0.033	0.000	0.000	0.000	0.000
	0.111	0.113	0.112	0.112	0.110	n/a	0.087	0.109	0.106	0.113	0.112	0.111				
	11	3	1	2	18		124	23	38	3	2	10	0	0	0	0
	9	3	1	2	17		41	16	26	3	2	7	0	0	0	0
	1.2	1.0	1.0	1.0	1.1		3.0	1.4	1.5	1.0	1.0	1.4	0.0	0.0	0.0	0.0
26	0.004	0.000	0.002	0.002	0.007	0.297		0.146	0.395	0.022	0.013	0.002	0.004	0.000	0.000	0.009
	0.092	0	0.092	0.092	0.092	0.077	n/a	0.085	0.071	0.091	0.091	0.092	0.092			0.093
	2	0	1	1	3	136		67	181	10	6	1	2	0	0	4
	2	0	1	1	3	38		29	47	10	6	1	2	0	0	4
	1.0	0.0	1.0	1.0	1.0	3.6		2.3	3.9	1.0	1.0	1.0	1.0	0.0	0.0	1.0
27	0.007	0.007	0.002	0.435	0.007	0.019	0.216		0.019	0.075	0.095	0.032	0.013	0.011	0.000	0.013
	0.091	0.091	0.092	0.068	0.091	0.090	0.081	n/a	0.090	0.087	0.087	0.089	0.090	0.091		0.090
	3	3	1	202	3	9	100		9	35	44	15	6	5	0	6
	3	3	1	32	3	8	33		9	19	34	10	6	5	0	6
	1.0	1.0	1.0	6.3	1.0	1.1	3.0		1.0	1.8	1.3	1.5	1.0	1.0	0.0	1.0
28	0.013	0.007	0.003	0.023	0.036	0.162	0.436	0.033		0.000	0.010	0.003	0.003	0.007	0.000	0.026
	0.112	0.112	0.112	0.111	0.111	0.103	0.085	0.111	n/a	0	0.112	0.112	0.112	0.112		0.110
	4	2	1	7	11	49	132	10		0	3	1	1	2	0	8
	4	2	1	7	9	27	40	10		0	3	1	1	2	0	8
	1.0	1.0	1.0	1.0	1.2	1.8	3.3	1.0		0.0	1.0	1.0	1.0	1.0	0.0	1.0
29	0.000	0.000	0.000	0.000	0.000	0.000	0.002	0.004	0.000		0.002	0.000	0.990	0.000	0.000	0.001
	0	0.020	0	0.020	0	0	0.020	0.020	0.020	n/a	0.020	0.020	0.002	0.020		0.022
	0	1	0	1	0	0	22	41	4		20	1	9774	1	0	8
	0	1	0	1	0	0	16	21	4		17	1	40	1	0	8
	0.0	1.0	0.0	1.0	0.0	0.0	1.4	2.0	1.0		1.2	1.0	244.4	1.0	0.0	1.0

80

Appendix F. Movement Probabilities for Radio-Tagged Steelhead between Individual Antennas from the Residence Dataset at Cowlitz Falls Dam during 2011.—Continued

[Each cell contains five rows of data including the probability of movement (row 1), the 95-percent confidence interval for the probability estimate (row 2) the number of movements (row 3), the number of fish that made movements (row 4), and the average number of movements per fish (row 5)]

Current location		Antenna																
		2	3	4	5	6	7	8	9	10	11	13	14	15	16	17	18	19
30	Prob.	0.000	0.000	0.000	0.000	0.000	0.000	0.000	0.000	0.001	0.000	0.001	0.000	0.000	0.000	0.000	0.000	0.001
	95% CI	0	0.044	0	0	0	0	0	0	0.044	0	0.044	0	0	0	0	0	0.044
	Movements	0	0	0	0	0	0	0	0	1	0	1	0	0	0	0	0	1
	Fish	0	0	0	0	0	0	0	0	1	0	1	0	0	0	0	0	1
	Avg/fish	0.0	0.0	0.0	0.0	0.0	0.0	0.0	0.0	1.0	0.0	1.0	0.0	0.0	0.0	0.0	0.0	1.0
31	Prob.	0.000	0.000	0.000	0.003	0.000	0.000	0.000	0.003	0.003	0.000	0.010	0.013	0.003	0.007	0.043	0.000	0.053
	95% CI	0.112	0	0	0.112	0	0	0	0.112	0.112	0	0.113	0.112	0.112	0.113	0.111	0	0.110
	Movements	0	0	0	1	0	0	0	1	1	0	3	4	1	2	13	0	16
	Fish	0	0	0	1	0	0	0	1	1	0	3	4	1	2	10	0	12
	Avg/fish	0.0	0.0	0.0	1.0	0.0	0.0	0.0	1.0	1.0	0.0	1.0	1.0	1.0	1.0	1.3	0.0	1.3
32	Prob.	0.000	0.000	0.000	0.000	0.000	0.000	0.000	0.000	0.000	0.000	0.000	0.000	0.000	0.000	0.000	0.000	0.000
	95% CI	0	0	0	0	0	0	0	0	0	0	0	0	0	0	0	0	0
	Movements	0	0	0	0	0	0	0	0	0	0	0	0	0	0	0	0	0
	Fish	0	0	0	0	0	0	0	0	0	0	0	0	0	0	0	0	0
	Avg/fish	0.0	0.0	0.0	0.0	0.0	0.0	0.0	0.0	0.0	0.0	0.0	0.0	0.0	0.0	0.0	0.0	0.0
33	Prob.	0.000	0.000	0.000	0.000	0.000	0.000	0.000	0.000	0.000	0.000	0.000	0.000	0.000	0.000	0.000	0.000	0.000
	95% CI	0	0	0	0	0	0	0	0	0	0	0	0	0	0	0	0	0
	Movements	0	0	0	0	0	0	0	0	0	0	0	0	0	0	0	0	0
	Fish	0	0	0	0	0	0	0	0	0	0	0	0	0	0	0	0	0
	Avg/fish	0.0	0.0	0.0	0.0	0.0	0.0	0.0	0.0	0.0	0.0	0.0	0.0	0.0	0.0	0.0	0.0	0.0

Current location		Antenna															
		20	21	22	23	24	25	26	27	28	29	30	31	32	33	Facility	Tailrace
30	Prob.	0.000	0.001	0.000	0.002	0.001	0.001	0.003	0.019	0.001	0.009	n/a	0.005	0.002	0.949	0.004	0.005
	95% CI	0	0.044	0	0.045	0.044	0.046	0.045	0.045	0.044	0.045		0.045	0.045	0.010	0.055	0.049
	Movements	0	1	0	3	1	2	5	36	1	17		10	4	1795	5	8
	Fish	0	1	0	2	1	1	5	26	1	14		10	4	55	5	8
	Avg/fish	0.0	1.0	0.0	1.5	1.0	2.0	1.0	1.4	1.0	1.2		1.0	1.0	32.6	1.0	1.0
31	Prob.	0.013	0.020	0.030	0.507	0.077	0.007	0.030	0.090	0.013	0.023	0.023	n/a	0.007	0.007	0.003	0.010
	95% CI	0.112	0.112	0.111	0.079	0.109	0.113	0.111	0.108	0.112	0.112	0.112		0.113	0.113	0.107	0.113
	Movements	4	6	9	152	23	2	9	27	4	7	7		2	2	1	3
	Fish	4	6	7	47	17	2	8	18	3	6	6		2	2	1	3
	Avg/fish	1.0	1.0	1.3	3.2	1.4	1.0	1.1	1.5	1.3	1.2	1.2		1.0	1.0	1.0	1.0
32	Prob.	0.000	0.000	0.000	0.000	0.000	0.000	0.000	0.000	0.000	0.999	0.000	0.000	n/a	0.000	0.000	0.001
	95% CI	0	0	0	0	0	0	0	0.020	0.020	0.001	0.020	0		0.020	0.000	0.023
	Movements	0	0	0	0	0	0	0	1	1	9782	2	0		1	1	7
	Fish	0	0	0	0	0	0	0	1	1	39	2	0		1	1	7
	Avg/fish	0.0	0.0	0.0	0.0	0.0	0.0	0.0	1.0	1.0	250.8	1.0	0.0		1.0	1.0	1.0
33	Prob.	0.000	0.000	0.000	0.000	0.000	0.000	0.000	0.000	0.000	0.000	0.980	0.000	0.001	n/a	0.016	0.004
	95% CI	0	0	0	0	0	0	0	0	0	0	0.007	0	0.048		0.046	0.047
	Movements	0	0	0	0	0	0	0	0	0	0	1775	0	1		29	7
	Fish	0	0	0	0	0	0	0	0	0	0	54	0	1		29	6
	Avg/fish	0.0	0.0	0.0	0.0	0.0	0.0	0.0	0.0	0.0	0.0	32.9	0.0	1.0		1.0	1.2

Appendix G. Movement Probabilities for Radio-Tagged Coho Salmon between Individual Antennas from the Residence Dataset at Cowlitz Falls Dam during 2011.

[Each cell contains five rows of data including the probability of movement (row 1), the 95-percent confidence interval for the probability estimate (row 2) the number of movements (row 3), the number of fish that made movements (row 4), and the average number of movements per fish (row 5)]

Cell format: probability / 95% CI / number of movements / number of fish / average movements per fish

Current location		Antenna															
	2	3	4	5	6	7	8	9	10	11	13	14	15	16	17	18	19
2	n/a	0.750 / 0.490 / 3 / 2 / 1.5	0.000 / 0 / 0 / 0.0	0.000 / 0 / 0 / 0.0	0.000 / 0 / 0 / 0.0	0.000 / 0 / 0 / 0.0	0.000 / 0 / 0 / 0.0	0.000 / 0 / 0 / 0.0	0.000 / 0 / 0 / 0.0	0.250 / 0.849 / 1 / 1 / 1.0	0.000 / 0 / 0 / 0.0	0.000 / 0 / 0 / 0.0	0.000 / 0 / 0 / 0.0	0.000 / 0 / 0 / 0.0	0.000 / 0 / 0 / 0.0	0.000 / 0 / 0 / 0.0	0.000 / 0 / 0 / 0.0
3	0.118 / 0.446 / 2 / 2 / 1.0	n/a	0.235 / 0.416 / 4 / 3 / 1.3	0.000 / 0 / 0 / 0.0	0.118 / 0.446 / 2 / 2 / 1.0	0.000 / 0 / 0 / 0.0	0.118 / 0.446 / 2 / 2 / 1.0	0.118 / 0.446 / 2 / 2 / 1.0	0.059 / 0.461 / 1 / 1 / 1.0	0.000 / 0 / 0 / 0.0	0.000 / 0 / 0 / 0.0	0.177 / 0.431 / 3 / 2 / 1.5	0.000 / 0 / 0 / 0.0	0.000 / 0 / 0 / 0.0	0.000 / 0 / 0 / 0.0	0.000 / 0 / 0 / 0.0	0.000 / 0 / 0 / 0.0
4	0.000 / 0 / 0 / 0.0	0.188 / 0.442 / 3 / 3 / 1.0	n/a	0.000 / 0 / 0 / 0.0	0.063 / 0.474 / 1 / 1 / 1.0	0.000 / 0 / 0 / 0.0	0.000 / 0 / 0 / 0.0	0.125 / 0.458 / 2 / 2 / 1.0	0.125 / 0.458 / 2 / 2 / 1.0	0.000 / 0 / 0 / 0.0	0.000 / 0 / 0 / 0.0	0.000 / 0 / 0 / 0.0	0.313 / 0.406 / 5 / 3 / 1.7	0.063 / 0.474 / 1 / 1 / 1.0	0.000 / 0 / 0 / 0.0	0.000 / 0 / 0 / 0.0	0.063 / 0.474 / 1 / 1 / 1.0
5	0.000 / 0 / 0 / 0.0	0.000 / 0 / 0 / 0.0	0.111 / 0.616 / 1 / 1 / 1.0	n/a	0.222 / 0.576 / 2 / 2 / 1.0	0.000 / 0 / 0 / 0.0	0.000 / 0 / 0 / 0.0	0.000 / 0 / 0 / 0.0	0.222 / 0.576 / 2 / 1 / 2.0	0.000 / 0 / 0 / 0.0	0.000 / 0 / 0 / 0.0	0.000 / 0 / 0 / 0.0	0.111 / 0.616 / 1 / 1 / 1.0	0.000 / 0 / 0 / 0.0	0.111 / 0.616 / 1 / 1 / 1.0	0.000 / 0 / 0 / 0.0	0.000 / 0 / 0 / 0.0
6	0.000 / 0 / 0 / 0.0	0.000 / 0 / 0 / 0.0	0.105 / 0.425 / 2 / 1 / 2.0	0.105 / 0.425 / 2 / 1 / 2.0	n/a	0.000 / 0 / 0 / 0.0	0.000 / 0 / 0 / 0.0	0.000 / 0 / 0 / 0.0	0.053 / 0.438 / 1 / 1 / 1.0	0.053 / 0.438 / 1 / 1 / 1.0	0.000 / 0 / 0 / 0.0	0.000 / 0 / 0 / 0.0	0.000 / 0 / 0 / 0.0	0.000 / 0 / 0 / 0.0	0.105 / 0.425 / 2 / 2 / 1.0	0.158 / 0.413 / 3 / 3 / 1.0	0.158 / 0.413 / 3 / 3 / 1.0
7	1.000 / - / 1 / 1 / 1.0	0.000 / 0 / 0 / 0.0	0.000 / 0 / 0 / 0.0	0.000 / 0 / 0 / 0.0	0.000 / 0 / 0 / 0.0	n/a	0.000 / 0 / 0 / 0.0	0.000 / 0 / 0 / 0.0	0.000 / 0 / 0 / 0.0	0.000 / 0 / 0 / 0.0	0.000 / 0 / 0 / 0.0	0.000 / 0 / 0 / 0.0	0.000 / 0 / 0 / 0.0	0.000 / 0 / 0 / 0.0	0.000 / 0 / 0 / 0.0	0.000 / 0 / 0 / 0.0	0.000 / 0 / 0 / 0.0
8	0.000 / 0 / 0 / 0.0	0.400 / 0.679 / 2 / 2 / 1.0	0.000 / 0 / 0 / 0.0	0.000 / 0 / 0 / 0.0	0.000 / 0 / 0 / 0.0	0.000 / 0 / 0 / 0.0	n/a	0.000 / 0 / 0 / 0.0	0.000 / 0 / 0 / 0.0	0.000 / 0 / 0 / 0.0	0.000 / 0 / 0 / 0.0	0.200 / 0.784 / 1 / 1 / 1.0	0.000 / 0 / 0 / 0.0	0.000 / 0 / 0 / 0.0	0.000 / 0 / 0 / 0.0	0.000 / 0 / 0 / 0.0	0.000 / 0 / 0 / 0.0
9	0.000 / 0 / 0 / 0.0	0.071 / 0.505 / 1 / 1 / 1.0	0.214 / 0.464 / 3 / 3 / 1.0	0.000 / 0 / 0 / 0.0	0.000 / 0 / 0 / 0.0	0.000 / 0 / 0 / 0.0	0.000 / 0 / 0 / 0.0	n/a	0.357 / 0.420 / 5 / 4 / 1.3	0.071 / 0.505 / 1 / 1 / 1.0	0.000 / 0 / 0 / 0.0	0.000 / 0 / 0 / 0.0	0.214 / 0.464 / 3 / 2 / 1.5	0.071 / 0.505 / 1 / 1 / 1.0	0.000 / 0 / 0 / 0.0	0.000 / 0 / 0 / 0.0	0.000 / 0 / 0 / 0.0
10	0.000 / 0 / 0 / 0.0	0.000 / 0 / 0 / 0.0	0.097 / 0.335 / 3 / 2 / 1.5	0.129 / 0.328 / 4 / 3 / 1.3	0.194 / 0.316 / 6 / 4 / 1.5	0.000 / 0 / 0 / 0.0	0.000 / 0 / 0 / 0.0	0.032 / 0.347 / 1 / 1 / 1.0	n/a	0.000 / 0 / 0 / 0.0	0.000 / 0 / 0 / 0.0	0.065 / 0.340 / 2 / 2 / 1.0	0.065 / 0.340 / 2 / 2 / 1.0	0.161 / 0.322 / 5 / 3 / 1.7	0.129 / 0.328 / 4 / 3 / 1.3	0.000 / 0 / 0 / 0.0	0.000 / 0 / 0 / 0.0

Appendix G. Movement Probabilities for Radio-Tagged Coho Salmon between Individual Antennas from the Residence Dataset at Cowlitz Falls Dam during 2011.—Continued

[Each cell contains five rows of data including the probability of movement (row 1), the 95-percent confidence interval for the probability estimate (row 2) the number of movements (row 3), the number of fish that made movements (row 4), and the average number of movements per fish (row 5)]

Each cell is given as: probability / 95% CI / number of movements / number of fish / average movements per fish. Empty cells are shown as "0.000 / 0 / 0 / 0.0".

Current location	20	21	22	23	24	25	26	27	28	29	30	31	32	33	Facility	Tailrace
2	0.000 / 0 / 0 / 0.0	0.000 / 0 / 0 / 0.0	0.000 / 0 / 0 / 0.0	0.000 / 0 / 0 / 0.0	0.000 / 0 / 0 / 0.0	0.000 / 0 / 0 / 0.0	0.000 / 0 / 0 / 0.0	0.000 / 0 / 0 / 0.0	0.000 / 0 / 0 / 0.0	0.000 / 0 / 0 / 0.0	0.000 / 0 / 0 / 0.0	0.000 / 0 / 0 / 0.0	0.000 / 0 / 0 / 0.0	0.000 / 0 / 0 / 0.0	0.000 / 0 / 0 / 0.0	0.000 / 0 / 0 / 0.0
3	0.000 / 0 / 0 / 0.0	0.000 / 0 / 0 / 0.0	0.000 / 0 / 0 / 0.0	0.063 / 0.474 / — / 1 / 1.0	0.000 / 0 / 0 / 0.0	0.000 / 0 / 0 / 0.0	0.059 / 0.461 / — / 1 / 1.0	0.000 / 0 / 0 / 0.0	0.000 / 0 / 0 / 0.0	0.000 / 0 / 0 / 0.0	0.000 / 0 / 0 / 0.0	0.000 / 0 / 0 / 0.0	0.000 / 0 / 0 / 0.0	0.000 / 0 / 0 / 0.0	0.000 / 0 / 0 / 0.0	0.000 / 0 / 0 / 0.0
4	0.000 / 0 / 0 / 0.0	0.000 / 0 / 0 / 0.0	0.000 / 0 / 0 / 0.0	1 / — / 1 / 1.0	0.000 / 0 / 0 / 0.0	0.000 / 0 / 0 / 0.0	1 / — / 1 / 1.0	0.000 / 0 / 0 / 0.0	0.000 / 0 / 0 / 0.0	0.000 / 0 / 0 / 0.0	0.000 / 0 / 0 / 0.0	0.000 / 0 / 0 / 0.0	0.000 / 0 / 0 / 0.0	0.000 / 0 / 0 / 0.0	0.000 / 0 / 0 / 0.0	0.000 / 0 / 0 / 0.0
5	0.000 / 0 / 0 / 0.0	0.053 / 0.438 / — / 1 / 1.0	0.000 / 0 / 0 / 0.0	0.053 / 0.438 / — / 1 / 1.0	0.000 / 0 / 0 / 0.0	0.053 / 0.438 / — / 1 / 1.0	0.000 / 0 / 0 / 0.0	0.000 / 0 / 0 / 0.0	0.053 / 0.438 / — / 1 / 1.0	0.000 / 0 / 0 / 0.0	0.000 / 0 / 0 / 0.0	0.111 / 0.616 / — / 1 / 1.0	0.000 / 0 / 0 / 0.0	0.000 / 0 / 0 / 0.0	0.000 / 0 / 0 / 0.0	0.111 / 0.616 / — / 1 / 1.0
6	0.000 / 0 / 0 / 0.0	1 / — / 1 / 1.0	0.000 / 0 / 0 / 0.0	1 / — / 1 / 1.0	0.000 / 0 / 0 / 0.0	1 / — / 1 / 1.0	0.000 / 0 / 0 / 0.0	0.000 / 0 / 0 / 0.0	1 / — / 1 / 1.0	0.000 / 0 / 0 / 0.0	0.000 / 0 / 0 / 0.0	1 / — / 1 / 1.0	0.000 / 0 / 0 / 0.0	0.000 / 0 / 0 / 0.0	0.000 / 0 / 0 / 0.0	0.000 / 0 / 0 / 0.0
7	0.000 / 0 / 0 / 0.0	0.000 / 0 / 0 / 0.0	0.000 / 0 / 0 / 0.0	0.000 / 0 / 0 / 0.0	0.000 / 0 / 0 / 0.0	0.000 / 0 / 0 / 0.0	0.000 / 0 / 0 / 0.0	0.000 / 0 / 0 / 0.0	0.000 / 0 / 0 / 0.0	0.000 / 0 / 0 / 0.0	0.000 / 0 / 0 / 0.0	0.000 / 0 / 0 / 0.0	0.000 / 0 / 0 / 0.0	0.000 / 0 / 0 / 0.0	0.000 / 0 / 0 / 0.0	0.000 / 0 / 0 / 0.0
8	0.000 / 0 / 0 / 0.0	0.000 / 0 / 0 / 0.0	0.000 / 0 / 0 / 0.0	0.000 / 0 / 0 / 0.0	0.000 / 0 / 0 / 0.0	0.000 / 0 / 0 / 0.0	0.000 / 0 / 0 / 0.0	0.000 / 0 / 0 / 0.0	0.000 / 0 / 0 / 0.0	0.000 / 0 / 0 / 0.0	0.000 / 0 / 0 / 0.0	0.000 / 0 / 0 / 0.0	0.000 / 0 / 0 / 0.0	0.000 / 0 / 0 / 0.0	0.000 / 0 / 0 / 0.0	0.200 / 0.784 / — / 1 / 1.0
9	0.000 / 0 / 0 / 0.0	0.000 / 0 / 0 / 0.0	0.000 / 0 / 0 / 0.0	0.000 / 0 / 0 / 0.0	0.000 / 0 / 0 / 0.0	0.000 / 0 / 0 / 0.0	0.000 / 0 / 0 / 0.0	0.032 / 0.347 / 1 / 1 / 1.0	0.000 / 0 / 0 / 0.0	0.000 / 0 / 0 / 0.0	0.000 / 0 / 0 / 0.0	0.000 / 0 / 0 / 0.0	0.000 / 0 / 0 / 0.0	0.000 / 0 / 0 / 0.0	0.000 / 0 / 0 / 0.0	0.000 / 0 / 0 / 0.0
10	0.032 / 0.347 / 1 / 1 / 1.0	0.000 / 0 / 0 / 0.0	0.000 / 0 / 0 / 0.0	0.032 / 0.347 / 1 / 1 / 1.0	0.000 / 0 / 0 / 0.0	0.000 / 0 / 0 / 0.0	0.000 / 0 / 0 / 0.0	0.032 / 0.347 / 1 / 1 / 1.0	0.000 / 0 / 0 / 0.0	0.000 / 0 / 0 / 0.0	0.000 / 0 / 0 / 0.0	0.000 / 0 / 0 / 0.0	0.000 / 0 / 0 / 0.0	0.000 / 0 / 0 / 0.0	0.000 / 0 / 0 / 0.0	0.032 / 0.347 / 1 / 1 / 1.0

Appendix G. Movement Probabilities for Radio-Tagged Coho Salmon between Individual Antennas from the Residence Dataset at Cowlitz Falls Dam during 2011.—Continued

[Each cell contains five rows of data including the probability of movement (row 1), the 95-percent confidence interval for the probability estimate (row 2) the number of movements (row 3), the number of fish that made movements (row 4), and the average number of movements per fish (row 5)]

Current location	Antenna																
	2	3	4	5	6	7	8	9	10	11	13	14	15	16	17	18	19
11	0.000	0.000	0.000	0.000	0.333	0.000	0.000	0.000	0.000	n/a	0.000	0.083	0.000	0.000	0.333	0.000	0.083
					0.462							0.542			0.462		0.542
	0	0	0	0	4	0	0	0	0		0	1	0	0	4	0	1
	0	0	0	0	4	0	0	0	0		0	1	0	0	4	0	1
	0.0	0.0	0.0	0.0	1.0	0.0	0.0	0.0	0.0		0.0	1.0	0.0	0.0	1.0	0.0	1.0
13	0.000	0.000	0.000	0.000	0.000	0.167	0.000	0.000	0.000	0.000	n/a	0.833	0.000	0.000	0.000	0.000	0.000
						0.731						0.327					
	0	0	0	0	0	1	0	0	0	0		5	0	0	0	0	0
	0	0	0	0	0	1	0	0	0	0		4	0	0	0	0	0
	0.0	0.0	0.0	0.0	0.0	1.0	0.0	0.0	0.0	0.0		1.3	0.0	0.0	0.0	0.0	0.0
14	0.000	0.200	0.000	0.000	0.000	0.000	0.040	0.040	0.000	0.000	0.240	n/a	0.200	0.000	0.080	0.000	0.000
		0.351					0.384	0.384			0.342		0.351		0.376		
	0	5	0	0	0	0	1	1	0	0	6		5	0	2	0	0
	0	4	0	0	0	0	1	1	0	0	4		4	0	2	0	0
	0.0	1.3	0.0	0.0	0.0	0.0	1.0	1.0	0.0	0.0	1.5		1.3	0.0	1.0	0.0	0.0
15	0.033	0.033	0.067	0.000	0.000	0.000	0.000	0.200	0.100	0.000	0.000	0.133	n/a	0.267	0.067	0.000	0.033
	0.352	0.350	0.346					0.320	0.339			0.333		0.306	0.346		0.350
	1	1	2	0	0	0	0	6	3	0	0	4		8	2	0	1
	1	1	2	0	0	0	0	5	2	0	0	3		6	1	0	1
	1.0	1.0	1.0	0.0	0.0	0.0	0.0	1.2	1.5	0.0	0.0	1.3		1.3	2.0	0.0	1.0
16	0.000	0.000	0.000	0.000	0.000	0.000	0.000	0.000	0.423	0.000	0.000	0.039	0.000	n/a	0.231	0.000	0.039
									0.292			0.377			0.337		0.377
	0	0	0	0	0	0	0	0	11	0	0	1	0		6	0	1
	0	0	0	0	0	0	0	0	6	0	0	1	0		5	0	1
	0.0	0.0	0.0	0.0	0.0	0.0	0.0	0.0	1.8	0.0	0.0	1.0	0.0		1.2	0.0	1.0
17	0.000	0.000	0.020	0.020	0.059	0.000	0.000	0.020	0.020	0.157	0.000	0.000	0.020	0.118	n/a	0.020	0.157
			0.272	0.272	0.266			0.272	0.272	0.252			0.272	0.258		0.272	0.252
	0	0	1	1	3	0	0	1	1	8	0	0	1	6		1	8
	0	0	1	1	2	0	0	1	1	6	0	0	1	5		1	5
	0.0	0.0	1.0	1.0	1.5	0.0	0.0	1.0	1.0	1.3	0.0	0.0	1.0	1.2		1.0	1.6
18	0.000	0.000	0.000	0.000	0.042	0.000	0.000	0.000	0.000	0.042	0.000	0.000	0.042	0.000	0.083	n/a	0.458
					0.392					0.392			0.392		0.383		0.294
	0	0	0	0	1	0	0	0	0	1	0	0	1	0	2		11
	0	0	0	0	1	0	0	0	0	1	0	0	1	0	2		5
	0.0	0.0	0.0	0.0	1.0	0.0	0.0	0.0	0.0	1.0	0.0	0.0	1.0	0.0	1.0		2.2
19	0.000	0.000	0.000	0.000	0.000	0.000	0.000	0.000	0.000	0.000	0.000	0.000	0.000	0.000	0.283	0.304	n/a
															0.245	0.241	
	0	0	0	0	0	0	0	0	0	0	0	0	0	0	13	14	
	0	0	0	0	0	0	0	0	0	0	0	0	0	0	10	8	
	0.0	0.0	0.0	0.0	0.0	0.0	0.0	0.0	0.0	0.0	0.0	0.0	0.0	0.0	1.3	1.8	
20	0.000	0.028	0.000	0.028	0.000	0.000	0.000	0.000	0.000	0.000	0.000	0.000	0.000	0.000	0.000	0.139	0.389
		0.322		0.322												0.303	0.255
	0	1	0	1	0	0	0	0	0	0	0	0	0	0	0	5	14
	0	1	0	1	0	0	0	0	0	0	0	0	0	0	0	4	8
	0.0	1.0	0.0	1.0	0.0	0.0	0.0	0.0	0.0	0.0	0.0	0.0	0.0	0.0	0.0	1.3	1.8

Appendix G. Movement Probabilities for Radio-Tagged Coho Salmon between Individual Antennas from the Residence Dataset at Cowlitz Falls Dam during 2011.—Continued

[Each cell contains five rows of data including the probability of movement (row 1), the 95-percent confidence interval for the probability estimate (row 2) the number of movements (row 3), the number of fish that made movements (row 4), and the average number of movements per fish (row 5)]

Current location	Antenna														Facility	Tailrace
	20	21	22	23	24	25	26	27	28	29	30	31	32	33	Facility	Tailrace
11	0.000	0.000	0.000	0.000	0.083	0.000	0.000	0.000	0.000	0.000	0.000	0.083	0.000	0.000	0.000	0.000
	0	0	0	0	0.542	0	0	0	0	0	0	0.542	0	0	0	0
	0	0	0	0	1	0	0	0	0	0	0	1	0	0	0	0
	0	0	0	0	1	0	0	0	0	0	0	1	0	0	0	0
	0.0	0.0	0.0	0.0	1.0	0.0	0.0	0.0	0.0	0.0	0.0	1.0	0.0	0.0	0.0	0.0
13	0.000	0.000	0.000	0.000	0.000	0.120	0.080	0.000	0.000	0.000	0.000	0.000	0.000	0.000	0.000	0.000
	0	0	0	0	0	0.368	0.376	0	0	0	0	0	0	0	0	0
	0	0	0	0	0	3	2	0	0	0	0	0	0	0	0	0
	0	0	0	0	0	3	2	0	0	0	0	0	0	0	0	0
	0.0	0.0	0.0	0.0	0.0	1.0	1.0	0.0	0.0	0.0	0.0	0.0	0.0	0.0	0.0	0.0
14	0.000	0.000	0.000	0.000	0.000	0.000	0.000	0.000	0.000	0.000	0.000	0.000	0.000	0.000	0.000	0.000
	0	0	0	0	0	0	0	0	0	0	0	0	0	0	0	0
	0	0	0	0	0	0	0	0	0	0	0	0	0	0	0	0
	0	0	0	0	0	0	0	0	0	0	0	0	0	0	0	0
	0.0	0.0	0.0	0.0	0.0	0.0	0.0	0.0	0.0	0.0	0.0	0.0	0.0	0.0	0.0	0.0
15	0.000	0.000	0.000	0.000	0.033	0.000	0.033	0.000	0.000	0.000	0.000	0.000	0.000	0.000	0.000	0.000
	0	0	0	0	0.350	0	0.350	0	0	0	0	0	0	0	0	0
	0	0	0	0	1	0	1	0	0	0	0	0	0	0	0	0
	0	0	0	0	1	0	1	0	0	0	0	0	0	0	0	0
	0.0	0.0	0.0	0.0	1.0	0.0	1.0	0.0	0.0	0.0	0.0	0.0	0.0	0.0	0.0	0.0
16	0.000	0.000	0.039	0.039	0.077	0.039	0.000	0.000	0.039	0.000	0.000	0.039	0.000	0.000	0.000	0.000
	0	0	0.377	0.377	0.369	0.377	0	0	0.377	0	0	0.377	0	0	0	0
	0	0	1	1	2	1	0	0	1	0	0	1	0	0	0	0
	0	0	1	1	2	1	0	0	1	0	0	1	0	0	0	0
	0.0	0.0	1.0	1.0	1.0	1.0	0.0	0.0	1.0	0.0	0.0	1.0	0.0	0.0	0.0	0.0
17	0.020	0.020	0.020	0.039	0.196	0.039	0.020	0.000	0.020	0.000	0.000	0.020	0.000	0.000	0.000	0.000
	0.272	0.272	0.272	0.269	0.246	0.269	0.272	0	0.272	0	0	0.272	0	0	0	0
	1	1	1	2	10	2	1	0	1	0	0	1	0	0	0	0
	1	1	1	2	7	2	1	0	1	0	0	1	0	0	0	0
	1.0	1.0	1.0	1.0	1.4	1.0	1.0	0.0	1.0	0.0	0.0	1.0	0.0	0.0	0.0	0.0
18	0.208	0.042	0.000	0.000	0.083	0.000	0.000	0.000	0.000	0.000	0.000	0.000	0.000	0.000	0.000	0.000
	0.356	0.392	0	0	0.383	0	0	0	0	0	0	0	0	0	0	0
	5	1	0	0	2	0	0	0	0	0	0	0	0	0	0	0
	4	1	0	0	2	0	0	0	0	0	0	0	0	0	0	0
	1.3	1.0	0.0	0.0	1.0	0.0	0.0	0.0	0.0	0.0	0.0	0.0	0.0	0.0	0.0	0.0
19	0.196	0.000	0.022	0.044	0.065	0.022	0.022	0.000	0.000	0.000	0.000	0.022	0.000	0.022	0.000	0.000
	0.259	0	0.286	0.283	0.279	0.286	0.286	0	0	0	0	0.286	0	0.286	0	0
	9	0	1	2	3	1	1	0	0	0	0	1	0	1	0	0
	5	0	1	2	3	1	1	0	0	0	0	1	0	1	0	0
	1.8	0.0	1.0	1.0	1.0	1.0	1.0	0.0	0.0	0.0	0.0	1.0	0.0	1.0	0.0	0.0
20	n/a	0.167	0.083	0.056	0.056	0.000	0.000	0.000	0.000	0.028	0.000	0.028	0.000	0.000	0.000	0.000
		0.298	0.313	0.318	0.318	0	0	0	0	0.322	0	0.322	0	0	0	0
		6	3	2	2	0	0	0	0	1	0	1	0	0	0	0
		5	3	2	1	0	0	0	0	1	0	1	0	0	0	0
		1.2	1.0	1.0	2.0	0.0	0.0	0.0	0.0	1.0	0.0	1.0	0.0	0.0	0.0	0.0

Appendix G. Movement Probabilities for Radio-Tagged Coho Salmon between Individual Antennas from the Residence Dataset at Cowlitz Falls Dam during 2011.—Continued

[Each cell contains five rows of data including the probability of movement (row 1), the 95-percent confidence interval for the probability estimate (row 2) the number of movements (row 3), the number of fish that made movements (row 4), and the average number of movements per fish (row 5)]

Current location	Antenna																
	2	3	4	5	6	7	8	9	10	11	13	14	15	16	17	18	19
21	0.000	0.000	0.000	0.000	0.000	0.000	0.067	0.000	0.000	0.000	0.000	0.000	0.000	0.000	0.067	0.000	0.000
	0	0	0	0	0	0	0.489	0	0	0	0	0	0	0	0.489	0	0
	0	0	0	0	0	0	1	0	0	0	0	0	0	0	1	0	0
	0	0	0	0	0	0	1	0	0	0	0	0	0	0	1	0	0
	0.0	0.0	0.0	0.0	0.0	0.0	1.0	0.0	0.0	0.0	0.0	0.0	0.0	0.0	1.0	0.0	0.0
22	0.000	0.000	0.000	0.000	0.000	0.000	0.000	0.000	0.000	0.000	0.000	0.000	0.000	0.000	0.000	0.000	0.040
	0	0	0	0	0	0	0	0	0	0	0	0	0	0	0	0	0.384
	0	0	0	0	0	0	0	0	0	0	0	0	0	0	0	0	1
	0	0	0	0	0	0	0	0	0	0	0	0	0	0	0	0	1
	0.0	0.0	0.0	0.0	0.0	0.0	1.0	0.0	0.0	0.0	0.0	0.0	0.0	0.0	0.0	0.0	1.0
23	0.000	0.000	0.000	0.000	0.000	0.000	0.000	0.000	0.007	0.000	0.000	0.000	0.000	0.000	0.007	0.000	0.015
	0	0	0	0	0	0	0	0	0.167	0	0	0	0	0	0.167	0	0.166
	0	0	0	0	0	0	0	0	1	0	0	0	0	0	1	0	2
	0	0	0	0	0	0	0	0	1	0	0	0	0	0	1	0	2
	0.0	0.0	0.0	0.0	0.0	0.0	0.0	0.0	1.0	0.0	0.0	0.0	0.0	0.0	1.0	0.0	1.0
24	0.000	0.000	0.000	0.000	0.000	0.000	0.000	0.013	0.000	0.000	0.000	0.013	0.013	0.000	0.064	0.013	0.013
	0	0	0	0	0	0	0	0.220	0	0	0	0.220	0.220	0	0.215	0.220	0.220
	0	0	0	0	0	0	0	1	0	0	0	1	1	0	5	1	1
	0	0	0	0	0	0	0	1	0	0	0	1	1	0	5	1	1
	0.0	0.0	0.0	0.0	0.0	0.0	0.0	1.0	0.0	0.0	0.0	1.0	1.0	0.0	1.0	1.0	1.0
25	0.000	0.000	0.000	0.022	0.000	0.000	0.000	0.000	0.022	0.000	0.000	0.000	0.044	0.044	0.044	0.000	0.000
	0	0	0	0.286	0	0	0	0	0.286	0	0	0	0.283	0.283	0.283	0	0
	0	0	0	1	0	0	0	0	1	0	0	0	2	2	2	0	0
	0	0	0	1	0	0	0	0	1	0	0	0	2	2	2	0	0
	0.0	0.0	0.0	1.0	0.0	0.0	0.0	0.0	1.0	0.0	0.0	0.0	1.0	1.0	1.0	0.0	0.0
26	0.000	0.006	0.000	0.000	0.000	0.000	0.000	0.000	0.006	0.000	0.000	0.011	0.011	0.006	0.011	0.000	0.000
	0	0.145	0	0	0	0	0	0	0.145	0	0	0.144	0.144	0.145	0.144	0	0
	0	1	0	0	0	0	0	0	1	0	0	2	2	1	2	0	0
	0	1	0	0	0	0	0	0	1	0	0	2	2	1	2	0	0
	0.0	1.0	0.0	0.0	0.0	0.0	0.0	0.0	1.0	0.0	0.0	1.0	1.0	1.0	1.0	0.0	0.0
27	0.000	0.000	0.000	0.000	0.000	0.000	0.000	0.000	0.000	0.000	0.000	0.000	0.011	0.000	0.000	0.000	0.000
	0	0	0	0	0	0	0	0	0	0	0	0	0.143	0	0	0	0
	0	0	0	0	0	0	0	0	0	0	0	0	2	0	0	0	0
	0	0	0	0	0	0	0	0	0	0	0	0	2	0	0	0	0
	0.0	0.0	0.0	0.0	0.0	0.0	0.0	0.0	0.0	0.0	0.0	0.0	1.0	0.0	0.0	0.0	0.0
28	0.000	0.000	0.000	0.000	0.000	0.000	0.000	0.000	0.015	0.000	0.000	0.037	0.030	0.015	0.030	0.000	0.007
	0	0	0	0	0	0	0	0	0.167	0	0	0.165	0.166	0.167	0.166	0	0.168
	0	0	0	0	0	0	0	0	2	0	0	5	4	2	4	0	1
	0	0	0	0	0	0	0	0	2	0	0	5	4	2	4	0	1
	0.0	0.0	0.0	0.0	0.0	0.0	0.0	0.0	1.0	0.0	0.0	1.0	1.0	1.0	1.0	0.0	1.0
29	0.000	0.000	0.000	0.000	0.000	0.000	0.000	0.000	0.000	0.000	0.000	0.000	0.039	0.000	0.000	0.000	0.000
	0	0	0	0	0	0	0	0	0	0	0	0	1	0	0	0	0
	0	0	0	0	0	0	0	0	0	0	0	0	1	0	0	0	0
	0.0	0.0	0.0	0.0	0.0	0.0	0.0	0.0	0.0	0.0	0.0	0.0	1.0	0.0	0.0	0.0	0.0

Appendix G. Movement Probabilities for Radio-Tagged Coho Salmon between Individual Antennas from the Residence Dataset at Cowlitz Falls Dam during 2011.—Continued

[Each cell contains five rows of data including the probability of movement (row 1), the 95-percent confidence interval for the probability estimate (row 2) the number of movements (row 3), the number of fish that made movements (row 4), and the average number of movements per fish (row 5)]

Current location	Antenna															
	20	21	22	23	24	25	26	27	28	29	30	31	32	33	Facility	Tailrace
21	0.133	n/a	0.467	0.000	0.067	0.000	0.000	0.000	0.000	0.000	0.000	0.200	0.000	0.000	0.000	0.000
	0.471		0.370		0.489							0.453				
	2		7	0	1	0	0	0	0	0	0	3	0	0	0	0
	2		3	0	1	0	0	0	0	0	0	3	0	0	0	0
	1.0		2.3	0.0	1.0	0.0	0.0	0.0	0.0	0.0	0.0	1.0	0.0	0.0	0.0	0.0
22	0.440	0.160	n/a	0.120	0.160	0.000	0.040	0.040	0.000	0.000	0.000	0.000	0.000	0.000	0.000	0.000
	0.293	0.359		0.368	0.359		0.384	0.384								
	11	4		3	4	0	1	1	0	0	0	0	0	0	0	0
	8	3		3	4	0	1	1	0	0	0	0	0	0	0	0
	1.4	1.3		1.0	1.0	0.0	1.0	1.0	0.0	0.0	0.0	0.0	0.0	0.0	0.0	0.0
23	0.000	0.000	0.007	n/a	0.102	0.007	0.015	0.394	0.000	0.029	0.073	0.299	0.000	0.000	0.000	0.044
			0.167		0.159	0.167	0.166	0.130		0.165	0.161	0.140				0.164
	0	0	1		14	1	2	54	0	4	10	41	0	0	0	6
	0	0	1		11	1	2	23	0	4	6	15	0	0	0	6
	0.0	0.0	1.0		1.3	1.0	1.0	2.3	0.0	1.0	1.7	2.7	0.0	0.0	0.0	1.0
24	0.026	0.000	0.064	0.231	n/a	0.115	0.039	0.167	0.026	0.022	0.064	0.128	0.000	0.000	0.000	0.044
	0.219		0.215	0.195		0.209	0.218	0.203	0.219	0.286	0.215	0.207				0.283
	2	0	5	18		9	3	13	2	1	5	10	0	0	0	2
	1	0	5	17		9	2	11	2	1	5	9	0	0	0	2
	2.0	0.0	1.0	1.1		1.0	1.5	1.2	1.0	1.0	1.0	1.1	0.0	0.0	0.0	1.0
25	0.044	0.000	0.022	0.022	0.044	n/a	0.370	0.152	0.087	0.022	0.000	0.000	0.000	0.000	0.000	0.006
	0.283		0.286	0.286	0.283		0.229	0.266	0.276	0.286						0.145
	2	0	1	1	2		17	7	4	1	0	0	0	0	0	1
	2	0	1	1	2		10	7	4	1	0	0	0	0	0	1
	1.0	0.0	1.0	1.0	1.0		1.7	1.0	1.0	1.0	0.0	0.0	0.0	0.0	0.0	1.0
26	0.000	0.006	0.000	0.000	0.006	0.071	n/a	0.230	0.601	0.011	0.006	0.016	0.000	0.000	0.000	0.006
		0.145			0.145	0.140		0.127	0.092	0.144	0.145	0.144				0.145
	0	1	0	0	1	13		42	110	2	1	3	0	0	0	1
	0	1	0	0	1	10		16	22	2	1	3	0	0	0	1
	0.0	1.0	0.0	0.0	1.0	1.3		2.6	5.0	1.0	1.0	1.0	0.0	0.0	0.0	1.0
27	0.000	0.000	0.000	0.241	0.016	0.011	0.267	n/a	0.027	0.102	0.225	0.048	0.005	0.000	0.000	0.048
				0.125	0.142	0.143	0.123		0.141	0.136	0.126	0.140	0.142			0.140
	0	0	0	45	3	2	50		5	19	42	9	1	0	0	9
	0	0	0	11	3	2	19		5	13	31	4	1	0	0	9
	0.0	0.0	0.0	4.1	1.0	1.0	2.6		1.0	1.5	1.4	2.3	1.0	0.0	0.0	1.0
28	0.000	0.000	0.000	0.015	0.022	0.022	0.674	0.082	n/a	0.000	0.000	0.000	0.007	0.000	0.000	0.044
				0.167	0.167	0.167	0.096	0.162					0.168			0.164
	0	0	0	2	3	3	91	11		0	0	0	1	0	0	6
	0	0	0	2	2	3	21	10		0	0	0	1	0	0	6
	0.0	0.0	0.0	1.0	1.5	1.0	4.3	1.1		0.0	0.0	0.0	1.0	0.0	0.0	1.0
29	0.000	0.000	0.000	0.000	0.000	0.000	0.001	0.003	0.000	n/a	0.001	0.000	0.993	0.000	0.000	0.003
							0.037	0.037			0.037		0.003			0.041
	0	0	0	0	0	0	4	7	0		2	0	2795	0	0	7
	0	0	0	0	0	0	3	5	0		0	0	17	0	0	7
	0.0	0.0	0.0	0.0	0.0	0.0	1.3	1.4	0.0		2.0	0.0	164.4	0.0	0.0	1.0

Appendix G. Movement Probabilities for Radio-Tagged Coho Salmon between Individual Antennas from the Residence Dataset at Cowlitz Falls Dam during 2011.—Continued

[Each cell contains five rows of data including the probability of movement (row 1), the 95-percent confidence interval for the probability estimate (row 2) the number of movements (row 3), the number of fish that made movements (row 4), and the average number of movements per fish (row 5)]

Current location	\	Antenna															
		2	3	4	5	6	7	8	9	10	11	13	14	15	16	17	18	19
30		0.000 0 0 0.0	0.000 0 0 0.0	0.000 0 0 0.0	0.000 0 0 0.0	0.000 0 0 0.0	0.000 0 0 0.0	0.000 0 0 0.0	0.000 0 0 0.0	0.000 0 0 0.0	0.000 0 0 0.0	0.000 0 0 0.0	0.000 0 0 0.0	0.000 0 0 0.0	0.000 0 0 0.0	0.000 0 0 0.0	0.000 0 0 0.0	0.000 0 0 0.0
31		0.000 0 0 0.0	0.000 0 0 0.0	0.000 0 0 0.0	0.000 0 0 0.0	0.000 0 0 0.0	0.000 0 0 0.0	0.000 0 0 0.0	0.000 0 0 0.0	0.000 0 0 0.0	0.000 0 0 0.0	0.000 0 0 0.0	0.000 0 0 0.0	0.000 0 0 0.0	0.000 0 0 0.0	0.000 0 0 0.0	0.000 0 0 0.0	0.010 0.193 1 1 1.0
32		0.000 0 0 0.0	0.000 0 0 0.0	0.000 0 0 0.0	0.000 0 0 0.0	0.000 0 0 0.0	0.000 0 0 0.0	0.000 0 0 0.0	0.000 0 0 0.0	0.000 0 0 0.0	0.000 0 0 0.0	0.000 0 0 0.0	0.000 0 0 0.0	0.000 0 0 0.0	0.000 0 0 0.0	0.000 0 0 0.0	0.000 0 0 0.0	0.000 0 0 0.0
33		0.000 0 0 0.0	0.000 0 0 0.0	0.000 0 0 0.0	0.000 0 0 0.0	0.000 0 0 0.0	0.000 0 0 0.0	0.000 0 0 0.0	0.000 0 0 0.0	0.000 0 0 0.0	0.000 0 0 0.0	0.000 0 0 0.0	0.000 0 0 0.0	0.000 0 0 0.0	0.000 0 0 0.0	0.000 0 0 0.0	0.000 0 0 0.0	0.000 0 0 0.0

Current location	\	Antenna															
		20	21	22	23	24	25	26	27	28	29	30	31	32	33	Facility	Tailrace
30		0.000 0 0 0.0	0.000 0 0 0.0	0.000 0 0 0.0	0.000 0 0 0.0	0.000 0 0 0.0	0.000 0 0 0.0	0.001 0.048 2 2 1.0	0.015 0.047 26 12 2.2	0.000 0 0 0.0	0.001 0.048 2 2 1.0	n/a	0.001 0.048 2 1 2.0	0.001 0.048 2 2 1.0	0.970 0.008 1658 34 48.8	0.000 0 0 0.0	0.010 0.047 17 17 1.0
31		0.029 0.191 3 3 1.0	0.010 0.193 1 1 1.0	0.049 0.189 5 5 1.0	0.480 0.140 49 23 2.1	0.118 0.182 12 11 1.1	0.000 0 0 0.0	0.020 0.192 2 2 1.0	0.177 0.176 18 10 1.8	0.000 0 0 0.0	0.010 0.193 1 1 1.0	0.059 0.188 6 6 1.0	n/a	0.000 0 0 0.0	0.000 0 0 0.0	0.000 0 0 0.0	0.039 0.190 4 4 1.0
32		0.000 0 0 0.0	0.000 0 0 0.0	0.000 0 0 0.0	0.000 0 0 0.0	0.000 0 0 0.0	0.000 0 0 0.0	0.000 0 0 0.0	0.000 0 0 0.0	0.000 0 0 0.0	0.995 0.003 2784 16 174.0	0.000 0 0 0.0	0.000 0 0 0.0	n/a	0.000 0.039 1 1 1.0	0.000 0 0 0.0	0.004 0.034 13 13 1.0
33		0.000 0 0 0.0	0.000 0 0 0.0	0.000 0 0 0.0	0.000 0 0 0.0	0.000 0 0 0.0	0.000 0 0 0.0	0.000 0 0 0.0	0.000 0 0 0.0	0.000 0 0 0.0	0.000 0 0 0.0	0.989 0.005 1640 32 51.3	0.000 0 0 0.0	0.000 0 0 0.0	n/a	0.008 0.050 12 12 1.0	0.005 0.052 7 7 1.0

Appendix H. Movement Probabilities for Radio-Tagged Chinook Salmon between Individual Antennas from the Residence Dataset at Cowlitz Falls Dam during 2011.

[Each cell contains five rows of data including the probability of movement (row 1), the 95-percent confidence interval for the probability estimate (row 2) the number of movements (row 3), the number of fish that made movements (row 4), and the average number of movements per fish (row 5)]

Current location		2	3	4	5	6	7	8	9	10	11	13	14	15	16	17	18	19
2	prob	n/a	0.287	0.034	0.048	0.043	0.234	0.024	0.034	0.014	0.005	0.115	0.024	0.014	0.005	0.010	0.048	0.000
	CI		0.114	0.133	0.132	0.133	0.119	0.134	0.133	0.135	0.135	0.128	0.134	0.135	0.135	0.135	0.132	0
	n mov		60	7	10	9	49	5	7	3	1	24	5	3	1	2	10	0
	n fish		36	7	9	9	29	5	5	3	1	15	5	3	1	2	9	0
	avg		1.7	1.0	1.1	1.0	1.7	1.0	1.4	1.0	1.0	1.6	1.0	1.0	1.0	1.0	1.1	0.0
3	prob	0.157	n/a	0.270	0.048	0.039	0.017	0.139	0.057	0.004	0.000	0.044	0.096	0.048	0.000	0.017	0.013	0.000
	CI	0.119		0.110	0.126	0.127	0.128	0.120	0.126	0.128	0	0.126	0.123	0.126	0	0.128	0.128	0
	n mov	36		62	11	9	4	32	13	1	0	10	22	11	0	4	3	0
	n fish	22		37	10	8	4	27	12	1	0	10	20	9	0	4	3	0
	avg	1.6		1.7	1.1	1.1	1.0	1.2	1.1	1.0	0.0	1.0	1.1	1.2	0.0	1.0	1.0	0
4	prob	0.024	0.183	n/a	0.301	0.038	0.005	0.014	0.249	0.028	0.000	0.005	0.005	0.061	0.009	0.014	0.024	0.005
	CI	0.133	0.121		0.112	0.132	0.134	0.133	0.116	0.132	0	0.134	0.134	0.130	0.134	0.133	0.133	0.134
	n mov	5	39		64	8	1	3	53	6	0	1	1	13	2	3	5	1
	n fish	5	22		32	7	1	3	36	6	0	1	1	11	2	3	5	–
	avg	1.0	1.8		2.0	1.1	1.0	1.0	1.5	1.0	0.0	1.0	1.0	1.2	1.0	1.0	1.0	1.0
5	prob	0.027	0.024	0.109	n/a	0.289	0.010	0.003	0.010	0.204	0.010	0.007	0.000	0.007	0.102	0.136	0.020	0.007
	CI	0.113	0.113	0.108		0.096	0.114	0.114	0.114	0.102	0.114	0.114	0	0.114	0.108	0.106	0.113	0.114
	n mov	8	7	32		85	3	1	3	60	3	2	0	2	30	40	6	2
	n fish	8	5	19		45	3	1	3	32	2	1	0	2	17	25	6	2
	avg	1.0	1.4	1.7		1.9	1.0	1.0	1.0	1.9	1.5	2.0	0.0	1.0	1.8	1.6	1.0	1.0
6	prob	0.013	0.010	0.025	0.145	n/a	0.000	0.005	0.003	0.027	0.090	0.005	0.003	0.005	0.008	0.247	0.259	0.067
	CI	0.097	0.098	0.097	0.091		0	0.098	0.098	0.096	0.093	0.098	0.098	0.098	0.098	0.085	0.084	0.095
	n mov	5	4	10	58		0	2	1	11	36	2	1	2	3	99	104	27
	n fish	5	4	10	38		0	2	1	11	24	2	1	2	3	44	50	22
	avg	1.0	1.0	1.0	1.5		0.0	1.0	1.0	1.0	1.5	1.0	1.0	1.0	1.0	2.3	2.1	1.2
7	prob	0.394	0.068	0.008	0.008	0.038	n/a	0.000	0.000	0.008	0.000	0.447	0.000	0.000	0.000	0.008	0.000	0.000
	CI	0.133	0.165	0.170	0.170	0.167		0	0	0.170	0	0.127	0	0	0	0.170	0	0
	n mov	52	9	1	1	5		0	0	1	0	59	0	0	0	1	0	0
	n fish	31	8	1	1	5		0	0	1	0	33	0	0	0	–	0	0
	avg	1.7	1.1	1.0	1.0	1.0		0.0	0.0	1.0	0.0	1.8	0.0	0.0	0.0	1.0	0.0	0.0
8	prob	0.075	0.188	0.030	0.008	0.008	0.008	n/a	0.030	0.000	0.000	0.158	0.414	0.023	0.015	0.008	0.000	0.008
	CI	0.163	0.153	0.167	0.169	0.169	0.169		0.167	0	0	0.156	0.130	0.168	0.168	0.169	0	0.169
	n mov	10	25	4	1	1	1		4	0	0	21	55	3	2	1	0	1
	n fish	9	18	4	1	1	1		4	0	0	19	36	3	2	–	0	–
	avg	1.1	1.4	1.0	1.0	1.0	1.0		1.0	0.0	0.0	1.1	1.5	1.0	1.0	1.0	0.0	1.0
9	prob	0.011	0.047	0.178	0.036	0.018	0.004	0.029	n/a	0.051	0.000	0.004	0.065	0.344	0.109	0.033	0.007	0.000
	CI	0.117	0.115	0.107	0.116	0.117	0.117	0.116		0.115	0	0.117	0.114	0.096	0.111	0.116	0.117	0
	n mov	3	13	49	10	5	1	8		14	0	1	18	95	30	9	2	0
	n fish	2	12	28	9	5	1	8		12	0	1	16	42	23	8	2	0
	avg	1.5	1.1	1.8	1.1	1.0	1.0	1.0		1.2	0.0	1.0	1.1	2.3	1.3	1.1	1.0	1.0
10	prob	0.015	0.005	0.035	0.285	0.115	0.000	0.000	0.025	n/a	0.020	0.000	0.010	0.020	0.180	0.195	0.005	0.010
	CI	0.138	0.138	0.136	0.117	0.130	0	0	0.137		0.137	0	0.138	0.137	0.126	0.124	0.138	0.138
	n mov	3	1	7	57	23	0	0	5		4	0	2	4	36	39	1	2
	n fish	3	1	7	37	17	0	0	4		4	0	2	4	25	28	1	2
	avg	1.0	1.0	1.0	1.5	1.4	0.0	0.0	1.3		1.0	0.0	1.0	1.0	1.4	1.4	1.0	1.0

Appendix H. Movement Probabilities for Radio-Tagged Chinook Salmon between Individual Antennas from the Residence Dataset at Cowlitz Falls Dam during 2011.—Continued

[Each cell contains five rows of data including the probability of movement (row 1), the 95-percent confidence interval for the probability estimate (row 2) the number of movements (row 3), the number of fish that made movements (row 4), and the average number of movements per fish (row 5)]

Current location	Antenna 20	21	22	23	24	25	26	27	28	29	30	31	32	33	Facility	Tailrace
2	0.019	0.014	0.010	0.000	0.010	0.000	0.000	0.000	0.000	0.000	0.000	0.000	0.000	0.000	0.000	0.000
	0.134	0.135	0.135	0	0.135	0	0	0	0	0	0	0	0	0	0	0
	4	3	2	0	2	0	0	0	0	0	0	0	0	0	0	0
	4	3	2	0	1	0	0	0	0	0	0	0	0	0	0	0
	1.0	1.0	1.0	0.0	2.0	0.0	0.0	0.0	0.0	0.0	0.0	0.0	0.0	0.0	0.0	0.0
3	0.004	0.013	0.004	0.000	0.000	0.000	0.009	0.000	0.004	0.000	0.000	0.000	0.000	0.000	0.000	0.000
	0.128	0.128	0.128	0	0	0	0.129	0	0.128	0	0	0	0	0	0	0
	1	3	1	0	0	0	2	0	1	0	0	0	0	0	0	0
	1	2	1	0	0	0	2	0	1	0	0	0	0	0	0	0
	1.0	1.5	1.0	0.0	0.0	0.0	1.0	0.0	1.0	0.0	0.0	0.0	0.0	0.0	0.0	0.0
4	0.009	0.005	0.000	0.005	0.000	0.014	0.000	0.000	0.000	0.000	0.000	0.000	0.000	0.000	0.000	0.000
	0.134	0.134	0	0.134	0	0.133	0	0	0	0	0	0	0	0	0	0
	2	1	0	1	0	3	0	0	0	0	0	0	0	0	0	0
	2	1	0	1	0	3	0	0	0	0	0	0	0	0	0	0
	1.0	1.0	0.0	1.0	0.0	1.0	0.0	0.0	0.0	0.0	0.0	0.0	0.0	0.0	0.0	0.0
5	0.007	0.007	0.003	0.000	0.007	0.000	0.000	0.000	0.007	0.000	0.000	0.000	0.000	0.000	0.000	0.000
	0.114	0.114	0.114	0	0.114	0	0	0	0.114	0	0	0	0	0	0	0
	2	2	1	0	2	0	0	0	2	0	0	0	0	0	0	0
	2	2	1	0	1	0	0	0	2	0	0	0	0	0	0	0
	1.0	1.0	1.0	0.0	2.0	0.0	0.0	0.0	1.0	0.0	0.0	0.0	0.0	0.0	0.0	0.0
6	0.025	0.027	0.003	0.005	0.010	0.000	0.000	0.010	0.000	0.000	0.000	0.008	0.000	0.000	0.000	0.000
	0.097	0.096	0.098	0.098	0.098	0	0	0.098	0	0	0	0.098	0	0	0	0
	10	11	1	2	4	0	0	4	0	0	0	3	0	0	0	0
	8	10	1	1	3	0	0	4	0	0	0	1	0	0	0	0
	1.3	1.1	1.0	2.0	1.3	0.0	0.0	1.0	0.0	0.0	0.0	3.0	0.0	0.0	0.0	0.0
7	0.000	0.000	0.000	0.000	0.000	0.000	0.000	0.008	0.000	0.000	0.000	0.000	0.000	0.000	0.000	0.000
	0	0	0	0	0	0	0	0.170	0	0	0	0	0	0	0	0
	0	0	0	0	0	0	0	1	0	0	0	0	0	0	0	0
	0	0	0	0	0	0	0	1	0	0	0	0	0	0	0	0
	0.0	0.0	0.0	0.0	0.0	0.0	0.0	1.0	0.0	0.0	0.0	0.0	0.0	0.0	0.0	0.0
8	0.000	0.000	0.000	0.000	0.000	0.008	0.000	0.000	0.015	0.000	0.000	0.008	0.000	0.000	0.000	0.000
	0	0	0	0	0	0.169	0	0	0.168	0	0	0.169	0	0	0	0
	0	0	0	0	0	1	0	0	2	0	0	1	0	0	0	0
	0	0	0	0	0	1	0	0	2	0	0	1	0	0	0	0
	0.0	0.0	0.0	0.0	0.0	1.0	0.0	0.0	1.0	0.0	0.0	1.0	0.0	0.0	0.0	0.0
9	0.000	0.004	0.004	0.004	0.007	0.018	0.007	0.000	0.015	0.000	0.000	0.004	0.000	0.000	0.000	0.004
	0	0.117	0.117	0.117	0.117	0.117	0.117	0	0.117	0	0	0.117	0	0	0	0.117
	0	1	1	1	2	5	2	0	4	0	0	1	0	0	0	1
	0	1	1	1	2	5	2	0	4	0	0	1	0	0	0	1
	0.0	1.0	1.0	1.0	1.0	1.0	1.0	0.0	1.0	0.0	0.0	1.0	0.0	0.0	0.0	1.0
10	0.005	0.000	0.005	0.000	0.020	0.020	0.005	0.005	0.005	0.000	0.000	0.015	0.000	0.000	0.000	0.000
	0.138	0	0.138	0	0.137	0.137	0.138	0.138	0.138	0	0	0.138	0	0	0	0
	1	0	1	0	4	4	1	1	1	0	0	3	0	0	0	0
	1	0	1	0	3	4	1	1	1	0	0	2	0	0	0	0
	1.0	0.0	1.0	0.0	1.3	1.0	1.0	1.0	1.0	0.0	0.0	1.5	0.0	0.0	0.0	0.0

Appendix H. Movement Probabilities for Radio-Tagged Chinook Salmon between Individual Antennas from the Residence Dataset at Cowlitz Falls Dam during 2011.—Continued

[Each cell contains five rows of data including the probability of movement (row 1), the 95-percent confidence interval for the probability estimate (row 2) the number of movements (row 3), the number of fish that made movements (row 4), and the average number of movements per fish (row 5)]

Current location	Antenna																
	2	3	4	5	6	7	8	9	10	11	13	14	15	16	17	18	19
11	0.006	0.000	0.000	0.006	0.159	0.000	0.000	0.000	0.017	n/a	0.006	0.000	0.000	0.006	0.604	0.028	0.077
	0.145			0.145	0.133				0.144	n/a	0.145			0.145	0.091	0.143	0.140
	1	0	0	1	29	0	0	0	3		1	0	0	1	110	5	14
	1	0	0	1	20	0	0	0	3		1	0	0	-	40	4	12
	1.0	0.0	0.0	1.0	1.5	0.0	0.0	0.0	1.0		1.0	0.0	0.0	1.0	2.8	1.3	1.2
13	0.160	0.038	0.000	0.000	0.000	0.214	0.044	0.009	0.003	0.000	n/a	0.403	0.050	0.006	0.006	0.000	0.003
	0.101	0.108				0.097	0.107	0.109	0.109		n/a	0.085	0.107	0.110	0.110		0.109
	51	12	0	0	0	68	14	3	1	0		128	16	2	2	0	1
	31	11	0	0	0	41	12	3	1	0		50	13	2	2	0	1
	1.6	1.1	0.0	0.0	0.0	1.7	1.2	1.0	1.0	0.0		2.6	1.2	1.0	1.0	0.0	1.0
14	0.018	0.069	0.013	0.005	0.000	0.000	0.131	0.062	0.000	0.000	0.417	n/a	0.144	0.021	0.010	0.003	0.000
	0.098	0.096	0.099	0.099			0.093	0.096			0.076	n/a	0.092	0.098	0.099	0.100	
	7	27	5	2	0	0	51	24	0	0	162		56	8	4	1	0
	7	20	5	2	0	0	31	20	0	0	63		37	8	4	1	0
	1.0	1.4	1.0	1.0	0.0	0.0	1.6	1.2	0.0	0.0	2.6		1.5	1.0	1.0	1.0	0.0
15	0.006	0.027	0.058	0.012	0.000	0.000	0.030	0.352	0.006	0.000	0.015	0.194	n/a	0.170	0.015	0.000	0.009
	0.108	0.106	0.105	0.107			0.106	0.087	0.108		0.107	0.097	n/a	0.098	0.107		0.107
	2	9	19	4	0	0	10	116	2	0	5	64		56	5	0	3
	2	9	19	4	0	0	9	44	2	0	5	39		37	5	0	3
	1.0	1.0	1.0	1.0	0.0	0.0	1.1	2.6	1.0	0.0	1.0	1.6		1.5	1.0	0.0	1.0
16	0.000	0.000	0.006	0.071	0.009	0.000	0.000	0.056	0.156	0.000	0.000	0.032	0.156	n/a	0.321	0.000	0.021
			0.106	0.102	0.106			0.103	0.098			0.105	0.098	n/a	0.088		0.105
	0	0	2	24	3	0	0	19	53	0	0	11	53		109	0	7
	0	0	2	19	3	0	0	17	37	0	0	8	34		39	0	7
	0.0	0.0	1.0	1.3	1.0	0.0	0.0	1.1	1.4	0.0	0.0	1.4	1.6		2.8	0.0	1.0
17	0.004	0.007	0.003	0.038	0.167	0.002	0.000	0.006	0.048	0.167	0.004	0.010	0.018	0.149	n/a	0.025	0.146
	0.075	0.075	0.075	0.073	0.068	0.076		0.074	0.073	0.068	0.075	0.074	0.074	0.069	n/a	0.074	0.069
	3	5	2	26	114	1	0	4	33	114	3	7	12	102		17	100
	2	4	2	21	47	1	0	4	21	41	3	7	12	41		15	49
	1.5	1.3	1.0	1.2	2.4	1.0	0.0	1.0	1.6	2.8	1.0	1.0	1.0	2.5		1.1	2.0
18	0.022	0.013	0.009	0.024	0.164	0.000	0.002	0.000	0.004	0.011	0.002	0.000	0.000	0.002	0.018	n/a	0.276
	0.091	0.092	0.092	0.091	0.084		0.092		0.092	0.092	0.092			0.092	0.092	n/a	0.079
	10	6	4	11	74	0	1	0	2	5	1	0	0	1	8		124
	10	6	4	8	41	0	1	0	2	5	1	0	0	1	8		50
	1.0	1.0	1.0	1.4	1.8	0.0	1.0	0.0	1.0	1.0	1.0	0.0	0.0	1.0	1.0		2.5
19	0.002	0.000	0.000	0.002	0.032	0.002	0.002	0.004	0.004	0.022	0.002	0.002	0.004	0.009	0.215	0.252	n/a
	0.085			0.085	0.083	0.085	0.085	0.084	0.084	0.083	0.085	0.085	0.084	0.084	0.075	0.073	n/a
	1	0	0	1	17	1	1	2	2	12	1	1	2	5	116	136	
	1	0	0	1	14	1	1	2	2	10	1	1	2	5	53	55	
	1.0	0.0	0.0	1.0	1.2	1.0	1.0	1.0	1.0	1.2	1.0	1.0	1.0	1.0	2.2	2.5	
20	0.006	0.003	0.003	0.006	0.011	0.000	0.002	0.000	0.002	0.003	0.000	0.002	0.002	0.003	0.014	0.196	0.270
	0.078	0.078	0.078	0.078	0.078		0.078		0.078	0.078		0.078	0.078	0.078	0.078	0.070	0.067
	4	2	2	4	7	0	1	0	1	2	0	1	1	2	9	123	170
	4	2	2	3	6	0	1	0	1	2	0	1	1	2	9	51	64
	1.0	1.0	1.0	1.3	1.2	0.0	1.0	0.0	1.0	1.0	0.0	1.0	1.0	1.0	1.0	2.4	2.7

Appendix H. Movement Probabilities for Radio-Tagged Chinook Salmon between Individual Antennas from the Residence Dataset at Cowlitz Falls Dam during 2011.—Continued

[Each cell contains five rows of data including the probability of movement (row 1), the 95-percent confidence interval for the probability estimate (row 2) the number of movements (row 3), the number of fish that made movements (row 4), and the average number of movements per fish (row 5)]

Current location	__ Antenna	20	21	22	23	24	25	26	27	28	29	30	31	32	33	Facility	Tailrace
11		0.011	0.000	0.006	0.017	0.017	0.011	0.006	0.006	0.000	0.000	0.000	0.022	0.000	0.000	0.000	0.000
		0.145	0	0.145	0.144	0.144	0.145	0.145	0.145	0	0	0	0.144	0	0	0	0
		2	0	1	3	3	2	1	1	0	0	0	4	0	0	0	0
		2	0	1	3	3	2	1	1	0	0	0	4	0	0	0	0
		1.0	0.0	1.0	1.0	1.0	1.0	1.0	1.0	0.0	0.0	0.0	1.0	0.0	0.0	0.0	0.0
13		0.000	0.000	0.003	0.000	0.006	0.013	0.006	0.000	0.035	0.000	0.000	0.000	0.000	0.000	0.000	0.000
		0	0	0.109	0	0.110	0.109	0.110	0	0.108	0	0	0	0	0	0	0
		0	0	1	0	2	4	2	0	11	0	0	0	0	0	0	0
		0	0	1	0	1	3	2	0	10	0	0	0	0	0	0	0
		0.0	0.0	1.0	0.0	2.0	1.3	1.0	0.0	1.1	0.0	0.0	0.0	0.0	0.0	0.0	0.0
14		0.003	0.000	0.003	0.000	0.010	0.015	0.013	0.008	0.054	0.000	0.000	0.003	0.000	0.000	0.000	0.000
		0.100	0	0.100	0	0.099	0.099	0.099	0.099	0.097	0	0	0.100	0	0	0	0
		1	0	1	0	4	6	5	3	21	0	0	1	0	0	0	0
		1	0	1	0	4	6	5	3	21	0	0	1	0	0	0	0
		1.0	0.0	1.0	0.0	1.0	1.0	1.0	1.0	1.0	0.0	0.0	1.0	0.0	0.0	0.0	0.0
15		0.003	0.000	0.000	0.006	0.018	0.024	0.015	0.009	0.021	0.000	0.000	0.003	0.000	0.000	0.000	0.006
		0.107	0	0	0.108	0.107	0.106	0.107	0.107	0.107	0	0	0.107	0	0	0	0.107
		1	0	0	2	6	8	5	3	7	0	0	1	0	0	0	2
		1	0	0	2	4	7	5	2	6	0	0	1	0	0	0	2
		1.0	0.0	0.0	1.0	1.5	1.1	1.0	1.5	1.2	0.0	0.0	1.0	0.0	0.0	0.0	1.0
16		0.009	0.000	0.009	0.006	0.032	0.044	0.021	0.000	0.021	0.000	0.003	0.027	0.000	0.000	0.000	0.003
		0.106	0	0.106	0.106	0.105	0.104	0.105	0	0.105	0	0.105	0.105	0	0	0	0.105
		3	0	3	2	11	15	7	0	7	0	1	9	0	0	0	1
		3	0	3	2	8	11	7	0	6	0	1	8	0	0	0	1
		1.0	0.0	1.0	1.0	1.4	1.4	1.0	0.0	1.2	0.0	1.0	1.1	0.0	0.0	0.0	1.0
17		0.004	0.003	0.021	0.013	0.063	0.029	0.006	0.019	0.026	0.002	0.000	0.021	0.000	0.000	0.000	0.000
		0.075	0.075	0.074	0.075	0.073	0.074	0.074	0.074	0.074	0.076	0	0.074	0	0	0	0
		3	2	14	9	43	20	4	13	18	1	0	14	0	0	0	0
		3	2	12	9	29	18	4	12	16	1	0	13	0	0	0	0
		1.0	1.0	1.2	1.0	1.5	1.1	1.0	1.1	1.1	1.0	0.0	1.1	0.0	0.0	0.0	0.0
18		0.316	0.098	0.007	0.007	0.007	0.004	0.000	0.002	0.000	0.000	0.000	0.011	0.000	0.000	0.000	0.000
		0.076	0.088	0.092	0.092	0.092	0.092	0	0.092	0	0	0	0.092	0	0	0	0
		142	44	3	3	3	2	0	1	0	0	0	5	0	0	0	0
		54	27	3	3	2	1	0	1	0	0	0	1	0	0	0	0
		2.6	1.6	1.0	1.0	1.5	2.0	0.0	1.0	0.0	0.0	0.0	5.0	0.0	0.0	0.0	0.0
19		0.239	0.006	0.044	0.032	0.059	0.009	0.006	0.019	0.013	0.002	0.000	0.020	0.000	0.000	0.000	0.000
		0.074	0.084	0.082	0.083	0.082	0.084	0.084	0.084	0.084	0.268	0	0.084	0	0	0	0
		129	3	24	17	32	5	3	10	7	1	0	11	0	0	0	0
		57	3	17	16	23	5	3	10	7	1	0	9	0	0	0	0
		2.3	1.0	1.4	1.1	1.4	1.0	1.0	1.0	1.0	1.0	0.0	1.2	0.0	0.0	0.0	0.0
20		n/a	0.272	0.116	0.024	0.022	0.008	0.003	0.006	0.003	0.000	0.002	0.019	0.000	0.000	0.002	0.000
			0.067	0.073	0.077	0.077	0.078	0.078	0.078	0.078	0	0.078	0.077	0	0	0.078	0
			171	73	15	14	5	2	4	2	0	1	12	0	0	1	0
			58	44	13	13	4	2	3	2	0	1	10	0	0	1	0
			2.9	1.7	1.2	1.1	1.3	1.0	1.3	1.0	0.0	1.0	1.2	0.0	0.0	1.0	0.0

Appendix H. Movement Probabilities for Radio-Tagged Chinook Salmon between Individual Antennas from the Residence Dataset at Cowlitz Falls Dam during 2011.—Continued

[Each cell contains five rows of data including the probability of movement (row 1), the 95-percent confidence interval for the probability estimate (row 2) the number of movements (row 3), the number of fish that made movements (row 4), and the average number of movements per fish (row 5)]

Current location	Antenna																
	2	3	4	5	6	7	8	9	10	11	13	14	15	16	17	18	19
21	0.011	0.015	0.009	0.013	0.006	0.002	0.002	0.004	0.002	0.000	0.000	0.000	0.000	0.002	0.011	0.062	0.009
	0.090	0.090	0.090	0.090	0.090	0.090	0.090	0.091	0.090	0	0	0	0	0.090	0.090	0.088	0.090
	5	7	4	6	3	1	1	2	1	0	0	0	0	1	5	29	4
	4	6	4	6	3	1	1	2	1	0	0	0	0	1	5	24	3
	1.3	1.2	1.0	1.0	1.0	1.0	1.0	1.0	1.0	0.0	0.0	0.0	0.0	1.0	1.0	1.2	1.3
22	0.000	0.000	0.000	0.000	0.004	0.002	0.000	0.000	0.000	0.004	0.002	0.004	0.004	0.004	0.021	0.008	0.043
	0	0	0	0	0.085	0.085	0	0	0	0.085	0.085	0.085	0.085	0.085	0.084	0.085	0.083
	0	0	0	0	2	1	0	0	0	2	1	2	2	2	11	4	23
	0	0	0	0	2	1	0	0	0	2	1	2	2	2	11	4	19
	1.0	0.0	0.0	0.0	1.0	1.0	0.0	0.0	0.0	1.0	1.0	1.0	1.0	1.0	1.0	1.0	1.2
23	0.001	0.001	0.000	0.000	0.002	0.000	0.000	0.000	0.000	0.000	0.001	0.000	0.001	0.001	0.003	0.000	0.006
	0.052	0.052	0	0	0.051	0	0	0	0	0	0.052	0	0.052	0.050	0.050	0	0.050
	1	1	0	0	3	0	0	0	0	0	1	0	1	2	5	0	9
	1	1	0	0	2	0	0	0	0	0	1	0	1	2	5	0	7
	1.0	1.0	0.0	0.0	1.5	0.0	0.0	0.0	0.0	0.0	1.0	0.0	1.0	1.0	1.0	0.0	1.3
24	0.000	0.000	0.000	0.000	0.001	0.000	0.001	0.001	0.002	0.001	0.002	0.007	0.008	0.005	0.028	0.001	0.010
	0	0	0	0	0.052	0	0.052	0.052	0.051	0.052	0.051	0.051	0.051	0.051	0.050	0.052	0.051
	0	0	0	0	1	0	1	2	3	2	3	10	12	8	42	2	15
	0	0	0	0	1	0	1	2	3	2	3	10	11	8	28	2	12
	0.0	0.0	0.0	0.0	1.0	0.0	1.0	1.0	1.0	1.0	1.0	1.2	1.1	1.0	1.5	1.0	1.3
25	0.000	0.000	0.000	0.000	0.002	0.000	0.002	0.000	0.000	0.000	0.008	0.012	0.020	0.026	0.045	0.000	0.016
	0	0	0	0	0.088	0	0.088	0	0	0	0.088	0.088	0.087	0.087	0.086	0	0.087
	0	0	0	0	1	0	1	0	0	0	4	6	10	13	22	0	8
	0	0	0	0	1	0	1	0	0	0	4	6	10	13	17	0	8
	0.0	0.0	0.0	0.0	1.0	0.0	1.0	0.0	0.0	0.0	1.0	1.0	1.0	1.0	1.3	0.0	1.0
26	0.000	0.001	0.001	0.002	0.000	0.000	0.001	0.001	0.001	0.001	0.002	0.007	0.004	0.002	0.005	0.001	0.001
	0	0.048	0.048	0.047	0	0	0.048	0.048	0.048	0.048	0.047	0.047	0.047	0.047	0.047	0.048	0.048
	0	1	1	3	0	0	1	2	1	1	3	12	6	4	9	1	2
	0	1	1	3	0	0	1	2	1	1	3	10	6	4	8	1	2
	0.0	1.0	1.0	1.0	0.0	0.0	1.0	1.0	1.0	1.0	1.0	1.2	1.0	1.0	1.1	1.0	1.0
27	0.001	0.000	0.000	0.000	0.000	0.000	0.000	0.000	0.000	0.000	0.000	0.002	0.001	0.001	0.002	0.000	0.002
	0.034	0	0	0	0.034	0.034	0	0	0	0	0.034	0.033	0.032	0.033	0.033	0	0.033
	2	0	0	0	1	1	0	0	0	0	1	6	4	5	6	0	6
	2	0	0	0	1	1	0	0	0	0	1	6	4	5	6	0	6
	1.0	0.0	0.0	0.0	1.0	1.0	0.0	0.0	0.0	0.0	1.0	1.0	1.0	1.0	1.0	0.0	1.0
28	0.000	0.001	0.002	0.000	0.001	0.000	0.001	0.010	0.002	0.000	0.013	0.034	0.021	0.020	0.013	0.000	0.005
	0	0.062	0.062	0	0.062	0	0.062	0.062	0.062	0	0.062	0.061	0.061	0.062	0.062	0	0.062
	0	1	2	0	1	0	1	10	2	0	13	34	21	20	13	0	5
	0	1	2	0	1	0	1	9	2	0	12	27	17	17	11	0	5
	0.0	1.0	1.0	0.0	1.0	0.0	1.0	01.1	1.0	0.0	1.1	1.3	1.2	1.2	1.2	0.0	1.0
29	0.000	0.000	0.000	0.000	0.000	0.000	0.000	0.000	0.000	0.000	0.000	0.002	0.000	0.000	0.000	0.000	0.000
	0	0	0	0	0	0	0	0	0	0	0	0.055	0	0	0	0	0
	0	0	0	0	0	0	0	0	0	0	0	2	0	0	0	0	0
	0	0	0	0	0	0	0	0	0	0	0	2	0	0	0	0	0
	0.0	0.0	0.0	0.0	0.0	0.0	0.0	0.0	0.0	0.0	0.0	1.0	0.0	0.0	0.0	0.0	0.0

Appendix H. Movement Probabilities for Radio-Tagged Chinook Salmon between Individual Antennas from the Residence Dataset at Cowlitz Falls Dam during 2011.—Continued

[Each cell contains five rows of data including the probability of movement (row 1), the 95-percent confidence interval for the probability estimate (row 2) the number of movements (row 3), the number of fish that made movements (row 4), and the average number of movements per fish (row 5)]

Current location	20	21	22	23	24	25	26	27	28	29	30	31	32	33	Facility	Tailrace
21	0.345	n/a	0.415	0.017	0.013	0.000	0.000	0.006	0.004	0.000	0.002	0.051	0.000	0.000	0.000	0.000
	0.073		0.069	0.090	0.090	0	0	0.090	0.091	0	0.090	0.088	0	0	0	0
	162		195	8	6	0	0	3	2	0	1	24	0	0	0	0
	60		65	8	6	0	0	3	2	0	1	20	0	0	0	0
	2.7		3.0	1.0	1.0	0.0	0.0	1.0	1.0	0.0	1.0	1.2	0.0	0.0	0.0	0.0
22	0.206	0.394	n/a	0.043	0.068	0.013	0.006	0.026	0.000	0.000	0.004	0.145	0.000	0.000	0.000	0.000
	0.076	0.066		0.083	0.082	0.085	0.085	0.084	0	0	0.085	0.079	0	0	0	0
	109	209		23	36	7	3	14	0	0	2	77	0	0	0	0
	54	63		20	26	6	3	13	0	0	2	45	0	0	0	0
	2.0	3.3		1.2	1.4	1.2	1.0	1.1	0.0	0.0	1.0	1.7	0.0	0.0	0.0	0.0
23	0.006	0.003	0.032	n/a	0.193	0.003	0.003	0.378	0.004	0.009	0.040	0.310	0.000	0.001	0.000	0.002
	0.050	0.051	0.050		0.045	0.051	0.050	0.040	0.051	0.050	0.050	0.042	0	0.050	0	0.051
	9	4	48		290	4	5	567	6	14	60	465	0	2	0	3
	9	4	33		73	4	5	79	6	14	37	68	0	2	0	3
	1.0	1.0	1.5		4.0	1.0	1.0	7.2	1.0	1.0	1.6	6.8	0.0	1.0	0.0	1.0
24	0.007	0.001	0.016	0.156	n/a	0.055	0.019	0.605	0.020	0.005	0.003	0.043	0.000	0.000	0.000	0.002
	0.051	0.052	0.050	0.047		0.050	0.050	0.032	0.050	0.051	0.051	0.050	0	0	0	0.051
	11	2	23	231		81	28	895	30	7	5	63	0	0	0	3
	9	2	18	67		47	18	70	26	7	5	34	0	0	0	3
	1.2	1.0	1.3	3.4		1.7	1.6	12.8	1.2	1.0	1.0	1.9	0.0	0.0	0.0	1.0
25	0.018	0.002	0.024	0.016	0.177	n/a	0.280	0.181	0.124	0.000	0.006	0.024	0.000	0.000	0.000	0.004
	0.088	0.088	0.087	0.087	0.080		0.075	0.080	0.083	0	0.088	0.087	0	0	0	0.087
	9	1	12	8	87		138	89	61	0	3	12	0	0	0	2
	9	1	11	8	40		59	42	40	0	3	11	0	0	0	2
	1.0	1.0	1.1	1.0	2.2		2.3	2.1	1.5	0.0	1.0	1.1	0.0	0.0	0.0	1.0
26	0.002	0.001	0.002	0.004	0.012	0.115	n/a	0.272	0.429	0.123	0.008	0.004	0.000	0.000	0.000	0.003
	0.047	0.048	0.047	0.047	0.047	0.044		0.040	0.036	0.044	0.047	0.047	0	0	0	0.054
	4	1	3	7	20	200		471	744	214	13	7	0	0	0	4
	4	1	3	6	17	69		75	81	67	12	7	0	0	0	4
	1.0	1.0	1.0	1.2	1.8	2.9		6.3	9.2	3.2	1.1	1.0	0.0	0.0	0.0	1.0
27	0.002	0.001	0.004	0.178	0.223	0.020	0.159	n/a	0.014	0.110	0.242	0.034	0.000	0.002	0.000	0.002
	0.032	0.032	0.032	0.029	0.029	0.032	0.030		0.032	0.031	0.028	0.032	0	0.033	0	0.033
	7	4	15	645	811	73	577		51	401	877	125	0	6	0	7
	6	4	14	76	65	42	81		34	71	81	47	0	6	0	7
	1.2	1.0	1.1	8.5	12.5	1.7	7.1		1.5	5.6	10.8	2.7	0.0	1.0	0.0	1.0
28	0.001	0.001	0.002	0.005	0.016	0.037	0.721	0.070	n/a	0.009	0.003	0.008	0.000	0.000	0.000	0.003
	0.062	0.062	0.062	0.062	0.062	0.061	0.033	0.060		0.062	0.062	0.062	0	0	0	0.062
	1	1	2	5	16	37	718	70		9	3	8	0	0	0	3
	1	1	2	5	15	24	80	44		9	3	8	0	0	0	3
	1.0	1.0	1.0	1.0	1.1	1.5	9.0	1.6		1.0	1.0	1.0	0.0	0.0	0.0	1.0
29	0.000	0.000	0.000	0.008	0.002	0.000	0.163	0.306	0.003	n/a	0.202	0.012	0.300	0.002	0.000	0.001
	0	0	0	0.055	0.055	0	0.050	0.046	0.054		0.049	0.055	0.046	0.055	0	0.062
	0	0	0	10	2	0	207	389	4		257	15	382	3	0	1
	0	0	0	8	2	0	66	75	4		69	12	54	3	0	1
	0.0	0.0	0.0	1.3	1.0	0.0	3.1	5.2	1.0		3.7	1.3	7.1	1.0	0.0	1.0

Appendix H. Movement Probabilities for Radio-Tagged Chinook Salmon between Individual Antennas from the Residence Dataset at Cowlitz Falls Dam during 2011.—Continued

[Each cell contains five rows of data including the probability of movement (row 1), the 95-percent confidence interval for the probability estimate (row 2) the number of movements (row 3), the number of fish that made movements (row 4), and the average number of movements per fish (row 5)]

Current location	Antenna 2	3	4	5	6	7	8	9	10	11	13	14	15	16	17	18	19
30	0.000	0.000	0.000	0.000	0.000	0.000	0.000	0.000	0.000	0.000	0.000	0.000	0.000	0.000	0.000	0.000	0.000
								0.020				0.020		0.020			
	0	0	0	0	0	0	0	1	0	0	0	1	0	2	0	0	0
	0	0	0	0	0	0	0	1	0	0	0	1	0	2	0	0	0
	0.0	0.0	0.0	0.0	0.0	0.0	0.0	1.0	0.0	0.0	0.0	1.0	0.0	1.0	0.0	0.0	0.0
31	0.000	0.000	0.000	0.000	0.000	0.000	0.000	0.000	0.000	0.000	0.000	0.000	0.001	0.002	0.011	0.001	0.017
													0.065	0.063	0.063	0.065	0.063
	0	0	0	0	0	0	0	0	0	0	0	0	1	2	10	1	16
	0	0	0	0	0	0	0	0	0	0	0	0	1	2	7	1	15
	0.0	0.0	0.0	0.0	0.0	0.0	0.0	0.0	0.0	0.0	0.0	0.0	1.0	1.0	1.4	1.0	1.1
32	0.000	0.000	0.000	0.000	0.000	0.000	0.000	0.000	0.000	0.000	0.000	0.000	0.000	0.000	0.000	0.000	0.000
	0	0	0	0	0	0	0	0	0	0	0	0	0	0	0	0	0
	0	0	0	0	0	0	0	0	0	0	0	0	0	0	0	0	0
	0.0	0.0	0.0	0.0	0.0	0.0	0.0	0.0	0.0	0.0	0.0	0.0	0.0	0.0	0.0	0.0	0.0
33	0.000	0.000	0.000	0.000	0.000	0.000	0.000	0.000	0.000	0.000	0.000	0.000	0.000	0.000	0.000	0.000	0.000
	0	0	0	0	0	0	0	0	0	0	0	0	0	0	0	0	0
	0	0	0	0	0	0	0	0	0	0	0	0	0	0	0	0	0
	0.0	0.0	0.0	0.0	0.0	0.0	0.0	0.0	0.0	0.0	0.0	0.0	0.0	0.0	0.0	0.0	0.0

Current location	Antenna 20	21	22	23	24	25	26	27	28	29	30	31	32	33	Facility	Tailrace
30	0.017	0.000	0.000	0.007	0.000	0.000	0.001	0.094	0.000	0.023	n/a	0.007	0.000	0.867	0.001	0.000
	0.063		0.020	0.020	0.020		0.020	0.019	0.020	0.020		0.020		0.007	0.020	0.020
	16	0	1	66	2	0	8	893	1	221		69	0	8278	8	1
	13	0	1	39	1	0	8	77	1	74		45	0	87	8	1
	1.2	0.0	1.0	1.7	2.0	0.0	1.0	11.6	1.0	3.0		1.5	0.0	95.1	1.0	1.0
31	0.017	0.007	0.110	0.455	0.066	0.004	0.013	0.199	0.013	0.021	0.060	n/a	0.000	0.000	0.000	0.004
	0.063	0.063	0.060	0.047	0.061	0.063	0.063	0.057	0.063	0.063	0.062					0.062
	16	7	104	432	63	4	12	189	12	20	57		0	0	0	4
	13	6	50	67	36	4	9	63	12	14	41		0	0	0	4
	1.2	1.2	2.1	6.4	1.8	1.0	1.3	3.0	1.0	1.4	1.4		0.0	0.0	0.0	1.0
32	0.000	0.000	0.000	0.000	0.000	0.000	0.000	0.000	0.000	1.000	0.000	0.000	n/a	0.000	0.000	0.000
										0.000						
	0	0	0	0	0	0	0	0	0	382	0	0		0	0	0
	0	0	0	0	0	0	0	0	0	54	0	0		0	0	0
	0.0	0.0	0.0	0.0	0.0	0.0	0.0	0.0	0.0	7.1	0.0	0.0		0.0	0.0	0.0
33	0.000	0.000	0.000	0.000	0.000	0.000	0.000	0.001	0.000	0.000	0.998	0.000	0.000	n/a	0.002	0.000
								0.022	0.020	0.020	0.001				0.025	0.020
	0	0	0	0	0	0	0	4	1	2	8269	0	0		12	1
	0	0	0	0	0	0	0	4	1	2	87	0	0		12	1
	0.0	0.0	0.0	0.0	0.0	0.0	0.0	1.0	1.0	1.0	95.0	0.0	0.0		1.0	1.0

www.ingramcontent.com/pod-product-compliance
Lightning Source LLC
Chambersburg PA
CBHW080422290526
45791CB00008BA/2373